DATE DUE

EXPERIMENTS INVESTIGATING FUNDRAISING AND CHARITABLE CONTRIBUTORS

RESEARCH IN EXPERIMENTAL ECONOMICS

Series Editor: R. Mark Isaac

RESEARCH IN EXPERIMENTAL ECONOMICS   VOLUME 11

EXPERIMENTS INVESTIGATING FUNDRAISING AND CHARITABLE CONTRIBUTORS

EDITED BY

R. MARK ISAAC

Department of Economics, Florida State University, USA

DOUGLAS D. DAVIS

School of Business, Virginia Commonwealth University, USA

ELSEVIER
JAI

Amsterdam – Boston – Heidelberg – London – New York – Oxford
Paris – San Diego – San Francisco – Singapore – Sydney – Tokyo

JAI Press is an imprint of Elsevier

JAI Press is an imprint of Elsevier
The Boulevard, Langford Lane, Kidlington, Oxford OX5 1GB, UK
Radarweg 29, PO Box 211, 1000 AE Amsterdam, The Netherlands
525 B Street, Suite 1900, San Diego, CA 92101-4495, USA

First edition 2006

British Library Cataloguing in Publication Data
A catalogue record for this book is available from the British Library

ISBN-13:   978-0-7623-1301-3
ISBN-10:   0-7623-1301-3
ISSN: 0193-2306 (Series)

For information on all JAI Press publications
visit our website at books.elsevier.com

Printed and bound in The Netherlands

06 07 08 09 10 10 9 8 7 6 5 4 3 2 1

Working together to grow
libraries in developing countries

www.elsevier.com | www.bookaid.org | www.sabre.org

ELSEVIER   BOOK AID International   Sabre Foundation

CONTENTS

LIST OF CONTRIBUTORS

Rachel Croson	University of Pennsylvania, USA
Douglas D. Davis	Virginia Commonwealth University, USA
Catherine C. Eckel	University of Texas at Dallas, USA
Philip J. Grossman	St. Cloud State University, USA
Matthew A. Halloran	Kansas State University, USA
Glenn W. Harrison	University of Central Florida, USA
R. Mark Isaac	Florida State University, USA
Laurie T. Johnson	University of Denver, USA
Andreas Lange	University of Maryland, USA
John A. List	University of Chicago, USA
Robert Moir	University of New Brunswick (Saint John), Canada
Michael K. Price	University of Nevada, USA
Shannon M. Price	University of Nevada, USA
Laura Razzolini	Virginia Commonwealth University, USA
Robert J. Reilly	Virginia Commonwealth University, USA
Timothy C. Salmon	Florida State University, USA
Kurt Schnier	University of Rhode Island, USA
Jen Shang	Indiana University, USA
James M. Walker	Indiana University, USA
Arlington W. Williams	Indiana University, USA
Bart J. Wilson	George Mason University, USA

PREFACE

This is the fourth volume in the series *Research in Experimental Economics* that is organized as a compilation of papers on the same topic. Previous collections, on *Emissions Permit Trading* (volume 8), *Market Power* (volume 9) and *Field Experiments* (volume 10) have been well received, and it has become evident that the organization of these volumes into topical collections serves a useful function. The topic of the current volume, *Charitable Auctions and Fundraising*, has been a subject of intense policy interest. In recent years private, religious and state organizations have come to rely increasingly on fund-raising activities to generate revenues. Experimental methods provide an ideal context for conducting a dialog between economists, fund-raisers and policymakers regarding the revenue and social consequences of alternative fund-raising methods. The construction of this volume is largely the same as the previous themed volumes in this series. Rather than using an open submission process, we either knew of, or solicited contributions, and we provided the editorial reviews.

The papers are arranged into four themes, each with two or (in one instance) three papers. A first theme pertains to the structure of charity auctions. The first paper, "Revenue from the Saints, the Showoffs, and the Predators: Comparisons of Auctions with Price-Preference Values," by Tim Salmon and Mark Isaac uses theoretical and computational tools to analyze the effects of own and other price preferences for auctions on the revenue outcomes of first and second price sealed-bid auctions. Results of this analysis are interesting, and in some instances surprising. For example, in the case where participants bid with charitable intentions, Salmon and Isaac show that revenue predictions for the second-price auction continues its standard dominance of first-price auctions. However, when bidders derive utility from total auction revenues, these revenue considerations can make the predicted differences quite small. Salmon and Isaac further show that if bidders derive extra utility from being the auction winner (which the authors term "See and be Seen" preferences), predicted revenues for the first-price auction might actually exceed those for a comparable second-price auction. These results, combined with the repeatedly observed tendency for bidders to overbid in first-price auctions, suggest that first-price auctions may persistently yield higher revenues than second-price auctions in charitable contexts. Finally, the authors show that revenue considerations have implications that extend beyond charitable giving. In particular, they show that predatory efforts to raise rival's costs may have the unintended effect of reducing auction revenues.

A second paper, "Sealed Bid Variations on the Silent Charity Auction" by Mark Isaac and Kurt Schnier, considers interactions between the auction format and the way fund-raising auctions are often conducted, with offering multiple items for sale simultaneously. Specifically, these authors compare the efficiency and revenue effects of some previously reported ascending price auctions with results of some newly reported first- and second- price sealed bid auctions in an environment where multiple auctions are open at the same time. Isaac and Schneir find that when multiple items are simultaneously offered for sale, the sealed bid auction, particularly the first-price sealed bid auction, outperforms the ascending price auction with no obvious loss in efficiency. The intuition driving this result is that in the case of sealed-bid auctions bidders need not "guard" their more highly valued items against last minute bidding. Abstracting from the possibilities that bidders may have price preferences for auctions and that bidders may have affiliated values in the ascending price auctions, these results suggest that fund-raisers would do well to consider use of a sealed bid format.

The second theme considers the lottery, perhaps the most standard alternative to the charity auction at fund-raising events. In a first paper "Raising Revenues for Charity: Auctions versus Lotteries" by Douglas Davis, Laura Razzolini, Robert Reilly, and Bart Wilson, the authors analyze a simple stylized model to identify when charities should generate higher revenues than an ascending price auction. Bidders are assumed to be risk neutral with quasi-linear preferences for a homogenously valued public good. Rather unconventionally, the authors also assume that bidders have full information regarding the private values of all bidders. In this case, the authors predict that auctions should raise higher revenues than lotteries when the public component of the auction (the MPCR) is small, and when a single private valuation for the good is very heterogeneous. However, results of an associated experiment generate the surprising result that lottery revenues persistently exceed revenues in comparable auctions, suggesting that, abstracting from legal prohibitions and potential bidder preferences for participating in one institution rather than the other, lotteries may be a preferred mechanism.

A second paper on the lottery theme, "The Optimal Design of Charitable Lotteries: Theory and Experimental Evidence" by Andreas Lange, John

List, Michael Price, and Shannon Price, analyzes the trade-off between the optimal structure of prizes in a fund-raising lottery, and the risk-preferences of participants. The primary prediction of the authors' theoretical analysis is that the optimal prize structure shifts from a single prize to multiple prizes, as agent risk postures move from risk neutral (or risk-preferring) to risk averse. The paper also reports a laboratory experiment conducted to test this and other predictions. Experimental results indicate that lotteries generate higher revenues than does a comparable voluntary contributions mechanism, but that netting out the value of the prize weakens the dominance of lotteries as a fund-raising mechanism. The authors also find that a single prize structure generates higher revenues than a multiple prize structure when agents are risk neutral or risk preferring. However, evidence that shifting from a single to a multiple prize structure exerts the predicted revenue increasing effect when participants are risk averse is guarded at best.

A third paper on the lottery theme "Multiple Public Goods and Lottery Fundraising" by Robert Moir reports an experiment conducted to examine the capacity of a charity lottery to improve social well being when an alternative public good also exists. The policy question raised here is a quite interesting one. As government support for public goods has fallen, charitable organizations have turned to increasingly aggressive private methods for support. One should not expect that the most aggressive fund-raising agencies would be the ones offering the highest value public goods. Moir's reported experiment takes a step toward showing that a process of lottery adoptions by agencies offering low value goods can reduce social welfare, when the solicited contributions come at the expense of voluntary contributions to higher value goods. Using a simple linear environment, Moir observes that as a theoretical matter, a lottery, even one on a comparatively low value good, increases public welfare relative to the free-riding static Nash prediction. However, experimental evidence suggests that the addition of the lottery diverts voluntary contributions away from the high value good and thus reduces public welfare.

Although auctions and lotteries are used with increasing frequency to raise charitable revenues, the fund drive undoubtedly remains the primary means of generating public contributions. The third theme in this volume examines the revenue consequences of altering the way the fund-raisers solicit contributions. A first paper, "The Impact of Social Comparisons on Nonprofit Fundraising," by Rachel Croson and Jen Shang reports a field experiment examining the effects of introducing a "social comparison" on contributions to a public good. Specifically, the authors manipulate the response format to callers in a public radio station fund drive. Relative to a baseline condition, the authors find that providing high social comparison information ($600) significantly increases mean contributions. Closer inspection of the data suggests that this high social comparison increases contributions primarily by increasing donations made by a minority of high-contributing callers.

A second paper on the fund-raising theme, "Do Donors Care About Subsidy Type: An Experimental Study" by Catherine Eckel and Philip Grossman reports an experiment conducted to further assess a phenomenon previously discovered by these authors, that net charitable contributions are higher when subsidized by a matching contribution than when they are subsidized by a theoretically comparable rebate subsidy. Here the authors examine treatments designed to investigate two factors that might drive the observed result: first, that participants are averse to rebates, and thus contribute less when forced to make contributions under such schemes, and second that participants do not understand the differing effects of the two subsidies. The authors find no preference for rebates over matching subsidies. However, charitable contributions (after adjusting for the subsidies) remained twice as high under a matching subsidy as under a rebate subsidy. The authors' finding that individuals contribute more to charities under a matching subsidy than under a rebate subsidy is a provocative, and potentially important result. Results of this paper, and related research discussed therein suggest that this finding may be fairly robust.

The fourth and final theme includes a pair of papers that broadly address some issues underlying charitable behavior. The first paper, "Identifying Altruism in the Laboratory" by Glenn Harrison and Laurie Johnson first reviews some of the recent literature that attempts to assess confounding factors that underlie efforts to measure altruism in Dictator games. Then the authors construct a simple experiment that allows insight into two important potential effects: subject pool heterogeneity, and inefficiency aversion. The authors show that these confounds affect behavior substantially, but that they are controllable.

The final paper "The Voluntary Provision of a Public Good with Binding Multi-Round Commitments" by Matthew Halloran, James Walker, and Arlington Williams reports a public goods experiment where, in addition to standard within round allocation decisions, participants are given the opportunity to make binding multi-round commitments. The authors find that the opportunity to make multi-round commitments does not increase mean allocations to the group account relative to a control treatment. However, commitments do have implications for reciprocal behavior within groups. The multi-round commitments treatment increases outcome variances across groups.

REVENUE FROM THE SAINTS, THE SHOWOFFS AND THE PREDATORS: COMPARISONS OF AUCTIONS WITH PRICE-PREFERENCE VALUES

Timothy C. Salmon and R. Mark Isaac

ABSTRACT

Traditional auction theory assumes that bidders possess values defined solely on the auctioned object. There may, however, be cases in which bidders possess preferences over the revenue achieved by the auctioneer. We present here a comprehensive framework of price-preference valuations, unifying several phenomena ranging from preference for charitable giving to shill bidding. We compare expected efficiency and revenue of first- and second-price auctions for some specific cases of key interest. We also incorporate heterogeneous bidder preferences and examine the effects of mis-specified beliefs and show that both are crucial for understanding these situations.

Experiments Investigating Fundraising and Charitable Contributors
Research in Experimental Economics, Volume 11, 1–30
Copyright © 2006 by Elsevier Ltd.
ISSN: 0193-2306/doi:10.1016/S0193-2306(06)11001-7
1

1. INTRODUCTION

While traditional auction literature has focused almost exclusively on situations in which bidders possess preferences only over the items being auctioned, bidders in real auctions will quite often have preferences over more than just what they win. One sort of these preferences might be preferences over the revenue achieved by the auctioneer. In previous literature such preferences have been called "price-preference valuations." There are, however, a large number of different variations and applications of a model of this sort. Several such models have been explored in recent literature. We will show that these are all special cases of a more general model and we will extend this model to some additional applications.

In Section 2 of this paper we will construct a general framework of price preferences in auctions. In doing so, we will demonstrate the necessity of considering complicating factors such as asymmetry and heterogeneity among the bidders as well as bidders possessing mis-specified beliefs about the population they are bidding against. Section 3 will present the formal model along with some analytical results. This will set up Section 4, which will use a computational approach to analyze multiple different cases and environments for which analytical results are unavailable.

2. A UNIFIED MODEL OF PRICE PREFERENCE VALUATIONS

There are a number of different reasons why a bidder in an auction might derive additional utility based on the revenue of the auctioneer. When specifying some form of these alternative preferences, there are additions that must be made to the standard story of preferences in auctions. It is typically assumed in auction models that each bidder i possesses some value v_i of winning the object. The notion of price preferences supposes that bidders may also derive utility from the level of the final price. Engelbrecht-Wiggans (1994) (EW) introduces such a model in the context of bidding rings and using auctions to divide partnerships. He assumes that each individual bidder derives some amount of utility proportional to the final price with this parameter, β, constant across all bidders and symmetric in regard to whether or not a bidder wins or loses the auction.

There are, however, a number of alternative applications of a model of this sort beyond the examples in EW that require a more flexible specification of these preferences. The first addition to the specification is to allow asymmetric benefits to a bidder between winning and losing. This involves introducing a new parameter, α, such that when a bidder wins, his utility is increased by $\beta*p$, where p is the seller's revenue or price, but his utility is increased by $\alpha*p$ when the bidder loses. It is relatively straightforward to extend the results in EW to allow for this case and some of the details of doing so will be shown in the appendix.[1]

In many of the cases in which price preference valuations are an issue it is inherent to the motivation of the scenario that bidders have asymmetric or heterogenous values for these parameters. In certain cases it is also crucial to the story that this asymmetry will not be known during the bidding process. In the descriptions of different cases below we will note these issues, and most of our computational results in Section 4 will be aimed at dealing with these situations since they are the ones for which analytical results cannot be found. Introducing asymmetries across bidders means different bidders will have different values for β and α requiring the notation of β_i and α_i. Our analysis will focus on computing optimal bid functions in first- and second-price auctions in three different cases.

One detail to note is that we have not actually specified whether these preferences result from pecuniary (e.g. a payment from the seller) or non-pecuniary (e.g. a preference to see the seller collect more money) motivations. Either can be modeled in the same structure from the bidders' perspective, but this will prove to be an important distinction for seller revenue, which will be net of any direct payments to the bidders.

While our basic model of auctions with price preferences can be used to study a wide range of phenomena, in this paper we will concentrate our focus on three cases of particular interest. The first involves charity auctions. In auctions that are conducted to benefit a charity, one could well expect that participating bidders gain utility based on the total amount of money raised by the charity. This issue has been examined using field data from charity auctions in Isaac and Schnier (2005) to examine evidence in favor of such preferences. For modeling purposes, we will claim that pure preferences for charitable giving involve bidder preferences that are focused specifically on the revenue the seller raises and therefore we should have $\alpha_i = \beta_i$. There is, however, no reason to believe that all n bidders in an auction are alike in their charitable preferences, thus we allow for $\beta_i \neq \beta_j$. The source of these preferences could be either pecuniary or non-pecuniary, but the most likely story is that they are non-pecuniary.[2] This case is captured by EW, but restricted to the case of inter-personal symmetry.

A variant of these baseline preferences for charitable giving concerns bidders who gain utility from seller revenue only when they are the winning bidder. A more informal description of such motivations is that a bidder wishes to bid in the auction to be seen as a generous person. We will refer to such preferences as preferences to see and be seen (SBS). Such bidders would possess $\beta_i > \alpha_i \geq 0$. Isaac and Schnier discussed this concept, and Engers and McManus (2002) extended EW to allow for $\beta_i > \alpha_i$ but their model retains the assumption that parameters are identical across individuals. This specification implies that all bidders are attempting to be as demonstrative as everyone else. We believe a more useful and realistic representation is that some bidders are significantly more demonstrative than the others. Further, the demonstrative bidders may or may not be aware that they are "different from the norm" while the less demonstrative bidders may not be aware of the existence of these other bidders. We will capture this phenomenon by modelling a stark case in which $\alpha_i = 0$ for all bidders, and $\beta_i > 0$ for only a subset of bidders who "want to be seen" as being generous to the charity. We will also examine cases in which beliefs are mis-specified. The motivation of this phenomenon for charitable giving is again almost certainly non-pecuniary.

There are both theoretical and experimental evidences that casts doubt on the usefulness of our examination of winner-pay auction formats for charitable giving. Goeree, Maasland, Onderstal, and Turner (2004) argue that all-pay auctions and lotteries or raffles are substantially superior to winner-pay auctions in terms of raising revenue for charitable causes with all-pay auctions also dominating lotteries. Davis, Razzolini, Reilly, and Wilson (2003) provide experimental evidence that lotteries can be more successful at raising money than English auctions. The strongest argument to motivate why we are concerned with auctions instead of lotteries is that in many places around the country charity lotteries are either illegal or carry significant and perhaps prohibitive transactions costs due to legal restrictions regarding their use.[3] Moreover, charitable auctions are quite often conducted by religious institutions and many of these institutions object to lotteries on the basis that they represent a form of gambling. While all-pay auctions may not suffer the same legal and religious problems as lotteries, there still seems to be reluctance on the part of auctioneers to use them except on low-value items. Due to these issues and the prevalence of winner-pay auctions run on behalf of charities as discussed in Isaac and Schnier (2005), we feel justified in claiming that there is still value to be found in examining first- and second-price or ascending winner-pay auctions.

The last case we will examine involves preferences quite different from those to be given to charity, but rather preferences to damage a rival. We will refer to this case as preferences for raising a rival's cost (RRC). Part of the circumstantial evidence presented by the government in the 1946 decision against the three largest tobacco companies is that the companies deliberately acted to raise the cost of rivals through the ubiquitous auctions of leaf tobacco.[4] Similar concerns have reappeared with the expansion of B-to-B auction sites on the web: "If you can use your clout in a B-to-B exchange to force your competitors to pay more for a key component, making it impossible for them to compete effectively, you might have broken antitrust laws."[5] Such motivations have also been proposed to explain British Telecom 3G's bidding behavior in the UK's UMTS[6] auction by Klemperer (2002a). The structure of these preferences is almost certainly asymmetric across firms and it also stands to reason that "prey" firms may not realize they are being targeted and "predator" firms may not realize there are other predators in the population. We will model this case assuming $\beta_i = 0$ for all firms with $\alpha_i > 0$ for the predators but $\alpha_j = 0$ for the prey. Because the benefits to the predatory firm do not come directly from the seller, we classify the preference as "non-pecuniary" although the predator's preferences may be based upon the hope of future monetary payoffs through other channels. Morgan, Steiglitz, and Reis (2002) develop a model of purely spiteful behavior in auctions, which is a closely related, yet not the same, phenomenon. We will discuss this issue further in Section 4.

While these are the three cases that we will focus our analysis on, the model is easily generalizable to deal with several other sorts of situations. The bid functions we will examine under the SBS specification are identical to the bid functions one could derive for simple cases of auctions involving subsidized bidders. The Federal Communications Commission (FCC) regularly subsidizes bidders with βs as high as 0.45 for certain auctions. Shachat and Swarthout (2002) develop an alternative model of subsidized bidders in which the subsidy is a fixed amount rather than a percentage based on the bid level. Corns and Schotter construct a model of asymmetric bidders for procurement of contracts in which the disadvantaged or high cost bidders are given a bidding advantage that consists of modifying the bids placed by the advantaged bidder by some amount for the purposes of determining who wins the contract. Because the underlying motivation to subsidize bidders is typically to assist disadvantaged bidders,[7] modeling this phenomenon in the most interesting environment necessitates using asymmetric value distributions, which would require a substantial extension of what we will present under the SBS case. To keep our analysis consistent, we will therefore not specifically deal with this case below.

McAfee (1992) constructs a similar model and applies it to an environment consisting of two bidders in an auction attempting to divide a personal or professional partnership. The winner pays the loser one-half of the winning bid (which may be set by a first- or second-price rule). The McAfee (1992) specification is a special case of our model using the assumption that $\beta_1 = \alpha_1 = \beta_2 = \alpha_2 = \frac{1}{2}$ with the values of the bidders being drawn from the same distribution. The utility transfer in this case is clearly pecuniary. de Frutos (2000) extended this model to allow for asymmetric value distributions but still enforced $\beta_1 = \alpha_1 = \beta_2 = \alpha_2 = \frac{1}{2}$.

It is also possible to model shill bidding in this framework if one models a shill as a bidder who is paid a share of the seller revenue when he loses, as (purportedly) an incentive to bid up seller revenue. This case is equivalent to the RRC case, with the exception that the preference is now directly pecuniary. As in the case of RRC, this certainly involves asymmetric bidders with only a single bidder possessing $\alpha_i > 0$ and it would almost certainly be the case that the other bidders in the auction would not be aware of the existence of the shill. A shill-bidding arrangement might also involve reimbursing the shill completely upon winning or $\beta_i = 1$ for the shill where the v_i for the shill is some constant also set by the auctioneer to pay the shill in the event they win. Due to the special nature of how v is set for the shill, we will not examine this issue directly.

The next section will develop the specifics of a theoretical model that can be used to derive bid functions for some of these cases for a first- and second-price or ascending auction. The fourth section contains a detailed examination of the effect on revenue and efficiency of each of these cases and the final section incorporates concluding thoughts on the insights gained into practical auction design from our results.

3. MODEL

In this paper, we will be assuming a common structure throughout the theoretical analysis. Each auction will consist of n risk neutral bidders who each draw an independent and privately known value for winning the auction, v_i, from a commonly known distribution $F(v)$ with pdf $f(v)$, which will be assumed for convenience to have support over the range [0,1]. Each bidder will possess two parameters β_i and α_i which describe the utility the bidder gains for each additional unit of revenue the auctioneer raises when the bidder wins or loses the auction, respectively. We will be assuming that $\alpha_i, \beta_i \geq 0$ and it would seem quite unreasonable to assume anything other than $\alpha_i, \beta_i \leq 1$.

If we assume for the first-price auction that there exists some symmetric bid function $b_f^*(v, \beta_i, \alpha_i)$ that is monotonically increasing and differentiable in v and assume that $\alpha_i = \alpha_j$ and $\beta_i = \beta_j$ for all i and j, then we can show what such a bid function must look like and show that it exists. The fact that we are working with symmetric bid functions allows us to make use of the fact that the probability of winning if i bids as if his value were r is $\Pr(b_f^*(r, \beta_i, \alpha_i) > b_f^*(v_j, \beta_j, \alpha_i)$ for all $j) = \Pr(r > v_j$ for all $j) = F(r)^{n-1}$. This means that the first-price auction problem is defined as:

$$\max_r S(v_i,\ r) = (v_i - (1 - \beta_i)b_f^*(r, \beta_i, \alpha_i))F(r)^{n-1}$$

$$+ \alpha_i \int_r^1 b_f^*(t, \beta_i, \alpha_i)(n - 1)f(t)F(t)^{n-2}dt \qquad (1)$$

With the equilibrium condition as

$$\frac{\partial(S(v_i, r))}{\partial r}\Big|_{r=v_i} = 0 \qquad (2)$$

The first term represents the utility that the bidder receives when he wins the auction multiplied by the probability of that event. The second term is his utility when he loses the auction, which requires integrating over all possible prices that the actual winner of the auction might pay multiplied by the probability of each price occurring. This model is a straightforward extension of the one solved in EW and it can be solved with similar methods. We omit most of the proofs supporting these results to conserve space because they are similar to those in EW, but we have included some of the details of the derivation in the appendix. The solution can be shown to be

$$b_f^*(v_i, \beta_i, \alpha_i) = \frac{\int_0^{v_i} t(n - 1)f(t)F(t)^{(n+\beta_i(2-n)+\alpha_i(n-1)-2)/(1-\beta_i)}dt}{(1 - \beta_i)(F(v_i)^{n-1})^{(1-\beta_i+\alpha_i)/(1-\beta_i)}} \qquad (3)$$

In the case of the uniform distribution on the range [0,1], the bid function becomes

$$b_f^*(v_i, \beta_i, \alpha_i) = \frac{n - 1}{n(1 - \beta_i + \alpha_i) - \alpha_i} v_i \qquad (4)$$

Similarly, the second-price problem is

$$\max_r S(v_i, r) = \int_0^r (v_i - (1 - \beta_i)b_s^*(t, \beta_i, \alpha_i))(n - 1)f(t)F(t)^{n-2}dt$$

$$+ \alpha_i b_s^*(r, \beta_i, \alpha_i)(n - 1)F(r)^{n-2}(1 - F(r))$$

$$+ \alpha_i \left(\int_r^1 b_s^*(t, \beta_i, \alpha_i)(n - 2)(n - 1)F(t)^{n-3}(1 - F(t))f(t)dt \right) \qquad (5)$$

The first term represents the utility that bidder i gets in the event that he wins the auction and we must integrate over the possible prices he would pay, which are the bids an opponent would be expected to make as defined by $b_s^*(t, \beta_i, \alpha_i)$ multiplied by the probability of t being the second highest value. The second term defines the utility i would receive from placing second highest bid as he would set the price and would thus get $\alpha_i * b_s^*(r, \beta_i, \alpha_i)$ times the probability his bid is second highest. The final term represents the utility from coming in less than second as he will get α_i times whatever the second highest bidder bids. Solving this results in a general solution of

$$b_s^*(v_i, \beta_i, \alpha_i) = \begin{cases} \dfrac{1}{\alpha_i} \dfrac{\int_{v_i}^1 t(1-F(t))^{(1-\beta_i)/(\alpha_i)} f(t) dt}{(1-F(v_i))^{(1+\alpha_i-\beta_i)/(\alpha_i)}}, & \text{if } \alpha_i > 0 \\[2ex] \dfrac{v_i}{1-\beta_i}, & \text{if } \alpha_i = 0 \end{cases} \tag{6}$$

Again, if we simplify this to the case of the uniform distribution on the range [0,1], the bid function becomes

$$b_s^*(v_i, \beta_i, \alpha_i) = \frac{v_i(1 - \beta_i + \alpha_i) + \alpha_i}{(1 - \beta_i + 2\alpha_i)(1 - \beta_i + \alpha_i)} \tag{7}$$

Note that since the bid functions for the second-price auction do not depend on either n or the lower bound of the value distribution, this function can be used to find the equilibrium dropout prices for an English clock auction. This bid function could also be interpreted to deliver the highest price a bidder would be willing to stay in for in a non-clock English auction. It would be incorrect, however, to assert this dropout price as an equilibrium strategy for the non-clock ascending auction for the reasons discussed in Isaac, Salmon, and Zillante (2005).

For many of the cases we are interested in, however, these solutions will not be sufficient since not all bidders will possess the same preference parameters. This requires introducing asymmetry into the model and results in significant additional complications. In particular, we can no longer assume that probability of winning is just $F(r)^{n-1}$. Letting β_{-i} and α_{-i} reflect the vector of all bidders' preference parameters except i, i now wins if $b^*(v_i, \beta_i, \alpha_i, \beta_{-i}, \alpha_{-i}) > b^*(v_j, \beta_j, \alpha_j, \beta_{-j}, \alpha_{-j})$ for all j. We cannot simply invert both bid functions and be left only with values because the parameters may be different. Further, we must make additional assumptions on the amount of information that each i has in regard to the parameters of the other bidders. As discussed above, in certain situations the environment requires dropping a standard assumption that the bidders know either the exact values of the parameters in use or the distribution of possible parameters. Either of these assumptions would allow us to find the equilibrium bidding strategies by computationally solving n differential equations (as done in Corns & Schotter (1999) and other papers), but either would violate the fundamental premise of many of the issues we are interested in examining.

We will instead take an approach that will allow us to investigate issues that the more standard approach would not allow.[8] We will assume that each bidder assumes all other bidders have some commonly known parameters, $\bar{\alpha}$, $\bar{\beta}$, which might be assumed to be the collective beliefs about the average parameter values in the population. In the event that we use the actual averages, our approach will result in an approximation of the true Nash equilibrium bid functions for the auction. We can also investigate the empirically interesting possibility of mis-specified beliefs by setting $\bar{\alpha}$ and $\bar{\beta}$ to other values. For example, in the SBS case, it is quite reasonable to propose that bidders with high β_is underestimate the average value of β in the population. In the RRC case, it is quite probable that the non-predatory bidders are unaware of the existence of the predators and that even the predators might not suspect there are other predators around. These mis-specified beliefs also seem a reasonable assumption because many of the auctions we are interested in modeling would occur infrequently, making it difficult for bidders to learn the true parameters in the population or even the distribution. Bidders should, however, be able to form a vague model of what the average opponent they face will do and play a best response to that.

The bid functions we derive through this method will not necessarily be equilibrium bid functions (though in some of the cases we consider, the bid functions will be full equilibrium bid functions despite our simplification). While we are sensitive to this concern, we believe there is still substantial value to what we are doing. This is due in part to the oft-observed fact that bidding behavior in experiments has a tendency to diverge from straight equilibrium predictions (see Kagel (1995) for a good overview and discussion of this literature). Our intention is to derive a range of possible bidding behavior to explore the impacts of these potential biases in anticipation of observing data in which they might be present. Further, a similar approach was shown to work well in fitting empirical data in Ivanova-Stenzel and Salmon (2004) in regard to heterogeneous risk preferences in first-price auctions. Our approach here will allow us to investigate the implications of these potential biases in the beliefs of bidders, which we will argue have important consequences for the design and conduct of real auctions that would be overlooked with a more traditional investigation. Further, it will turn out that our results involving the uniform distribution are in virtually all cases true equilibrium results. The fact that they will show essentially the same pattern as the results using the normal distribution should increase the validity of the disequilibrium results for the normal case.

A disadvantage of this approach is that when assuming bidder heterogeneity, we will be unable to obtain analytical expressions for the bid functions for distributions other than uniform and we will be unable to derive expected revenue and expected efficiency equations even for uniformly distributed values. Thus, most of our results on expected revenue and efficiency will be based on computationally solving for the bid functions. It is important to note that even if we were to compute the full equilibrium bid functions, the process and the comparisons would still have to be done computationally. While this computational approach will limit the generalizability of our results, we believe that it will allow us to clearly demonstrate the general principles at work in these environments.

Solving for the bid functions in these cases involves finding bidder i's best response to the belief that he is bidding against $n-1$ bidders who possess parameters of $\bar{\alpha}$ and $\bar{\beta}$, and who believe that they themselves are facing $n-1$ bidders possessing parameters of $\bar{\alpha}$ and $\bar{\beta}$. This assumption allows us to assert that in a first-price auction, bidder i expects his $n-1$ opponents to bid according to the bid function $b_f^*(v_j, \bar{\beta}, \bar{\alpha})$ and $b_s^*(v_j, \bar{\beta}, \bar{\alpha})$ in a second-price auction. We then solve for the bid functions for each individual bidder in the asymmetric case, which we will denote as $B_F^*(v_i, \beta_i, \alpha_i, \bar{\beta}, \bar{\alpha})$ and $B_S^*(v_i, \beta_i, \alpha_i, \bar{\beta}, \bar{\alpha})$.

To find the probability of winning in this case, we can use the fact that if bidder i bids as if he had value of r, then his perceived probability of winning is $\Pr(B_F^*(r, \beta_i, \alpha_i, \bar{\beta}, \bar{\alpha}) > b_f^*(v_j, \bar{\beta}, \bar{\alpha}) \forall v_j) = \Pr(b_f^{*-1}(B_F^*(r, \beta_i, \alpha_i, \bar{\beta}, \bar{\alpha})) > v_j \forall v_j) = F(b_f^{*-1}(B_F^*(r, \beta_i, \alpha_i, \bar{\beta}, \bar{\alpha})))^{n-1}$. To simplify the notation we will let this be represented as just $\phi(r)$. The problem for the first-price auction becomes

$$\max_r S(v_i, r) = (v_i - (1-\beta)B_F^*(r, \beta_i, \alpha_i, \bar{\beta}, \bar{\alpha}))\phi(r) + \alpha \int_q^1 b_f^*(t, \bar{\beta}, \bar{\alpha}) d\phi(t) \quad (8)$$

where q is defined as the minimum value another bidder must have in order to beat $B_F^*(r, \beta_i, \alpha_i, \bar{\beta}, \bar{\alpha})$. This is the q that solves $b_f^*(q, \bar{\beta}, \bar{\alpha}) = B_F^*(r, \beta_i, \alpha_i, \bar{\beta}, \bar{\alpha})$ or $q = b_F^{*-1}(B_F^*(r, \beta_i, \alpha_i, \bar{\beta}, \bar{\alpha}))$. We can use the standard lower bound in solving this of $B_F^*(0, \beta_i, \alpha_i, \bar{\beta}, \bar{\alpha})$, but there will also be an upper bound equal to $b_f^*(1, \bar{\beta}, \bar{\alpha})$. This is because if a bidder places a bid of $b_f^*(1, \bar{\beta}, \bar{\alpha}) + \varepsilon$, they expect to win with probability of 1 since they never expect an opponent to bid above this level.

Solving this problem in the case of uniformly distributed values is fairly trivial and can be done analytically giving us $B_F^*(v_i, \beta_i, \alpha_i, \bar{\beta}, \bar{\alpha}) = (n - 1)/(n(1 - \beta_i + \alpha_i) - \alpha_i)v_i$ with an upper bound of $(n - 1)/(n(1 - \bar{\beta} + \bar{\alpha}) - \bar{\alpha})$. Except for the upper bound, this is exactly what we obtained in the symmetric case, indicating that beliefs about opponents' parameters are largely unimportant when values are distributed uniformly. For all other value distributions, we must solve this computationally, and beliefs about the parameters of others may play a larger role. The methods used are discussed below.

The problem that must be solved for the second-price auction also becomes more complex. If we let $w = b_s^{*-1}(B_S^*(r, \beta_i, \alpha_i, \bar{\beta}, \bar{\alpha}))$ then we can represent the basic problem as follows:

$$
\max_r S(v_i, r) = \int_0^w (v_i - (1 - \beta_i)b_s^*(t, \bar{\beta}, \bar{\alpha}))f(t)(n - 1)F(t)^{n-2}dt
$$
$$
+ \alpha_i B_S^*(r, \beta_i, \alpha_i, \bar{\beta}, \bar{\alpha})(n - 1)F(w)^{n-2}(1 - F(w))
$$
$$
+ \alpha_i \left(\int_w^1 b_s^*(t, \bar{\beta}, \bar{\alpha})(n - 2)(n - 1)F(t)^{n-3}(1 - F(t))f(t)dt \right) \quad (9)
$$

The general construction of this problem is identical to the previous second-price case, but allowing for the fact that in the event i does not come in second, he expects that the price will be set by a bidder bidding according to $b_s^*(t, \bar{\beta}, \bar{\alpha})$, while if i comes in second the price is set according to $B_S^*(r, \beta_i, \alpha_i, \bar{\beta}, \bar{\alpha})$. Also, the bounds of integration require a term, w, which is the lowest value a competitor can have and beat bidder i's bid.

At least this is the problem that must be solved if $\alpha_i > 0$. If $\alpha_i = 0$, then the solution is just $B_S^* = v_i/(1 - \beta_i)$ regardless of $F()$ and beliefs about the parameters of others. If $\alpha_i > 0$ then we do know one thing about the solution, which is that it has a lower bound of $b_s^*(0, \bar{\beta}, \bar{\alpha})$ as this is the minimum bid that i believes his opponent will ever make. Consequently, i believes that he can drive up the price to at least this price level. If $\alpha_i > 0$ then this lower bound is required. In the event that a bidder possesses $\alpha_i = 0$, he is indifferent between bidding any amount between this and $v_i/(1 - \beta_i)$ when the bound is above $v_i/(1 - \beta_i)$. Since a bidder might realize his beliefs are not perfect and there is no added value from bidding like this to someone with $\alpha_i = 0$, we will assume that such bidders ignore this lower bound and break the tie in favor of bidding $v_i/(1 - \beta_i)$.

Again, we can derive an analytical solution to the asymmetric problem assuming uniformly distributed values, which is similar to the solution for the symmetric case but with two changes. First is the addition that there will be a lower bound equal to $\tilde{\alpha}/(1 - \bar{\beta} + 2\tilde{\alpha})(1 - \bar{\beta} + \tilde{\alpha})$ for bidders possessing $\alpha_i > 0$. The second change is that some of the αs and βs in the sloped part of the bid function turn out to be the α and β believed to be held by the opponent. The complete bid function for uniformly distributed values is:

$$B_S^*(v_i, \beta_i, \alpha_i, \bar{\beta}, \tilde{\alpha}) = \begin{cases} v_i/(1 - \beta_i), & \text{if } \alpha_i = 0 \\ \max\left\{ \dfrac{\tilde{\alpha}}{(1-\bar{\beta}+2\tilde{\alpha})(1-\bar{\beta}+\tilde{\alpha})}, \dfrac{v_i(1-\bar{\beta}+\tilde{\alpha})+\alpha_i}{(1-\beta_i+2\alpha_i)(1-\bar{\beta}+\tilde{\alpha})} \right\}, & \text{if } \alpha_i > 0 \end{cases}$$

(10)

For the numerical examples below we will report results for the uniform distribution on the range [0,1] and also for the normal distribution with $\mu = 0.5$ and $\sigma = 0.15$ using the same bounds. While the technical bounds on this distribution are not [0,1], this range contains 99.91% of the mass, so we introduce very little error by using this simplification. We specifically chose a normal distribution as a second example that was very tight both to allow the use of these simple bounds but also to make a contrast with the uniform to ensure that a tighter value distribution does not yield markedly different results.

When computing revenue and efficiency for the cases with uniformly distributed values, we can use these analytical bid functions but cannot compute analytical expected efficiencies and revenues because the integrals are not continuous. For the normal distribution cases, we have computed approximations to the bid functions using the standard minimization procedures in Matlab by computing the best responses for a grid of values between 0 and 1 and then we fit a fourth-order polynomial (e.g. $\tilde{b}(v) = \gamma_1 + \gamma_2 v + \gamma_3 v^2 + \gamma_4 v^3 + \gamma_5 v^4$) to the points. This produces excellent fits to the best response curves with R^2 generally around 0.999 and with relatively little error when compared to cases for which there are analytically computable results. Expected revenue and efficiencies are then calculated by drawing 1,000 value vectors, generating bids according to these bid functions and computing the resulting average revenue and efficiency.

4. RESULTS

We will present results comparing the revenue and efficiency produced by first- and second-price auctions for the cases specified in Section 2. In regard to efficiency, we consider only allocative efficiency; in other words, an auction will be 100% efficient if the bidder with the highest v_i wins. We ignore the price-preference elements of a bidder's total value in this regard, because incorporating non-pecuniary preferences can lead to the efficient allocation requiring an infinite price. We first present the results achievable in the baseline charity case with comparisons to the standard non-charity case to determine the effects on revenue from the addition of these preferences. We will then examine the SBS and RRC cases.

4.1. Baseline Charity

To orient our discussion for this case, we note that EW and Engers and McManus (2002) prove that in the symmetric cases involving $\alpha_i = \beta_i$ or even $\alpha_i \neq \beta_i$ with the parameters symmetric across all bidders, the second price or ascending clock auction yields at least as much revenue as the first price. It is also easy to see that in these symmetric cases, efficiency will be theoretically 100% in all auctions and it will therefore be equal across institutions. The question is, how much larger will the second-price revenue be?

Figs. 1 and 2 contain results from the cases in which $\alpha_i = \beta_i = \alpha_j = \beta_j \in \{0, 0.15, 0.3\}$ for auctions involving 2, 4 and 6 bidders for the uniform and normal value distributions, respectively.[9] Fig. 2 contains more comparisons because with the assumption of normally distributed values we can investigate the effects of beliefs on the revenue. We only present results about mis-specified beliefs for the normal distribution because different belief specifications result in no important effects in the uniform case. In the second-price auction, although beliefs regarding the parameters of other bidders technically enter into the bid function it is clear from Eq. 10 that the beliefs cancel out and have no effect in the event that $\bar{\beta} = \bar{\alpha}$ except through the lower bound, which turns out to rarely bind. In the first-price auction with uniformly distributed values, beliefs about the parameters of others only figure in through the upper bound, which again rarely binds. There is no appreciable effect on revenue for the parameters tested. In Fig. 2, the "0" bar represents the case in which the bidder beliefs are that their opponents' parameters are their own multiplied by 0, while the "1" bar represents the case in which the bidders believe their opponents' parameters are their own multiplied by 1. We only present different revenue estimates under the different belief specifications for the first-price auction as they have no discernible effect on the revenue from the second-price auctions.

We see two important results from these graphs. The first is that while the claim that $E[R_S] \geq E[R_F]$ is indeed technically valid, the revenue difference between the first- and second-price auctions is quite small in most cases. The one case in which the second price does markedly better is the $n = 2$ case with uniform values, but the edge for the second-price auction disappears as

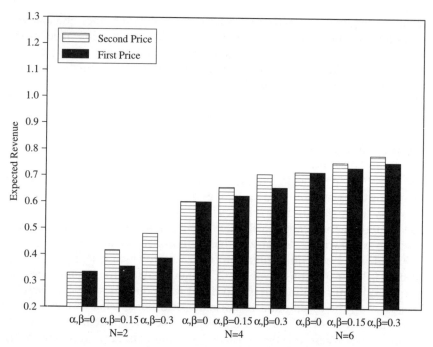

Fig. 1.   Revenue Comparisons between First- and Second-Price Auctions Assuming
Uniformly Distributed Values for 2, 4 and 6 Bidder Auctions. The Cases Considered
Involve Fully Symmetric Bidders with the Parameters Indicated.

more bidders are added. In the normally distributed case, the differences are
small across the entire range.[10] The small size of the difference is important
because it has been observed in countless laboratory experiments that bidders will bid higher than the risk-neutral Nash equilibrium prediction in
first-price auctions. Consequently, the size of these revenue differences could
easily be overwhelmed by such behavior.

   There is an important point embedded into this result that echoes a similar issue discussed in Klemperer (2002b). The argument in Klemperer
(2002b) is that auctioneers should not be heavily influenced in their choice of
auction designs based on the result found in Milgrom and Weber (1982) that
ascending auctions will raise more money than first-price auctions when
values are affiliated. The reason is that while the Milgrom and Weber (1982)
result is technically correct, Riley and Li (1999) show that even the theoretical revenue difference is of a very small magnitude. This means that if
there are any small deviations in the bidding strategies used or in the

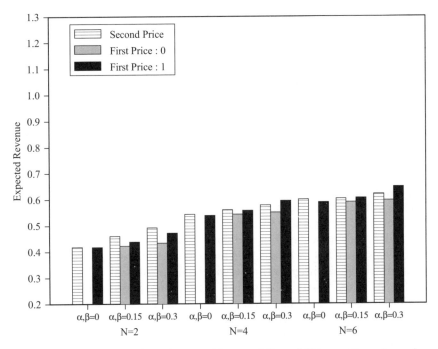

Fig. 2. Revenue Comparisons between First- and Second-Price auctions Assuming Normally Distributed Values for 2, 4 and 6 Bidder Auctions. The Cases Considered Involve Fully Symmetric Bidders with the Parameters Indicated. The First Price 0 and 1 Bars Represent Cases in which the Bidders Believe $\bar{\beta}$ and $\bar{\alpha}$ are Equal to 0 and 1 Times the True Parameters.

environment between the standard Milgrom and Weber (1982) theory and a field application, the revenue ranking could very easily be upset. Our claim is identical in that we show that while in the case of these charitable preferences it is possible to show theoretically that the second price raises at least as much money as the first, the theoretical difference is small and could be easily upset by other environmental factors not included in the basic theory.

Fig. 2 contains the second important result, which is that in the case of normally distributed values the revenue outcome from a first-price auction is highly contingent upon the beliefs of the bidders. The result is that revenue significantly decreases if the bidders underestimate the preferences for charitable giving among the rest of the population. The change in revenue caused by the change in beliefs is of approximately the same order as the change in revenue derived from changing auction formats.

4.2. See and Be Seen

The SBS model involves some bidders possessing $\beta_i > 0$, while others possess $\beta_j = 0$ and all bidders possess $\alpha_i = \alpha_j = 0$. This case is intended to represent cases of charitable bidding in which a bidder derives utility from having others see him as giving generously to support the charity while he derives no utility just from the fact that the charity gets more money. A straightforward application of the standard Revenue Equivalence Theorem will show that if all bidders possessed equal β_is with $\alpha_i = 0$, then expected revenue would be constant across both mechanisms. To see this clearly, consider the case of uniformly distributed values. The equilibrium bid functions for the second-price auction and first-price auctions are $v_i/(1 - \beta_i)$ and $((n - 1)/n)(v_i/(1 - \beta_i)$, respectively.[11] The effect of the β_i is just to make a bidder who has a value of v_i bid as if his true value were $v_i/(1 - \beta_i)$. Thus with symmetric β_is, all bidders inflate their bids by the same proportional amount over the case with all β_is equal to 0, which can be thought of as just an upward shift of the value distribution with people otherwise bidding "normally." No conditions of the RET are violated by such a monotonic transformation of values leading to both mechanisms yielding equivalent revenue and perfect efficiency. Of course with the upward shift in the value distribution, the revenues when $\beta_i > 0$ will not be equivalent to the case when $\beta_i = 0$.

Adding asymmetry to the bidders' parameters will break revenue equivalence and lead to inefficiency but interestingly enough, it will not break efficiency equivalence between the mechanisms. Efficiency equivalence is maintained because the effect of the β_is is effectively to just re-scale the value that a bidder is bidding as if they possess resulting in a new set of what might be considered "modified" values. Both auction formats turn out to be "efficient" with respect to these modified valuations as the bidder with the highest modified valuation will win in both. That bidder may not have the highest allocative value or v_is and since we are considering only the v_is for measuring true efficiency, we will measure the auctions as being occasionally inefficient.

Figs. 3 and 4 show the revenue comparisons between first- and second-price auctions for both low and high β cases for 2, 4 and 6 bidder auctions. Under both low and high[12] β cases, half of the bidders possess $\beta_i = 0.15$ or $\beta_i = 0.5$, while the other half possess $\beta_j = 0$. The results from the normal distribution include the results from three different belief specifications. The 0 case involves all bidders expecting their opponents to have parameters equal to 0 times the actual parameters of the bidders with $\beta_i > 0$. The 0.5 case involves beliefs where these values are multiplied by 0.5 and the 1 case,

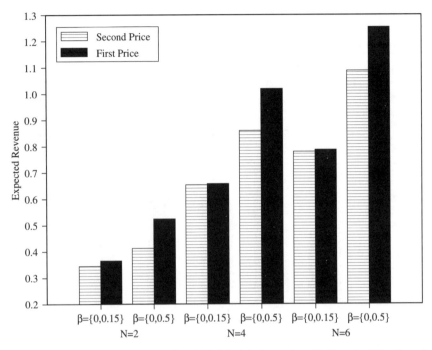

Fig. 3. Revenue Comparisons for SBS Model Assuming Uniformly Distributed Values for Auctions with 2, 4 and 6 Bidders. The Cases Shown Involve Half of the Bidders Possessing each of the Indicated βs while $\alpha_i = \alpha_j = 0$.

multiplied by 1. Seeing all of these cases allows us to examine what happens when people under and overestimate the average parameters in the population as well as get them approximately correct. Again, we only present the mis-specified belief revenue results for the first-price case in the normal distribution because there was no effect in the second-price revenue totals for either the uniform or normal distributions.

Fig. 3 contains the revenue comparison between the auction formats under the assumption of uniformly distributed values. In the low β case, $\beta_i = 0.15$, the first-price auction achieves slightly more revenue than does the second price but in the high β_i case, $\beta_i = 0.5$, the first price achieves strikingly more revenue than the second. The reason for this is that in both first- and second-price auctions, the bidders with $\beta_i > 0$ inflate their bids over what the $\beta_j = 0$ bidders would bid at the same values and these $\beta_i > 0$ bidders win much more often. In the first-price case, the auctioneer gets the full benefit of this inflated bid. In the second-price case, the auctioneer may see a

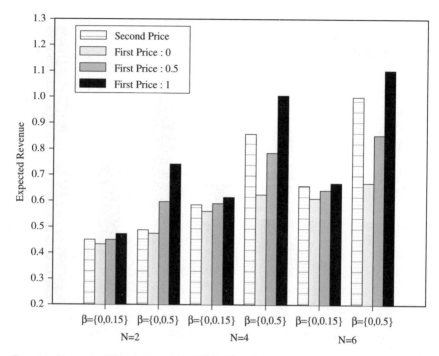

Fig. 4. Revenue Comparisons for SBS Model Assuming Normally Distributed Values for Auctions with 2, 4 and 6 Bidders. The Cases Shown Correspond to Half the Bidders Possessing each of the Noted βs while $\alpha_i = \alpha_j = 0$. For each Case, there are Three Belief Specifications with Bidders Believing that β is Equal to 1, 0.5 or 0 Times the High β.

very high bid from the $\beta_i > 0$ bidder, but the price the auctioneer receives might be set by the $\beta_j = 0$ bidder, which is not inflated. This can cause the revenue in the second-price auction to be significantly lower than the first price for large values of β_i. The effect is stronger in the 2 bidder case as it is almost always the $\beta_j = 0$ bidder setting the price in the second-price auction while in the 4 and 6 bidder cases, the prices are occasionally set by the other $\beta_i > 0$ bidders.

In the case of normally distributed values, the same effect holds to some extent, but as Fig. 4 shows, the beliefs on the part of the bidders are absolutely crucial to the revenue ranking. In the cases involving the bidders underestimating the charitable giving of their opponents, the revenue of the first price plummets to well below the revenue achieved by the second price. As the perceived preferences for charitable giving increase, revenue increases such that when this is overestimated, the revenue from the first price is significantly greater than the second price. When expectations are approximately accurate, the revenue ranking is indeterminate. In practical terms it appears that for the first-price auction to dominate the second, all participants must think that just about all of the other participants are "show-offs" or high β types.

The reason for this pattern is that in a first-price auction, a bidder bids by estimating the minimum amount he must bid in expectation to shut out his closest rival. If he believes his closest rival to have a low β, then he can shade his bid by much more than if he expects his opponent to have a high β. Bidders in second-price auctions again are unconcerned with the preferences of their opponents so long as their αs are zero and therefore revenue is unchanged across the changing beliefs. These results demonstrate that asymmetries across bidders and the beliefs possessed concerning the preferences of others can have important impacts on revenue that are completely overlooked by the revenue equivalence result obtainable with symmetric β_is.

While efficiency is identical across both institutions, the asymmetric parameters do introduce inefficiency. In the low β_i case, efficiencies are around 0.98, while the high β_i case drops the efficiencies down to around 0.91. These efficiency numbers are approximately equivalent for both value distributions and only drop slightly as the number of bidders increases.

4.3. Raising Rivals' Cost

When bidders are interested in RRC, it seems that simple "common sense" would lead one to suppose that this should lead to increased auction revenue. Our results will very clearly show the exact opposite, at least when this motivation is modeled as we have done here. Understanding the reason for this result will prove quite interesting.

Fig. 5 shows the revenue comparisons for the RRC case under the assumption of uniformly distributed values. We have again presented examples of low and high values of the parameters or $\alpha_i = 0.15$ and $\alpha_i = 0.5$. We have also constructed each case such that half of the bidders possess this $\alpha_i > 0$, while the other half possess $\alpha_j = 0$ and all bidders possess $\beta_i = \beta_j = 0$. This is the first time that the different belief structures have an effect on revenues in the second-price auction and thus we have included bars for the second-price revenue under the 0, 0.5 and 1 specifications. The different belief specifications, as usual, have no discernible impact on the revenue in the first-price auction when assuming uniformly distributed values. For ease of comparison, we have also included a baseline bar of the revenue achievable in a

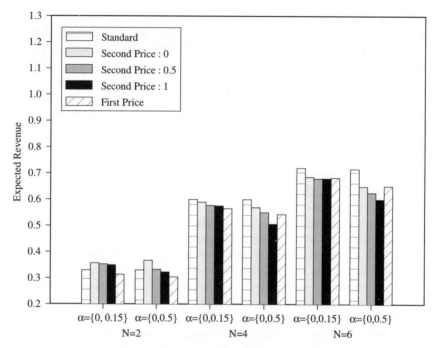

Fig. 5. Revenue Comparisons for RRC Model Assuming Uniformly Distributed Values for Auctions with 2, 4 and 6 Bidders. The Cases Shown Correspond to Half the Bidders Possessing the αs Indicated while $\beta_i = \beta_j = 0$. The Standard Bar is the Revenue Expected without Price Preferences while the Three Second-Price Bars Correspond to Expectations that $\bar{\alpha}$ is Equal to 0, 0.5 or 1 Times the High α.

standard auction with $\alpha_i = \beta_i = 0$ for all bidders. This allows us to see very clearly that when $n > 2$ revenue in both auctions is decreasing in α_i. When $n = 2$ and α_i is low, this can lead to slightly more revenue than the standard case. We can also clearly see that revenue is decreasing in the beliefs about the opponents' value of $\bar{\alpha}$ for the second-price auctions. This should be expected as $\partial\left((v_i(1 + \bar{\alpha}) + \alpha_i)/(1 + 2\alpha_i)(1 + \bar{\alpha})\right)/\partial\bar{\alpha} = -\alpha_i/(1 + 2\alpha_i)(1 + \bar{\alpha})^2 < 0$. Note that since all of the $\alpha_i > 0$ bidders will have $\alpha_i \geq \bar{\alpha}$ and all others have $\alpha_j = 0$, the lower bound is never an issue.

Neither auction format performs significantly better in insulating the auctioneer against this drop in revenue, though the best case for the auctioneer is for all bidders to believe that no other bidders possess a positive value of $\alpha > 0$. These results are echoed in the case of normally distributed values as shown in Fig. 6. This figure contains the revenue achievable by a

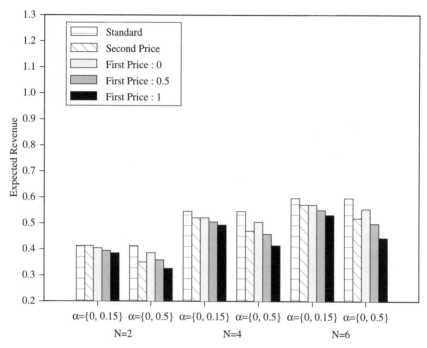

Fig. 6. Revenue Comparisons for RRC Model Assuming Normally Distributed Values for Auctions with 2, 4 and 6 Bidders. The Cases Shown Correspond to Half the Bidders Possessing the αs Indicated with $\beta_i = \beta_j = 0$. The Standard Bar is the Revenue Expected without Price Preferences while the Three First-Price Bars Correspond to Expectations that $\bar{\alpha}$ is Equal to 0, 0.5 or 1 Times the High α.

second-price auction and then that achievable by a first-price auction under three different belief conditions along with the standard revenue from assuming $\alpha_i = \beta_i = 0$. The different belief specifications had no effect on the revenue in the second-price auctions, but they did affect the first-price auctions. The results show again that revenue is generally decreasing in α and that the best case for the auctioneer in the event that positive αs exist is for all bidders to assume otherwise.

The reason for higher α_is reducing revenue in first-price auctions is fairly straightforward. In a first-price auction, if a bidder derives utility from his opponent paying a higher price, there is unfortunately nothing that bidder can do to make his opponent pay a higher price. The effect of the α term serves only to make losing more attractive. The higher the α, the more attractive is losing and thus the lower a bidder will bid in an attempt to win.

This effect is easy to show in the case of uniformly distributed values as $\partial\big(B_F^*(v_i, \beta_i, \alpha_i, \bar{\beta}, \bar{\alpha})\big)\big/\partial\alpha_i = -(n-1)^2\big/(\alpha_i - n - n\alpha_i + n\beta_i)^2 v_i < 0$.

In the second-price auction, the effect of α_i is more complex. For example, in the case of uniformly distributed values, $\partial\big(B_S^*(v_i, \beta_i, \alpha_i, \bar{\beta}, \bar{\alpha})\big)\big/\partial\alpha_i = (1 - 2v_i - 2v_i\bar{\alpha})\big/(1 + 2\alpha_i)^2(1 + \bar{\alpha})$ possesses an indeterminate sign. It is positive so long as $v_i \leq 1/(2 + 2\bar{\alpha})$ and negative otherwise. To see the effect under normally distributed values it is easier to examine some examples of bid functions. Fig. 7 contains sample bid functions for normally distributed values for $\alpha_i = 0$, $\alpha_i = 0.15$ and $\alpha_i = 0.5$ with the bidders assuming that $\bar{\alpha} = \alpha_i$.[13] These show that for values less than a threshold, the α causes the bidder to inflate their bid over what an $\alpha_i = 0$ bidder would use but for values greater than this point, the bids are lower. Also, the $\alpha_i = 0.5$ bids are the lowest.

The curious part is why this is so and whether or not this can be rationalized with the idea of a bidder being interested in RRC. The issue is made more complicated when viewed in light of the results in Morgan et al. (2002) (MSR). In MSR, the authors construct a model in which bidders are

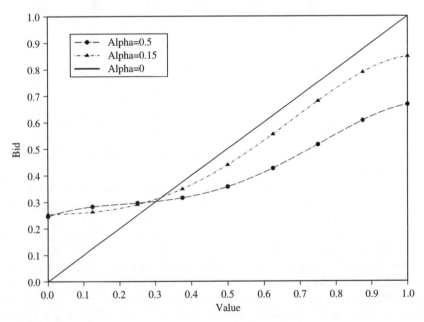

Fig. 7. Bid Functions for Second-Price Auctions Assuming Normally Distributed Values for Three Different Values of α with $\beta = 0$.

motivated by spite. Their model assumes that bidder i suffers a utility loss of $\alpha(v_j - p)$ when they lose the auction to bidder j. In other words, bidders have a goal of minimizing the surplus that their rival achieves. MSR shows that such a motivation leads bidders to regularly bid above their value in second-price and ascending auctions. This is a curious juxtaposition of results, as both our framework and the MSR framework would seem suited to modeling similar behavior. A careful understanding of the reasons the two approaches arrive at the different results reveals that the two approaches are modeling subtly different behavior.

In our framework, if a bidder has a low value and is likely to lose, he bids specifically to make his rival pay a higher price. For a bidder with a higher value who would likely win, his focus changes. As the price rises, losing becomes relatively more attractive. He ends up bidding under his value because if he bids a little less than v_i and loses but would have won bidding v_i, he does not decrease his expected value much because there are few such cases and the profit he would have made in them is small. The bidder instead gains higher utility from the $\alpha_i p$ term by allowing the other bidder to win at a high price. The predatory interpretation of this might be that they are avoiding the cases in which they win with little profit, preferring instead for their rival to win at a higher price. If one supposes that the motivation for having an $\alpha_i > 0$ is to harm a competitor the harm might be that if these two rivals are in repeated competition, the $\alpha_i > 0$ bidder has forced the other bidder to pay a high price in the current auction and perhaps tie up resources that the competitor might otherwise put into a subsequent auction. If true, that could allow the $\alpha_i > 0$ bidder to win the next auction at a higher surplus than otherwise possible. Thus, while the result of revenue decreasing in α_i is initially somewhat counterintuitive, it appears to be quite sensible in terms of what might motivate bidders to engage in such behavior.

It is interesting to note that this result is quite similar to the one shown in Pitchik and Schotter (1988). In that paper, the authors derive equilibria for sequential auctions with budget constrained bidders. One of the properties of their bid functions is

Property 2. Under Second price rules, bidder i strictly prefers to lose good 1 to bidder $j \neq i$ at higher prices rather than lower prices so long as the higher price is at least as great as c^i.

In this case, the incentive to raise rivals cost was derived endogenously into a multiple period auction model and the effect on the bidding strategy seems quite similar. The advantage of our method of modeling this motivation is that it can be applied to a broader range of situations. One could also think of using a framing like this as a heuristic for deriving approx-imately accurate bidding strategies for sequential auctions with longer time-lines than the two modeled in Pitchik and Schotter (1988). This is because solving for the truly optimal bid functions would get quite difficult as the number of items increases.

If we try to explain the MSR result in a similar manner, it is no longer necessarily true that as your value rises, the idea of losing at a price slightly below your value becomes attractive. If a bidder i bids below his value and if any bidder j wins, i has made j strictly better off. This in turn makes i strictly worse off. Thus it is not attractive to bid below one's value in the MSR framework. In fact, due to the possibility of making the eventual winner less happy, it becomes attractive to bid above your value. Subtly different ways of modeling similar phenomena, therefore, have substantially different effects on bidding behavior and revenue. It appears that the MSR frame-work is likely best suited to the notion of pure spite while our framework is better suited to an indirect pecuniary motivation to raise the price paid by a rival.

For an auctioneer concerned with efficiency, RRC is the first case that is not efficiency-equivalent. In practical terms, however, efficiency is approx-imately equivalent as neither format consistently outperforms the other.

5. CONCLUSION

We have investigated the consequences for auction outcomes stemming from situations in which bidders possess preferences over the revenue achieved by the auctioneer. In doing so, we have been careful to also in-vestigate the effects of different belief specifications on the outcome of such auctions. This allows us to point out several issues that may be important to those wishing to conduct auctions in such environments. Ultimately, the importance of these issues is an empirical phenomenon, which we will be seeking to carefully test in future work.

The first point to make is that despite the results in EW and Engers and McManus (2002), an auctioneer should be quite skeptical of the purported revenue benefits of using a second-price or ascending auction instead of a first-price auction for standard charity auctions. While it does seem the case that many charity auctions are run with a roughly ascending format, see Isaac and Schnier (2005) for more details, which should not be taken as *prima facia* evidence that they raise more revenue in the field. There may be many other institutional considerations that make them more attractive.

Alternatively, if there are revenue benefits from using them, they may well be derived from other issues such as bidders being more comfortable participating in them rather than sealed bid auctions, which is an effect demonstrated in Ivanova-Stenzel and Salmon (2004).

Second, the results based on different belief specifications are useful for practical auctioneers as they may indicate possibilities for the auctioneer to manipulate beliefs or expectations in their favor. For example, in the SBS case, it was found that revenue was strongly increasing in the belief bidders had about the βs of the other bidders and that first-price auctions could have a revenue edge over ascending. If an auctioneer can somehow transmit information to the bidders about how great the preference is of others to give to the charity or in some other way shift bidders' beliefs about the βs of their rivals, then this could benefit the auctioneer. Similarly, if bidders are deriving their utility from being seen as generous, the more the auctioneer can do to facilitate the visibility of such winners, the more willing they are likely to be to bid higher. A design change to take advantage of such preferences might be to have a number of sealed bid auctions that close at different times during the night of the charity auction in which the auctioneer makes public announcements after each auction, naming exactly who was the winning bidder and how much they bid. The general difficulty of running sealed bid auctions for such purposes is that some bidders might leave after placing their bids. Thus, doing things like holding several auctions over the course of the night or having other things going on to make sure bidders stay around to make the bid revelation more visible may be helpful.

If, however, an auctioneer believes that there may be bidders in their population who have an interest in raising their rivals' costs, our results suggest other important issues for the auctioneer to consider. At first thought, such bidders would seem helpful to an auctioneer who might be tempted to either encourage or at least not discourage such behavior. Our results suggest that the auctioneer should discourage such behavior as much as possible because revenue is decreasing in α_i for $n > 2$. The auctioneer should also work to convince bidders that such predatory bidders are rare.

In our introduction we briefly mentioned several other situations that are encompassed by our model but that we have not investigated here. Going through all of them is beyond the scope of the paper, but our methods can be extended to each of them. From preliminary investigations with the shill-bidding case, we can say that using a price-preference contract to motivate a shill is almost always revenue decreasing for the auctioneer. The auctioneer can almost always do better with a reserve price than they can with a shill.

The reasons should be fairly obvious from the results above based on the effect of raising α_i on the revenue of the auctioneer. This is a topic of further investigation.

NOTES

1. We note that, in the process of working on this project, we found that many of the results for this case have been separately derived in Engers and McManus (2002).

2. Pecuniary-based preferences in this case might be derived from charity auctions attended by parents held on behalf of their child's school. Part of the money raised by the auction may be used to benefit their child thus granting them pecuniary benefits from the auctioneer raising more money.

3. The types of regulatory costs include geographically restrictive, expensive, prolonged or discretionary licensure (e.g. Georgia and local option Illinois), licensing, training or bonding requirements for individuals in the organization (e.g. Colorado), duration of business requirements (e.g. Texas, Colorado, local option Illinois) restrictions on advertising (Texas), frequency limits (e.g. Georgia), restrictions on allowable prizes (e.g. Texas), reporting and record requirements (e.g. Arizona, Georgia), specifications for ticket printing (e.g. Colorado), gross receipts subject to sales tax (e.g. Iowa) and funds segregation (e.g. Colorado). And, of course, in any state there are federal record keeping and reporting requirements for tax purposes that may daunt smaller organizations. More specific citations on these legal issues are available from authors upon request.

4. *American Tobacco Company v. United States*, 328 U.S. 781 (1946).

5. David A. Price, American Antitrust Institute, http://www.antitrustinstitute.org/recent/82.cfm.

6. Universal Mobile Telecommunications System.

7. Most auctioneers would only consider subsidizing a proper subset of the bidders who are deemed to be disadvantaged in relation to another set. The FCC, however, has chosen to subsidize all of the bidders in some of their auctions.

8. Our approach has an attractive side benefit, which is that it is also more computationally tractable, but that is not our main motivation for using it.

9. We have chosen to use graphs in presenting these revenue comparisons to allow for easy visual comparisons in levels. We have prepared a separate appendix listing all of the numbers behind these tables and claims along with tests of significance available at http://garnet.acns.fsu.edu/tsalmon.

10. There are two of the high parameter value cases in the graph showing the first price achieving more revenue than the second. The actual differences are small, in the range of 0.01, and are largely from a small degree of rounding in some of the numerical calculations.

11. Recall that in the standard case, without price preference valuations, the bid functions are v_i and $((n-1)/n)v_i$.

12. We chose to use a higher value for the high β value for the SBS case and RRC case we will present later because of a belief that such extreme values are more plausible in these cases and we wanted to explore the effect of such extreme

preferences. We retained the same lower value for consistency with the baseline charity case.

13. This figure shows what might be thought of as a counterintuitive result, which is that both $\alpha_i = 0.15$ and $\alpha_i = 0.5$ bid functions possess approximately the same lower bound. This is not an error. The true lower bounds are 0.253 for the $\alpha_i = 0.15$ case and 0.249 for $\alpha_i = 0.5$, which can be derived from the analytical symmetric bid function.

REFERENCES

Corns, A., & Schotter, A. (1999). Can affirmative action be cost effective? An experimental examination of price-preference auctions. *American Economic Review, 89*(1), 291–305.

Davis, D. D., Razzolini, L., Reilly, R., & Wilson, B. J. (2003). *Raising revenue for charity: Auctions versus lotteries.* Working Paper, Virginia Commonwealth University.

de Frutos, M. A. (2000). Asymmetric price-benefits auctions. *Games and Economic Behavior, 33*, 48–71.

Engelbrecht-Wiggans, R. (1994). Auctions with price proportional benefits to bidders. *Games and Economic Behavior, 6*, 339–346.

Engers, M., & McManus, B. (2002). *Charity auctions.* Working Paper, University of Virginia.

Goeree, J. K., Maasland, E., Onderstal, S., & Turner, J. L. (2004). *How (not) to raise money.* CREED Working Paper.

Isaac, R. M., Salmon, T. C., & Zillante, A. (2006). A theory of jump bidding in ascending auctions. *Journal of Economic Behavior and Organization.*

Isaac, R. M., & Schnier, K. (2005). Silent charity auctions: Revenue effects of alternative bidding formats. *Economic Inquiry, 43*, 715–733.

Ivanova-Stenzel, R., & Salmon, T. C. (2004). Bidder preferences among auction institutions. *Economic Inquiry, 42*, 223–236.

Kagel, J. H. (1995). Auctions: A survey of experimental research. In: J. H. Kagel & A. E. Roth (Eds), *The handbook of experimental economics* (pp. 501–586). Princeton, NJ: Princeton University Press.

Klemperer, P. (2002a). Some observations on the British 3G telecom auction: Comments on Börgers and Dustmann. *ifo Studien, 48*, 115–120.

Klemperer, P. (2002b). *Using and abusing economic theory – lessons from auction design.* Working Paper, Oxford University.

McAfee, P. (1992). Amicable divorce: Dissolving a partnership with simple mechanisms. *Journal of Economic Theory, 56*, 266–293.

Milgrom, P. R., & Weber, R. J. (1982). A theory of auctions and competitive bidding. *Econometrica, 50*(5), 1089–1122.

Morgan, J., Steiglitz, K., & Reis, G. (2002). *The spite motive and equilibrium behavior in auctions.* Working Paper.

Pitchik, C., & Schotter, A. (1988). Perfect equilibria in budget-constrained sequential auctions: An experimental study. *RAND Journal of Economics, 19*(3), 363–388.

Riley, J. G., & Li, H. (1999). *Auction choice.* Mimeo, University of California, Los Angeles.

Shachat, J., & Swarthout, J. T. (2002). *Procurement auctions for differentiated goods.* Working Paper, IBM Research Labs.

APPENDIX. BIDDING STRATEGY IN SYMMETRIC FIRST-PRICE AUCTIONS

If we hypothesize the existence of the bid function $b_f^*(v_i, \beta, \alpha)$ that is used by the other $n - 1$ bidders each of whom possess the same parameters for β and α, we can find what its form must be by determining what value bidder i would choose to submit to such a bid function. Since in this case, the bid function will be symmetric, we can see that the probability of winning if i bids as if their value were r is $\Pr(b_f^*(r, \beta, \alpha) > b_f^*(v_j, \beta, \alpha)$ for all $j) = \Pr(r > v_j$ for all $j) = F(r)^{n-1}$. Letting $\rho(r) = F(r)^{n-1}$ define the probability of winning given that bidder i has bid according to value r, we have:

$$\max_r S(v_i, r) = (v_i - (1 - \beta)b_f^*(r, \beta, \alpha))\rho(r) + \alpha \int_r^1 b_f^*(t, \beta, \alpha)d\rho(t) \quad (11)$$

Equilibrium condition is

$$\frac{\partial(S(v_i, r))}{\partial r}\Big|_{r=v_i} = 0 \quad (12)$$

FOC: noting that $\dfrac{\partial\left(\int_p^y f(x)dx\right)}{\partial p} = -f(p)$

$$v_i\rho'(r) - (1 - \beta)b_f^*(r, \beta, \alpha)\rho'(r) - (1 - \beta)\rho(r)b_f^{*'}(r, \beta, \alpha) - \alpha b_f^*(r, \beta, \alpha)\rho(r) = 0 \quad (13)$$

$$(1 - \beta + \alpha)b_f^*(r, \beta, \alpha)\rho'(r) + (1 - \beta)\rho(r)b_f^{*'}(r, \beta, \alpha) = v_i\rho'(r) \quad (14)$$

If we multiply both sides by $\rho(r)^{(\alpha)/(1-\beta)}$, we get:

$$(1 - \beta + \alpha)b_f^*(r, \beta, \alpha)\rho(r)^{\frac{\alpha}{1-\beta}}\rho'(r) + (1 - \beta_i)\rho(r)^{\frac{1-\beta+\alpha}{1-\beta}}b_f^{*'}(r, \beta, \alpha) = v_i\rho'(r)\rho(r)^{\frac{\alpha}{1-\beta}} \quad (15)$$

Which allows us to write the left side as $\dfrac{\partial\left((1-\beta_i)b_f^*(r,\beta,\alpha)\rho(r)^{(1-\beta+\alpha)/(1-\beta)}\right)}{\partial r}$, and also noting that in equilibrium $r = v_i$ we have

$$\frac{\partial\left((1 - \beta)b_f^*(r, \beta, \alpha)\rho(r)^{(1-\beta+\alpha)/(1-\beta)}\right)}{\partial r} = v_i\rho'(v_i)\rho(v_i)^{\frac{\alpha}{1-\beta}} \quad (16)$$

Since this condition must hold for all values, we can integrate both sides between 0 and v_i:

$$\int_0^{v_i} \frac{\partial\left((1 - \beta)b^*(t, \beta, \alpha)\rho(t)^{(1-\beta+\alpha)/(1-\beta)}\right)}{\partial t}dt = \int_0^{v_i} t\rho'(t)\rho(t)^{\frac{\alpha_i}{1-\beta_i}}dt \quad (17)$$

Using boundary condition that $b_f^*(0, \beta, \alpha) = 0$, we get

$$(1 - \beta)b_f^*(v_i, \beta, \alpha)\rho(v_i)^{\frac{1-\beta+\alpha}{1-\beta}} = \int_0^{v_i} t\rho'(t)\rho(t)^{\frac{\alpha}{1-\beta}}dt \qquad (18)$$

$$b_f^*(v_i, \beta, \alpha) = \frac{\int_0^{v_i} t\rho'(t)\rho(t)^{\frac{\alpha}{1-\beta}}dt}{(1 - \beta)\rho(v_i)^{\frac{1-\beta+\alpha}{1-\beta}}} \qquad (19)$$

since $\rho(x) = F(x)^{n-1}$ then $\rho'(x) = (n - 1)f(x)F(x)^{n-2}$ so

$$b_f^*(v_i, \beta, \alpha) = \frac{\int_0^{v_i} t(n - 1)f(t)F(t)^{(n+\beta(2-n)+\alpha(n-1)-2)/(1-\beta)}dt}{(1 - \beta)(F(v_i)^{n-1})^{(1-\beta+\alpha)/(1-\beta)}} \qquad (20)$$

This will be a valid equilibrium bid function so long as it is differentiable and monotonically increasing, which can be shown by extension of Engelbrecht-Wiggans (1994) or as in Engers and McManus (2002).

BID FUNCTION IN SYMMETRIC SECOND-PRICE AUCTIONS

For this case we must consider three possibilities. First is what I expect to get if I win, second is what I get if I come in second and third is what I expect if I come in less than second. We again assume that some monotonic and differentiable bid function $b_s^*(v)$ exists and we wish to check to see if i wants to bid as if they possess some value r instead of v_i.

$$S(v_i, r) = \int_0^r (v_i - (1 - \beta)b_s^*(t, \beta, \alpha))dF(t)^{n-1} +$$

$$\alpha b_s^*(r, \beta, \alpha)(n - 1)F(r)^{n-2}(1 - F(r)) +$$

$$\alpha\left(\int_r^1 b_s^*(t, \beta, \alpha)(n - 2)(n - 1)F(t)^{n-3}(1 - F(t))dF(t)\right) \qquad (21)$$

Equilibrium condition is again that $\frac{\partial(S(v_i, r))}{\partial r}\big|_{r=v_i} = 0$

Taking the derivative we get:

$$v\frac{dF(r)^{n-1}}{dr} + b_s^*(r)(\beta-1)\frac{dF(r)^{n-1}}{dr} - b_s^*(r,\beta,\alpha)\alpha(1-F(r))F(r)(n-2)\frac{dF(r)^{n-1}}{dr}$$

$$+ b_s^*(r,\beta,\alpha)\alpha F^{n-2}(r)(n-1)(1-F(r)) - b_s^*(r)\alpha\frac{\partial F(r)^{n-1}}{\partial r}$$

$$+ b_s^*(r,\beta,\alpha)\alpha F(r)(1-F(r))(n-2)\frac{\partial F(r)^{n-1}}{\partial r} = 0 \tag{22}$$

This will simplify to

$$vf(r) = b_s^*(r,\beta,\alpha)(1-\beta+\alpha)f(r) - b_s^*(r,\beta,\alpha)\alpha(1-F(r)) \tag{23}$$

multiply everything by $-\frac{(1-F(r))^{(1-\beta)/(\alpha)}}{\alpha_i}$ and get

$$-vf(r)\frac{(1-F(r))^{(1-\beta)/(\alpha)}}{\alpha} = -b_s^*(r,\beta,\alpha)(1-\beta+\alpha)f(r)\frac{(1-F(r))^{(1-\beta)/(\alpha)}}{\alpha}$$

$$+ b_s^*(r,\beta,\alpha)(1-F(r))^{1+(1-\beta)/(\alpha)} \tag{24}$$

Notice that $(1-F(\bar{x})) = 0$ if $\bar{x}$ is the max of the distribution. Also, since this condition must hold for all v, we can integrate both sides:

$$\int_r^1 \frac{\partial(b_s^*(t,\beta,\alpha)(1-F(t))^{(1+\alpha-\beta)/(\alpha)})}{dt}dt = \int_r^1 \frac{t}{1+\alpha-\beta}\frac{\partial((1-F(t))^{(1+\alpha-\beta)/(\alpha)})}{\partial t}dt \tag{25}$$

In equilibrium $r = v$, and we also need an obvious correction for the case $\alpha_i = 0$

$$b_s^*(v,\beta,\alpha) = \begin{cases} \dfrac{1}{\alpha}\dfrac{\int_v^1 t(1-F(t))^{(1-\beta)/(\alpha)}\,dF(t)}{(1-F(v))^{(1+\alpha-\beta)/(\alpha)}}, & \text{if } \alpha > 0 \\[2ex] \dfrac{v}{1-\beta}, & \text{if } \alpha = 0 \end{cases} \tag{26}$$

SEALED BID VARIATIONS ON THE SILENT AUCTION

R. Mark Isaac and Kurt Schnier

ABSTRACT

Motivated by both prior experimental work and by field observations, we consider the performance of two different sealed bid versions of the silent auction. These are important institutional alternatives to the more familiar ascending price silent auction. In a new series of laboratory experiments, we investigate the effects of the different institutions both on aggregate efficiency and upon aggregate revenue generation.

1. INTRODUCTION

A silent auction is one in which a seller displays multiple items for sale, while potential buyers make open ascending (but written, and hence the term "silent") bids at each item's bidding station. The seller is usually, but not necessarily, a charitable organization. All auctions close by a clock, which is typically a common clock across many, if not all, of the items. The popularity of this institution appears to rest in part upon the attending social activity of the auction and also upon its low cost to the charity of selling a large number of donated items at low transactions cost. Isaac and Schnier (2005) reported on a combined field and experimental analysis of charitable

Experiments Investigating Fundraising and Charitable Contributors
Research in Experimental Economics, Volume 11, 31–46
Copyright © 2006 by Elsevier Ltd.
ISSN: 0193-2306/doi:10.1016/S0193-2306(06)11002-9

silent auctions. One of the surprising results of that study was that, although the auctions were quite efficient, revenue levels were less than what might have been expected. This has led us to consider the efficacy of altering the silent auction institution, specifically, changing the open, written, ascending bidding format to sealed bidding. In this paper, we pursue this line of inquiry.[1]

In Section 2, we provide more detail on the background to this research question. In Section 3, we provide the experimental design, and in Section 4 we discuss some relevant theory. The experimental results are presented and analyzed in Section 5 and Section 6 provides a brief conclusion summarizing the implications of our findings.

2. BACKGROUND

In the experimental part of Isaac and Schnier, the (ascending) silent auction performed well in its task of allocating a large number of items with relatively high efficiency (mean efficiency of 0.9488 in a treatment where the minimum bid increment was 25 cents, mean efficiency of 0.9687 in a treatment where the minimum bid increment was 50 cents).[2] What is perhaps surprising is the relatively poor performance of auctions on the revenue index (means of 0.8131 in the 25 cent minimum treatment and 0.9271 in the 50-cent treatment, where an index of 1.000 indicates the benchmark set by the sum of the second highest values).[3]

Our motivation for the research reported here stems both from these laboratory results and also from two empirical observations. Our first empirical observation is that, in discussing silent auctions with actual field participants, we frequently have heard some variation on the following. Participants report that, because of the geographic dispersion of the items, they pay less attention to their lower valued items in order to "guard" or "stand watch over" the bidding stations of their higher value items. If the subjects in the Isaac and Schnier experiments were following a similar strategy, then that could easily explain the dichotomy between the relatively high efficiencies versus the disappointing revenues. Bidders making sure to carefully follow the bidding on their high-value items should produce relatively high efficiencies. However, bidders not participating in or not carefully following the bidding on their lower value items would mean less aggressive bidding by bidders with values who are more likely to be setting the price than winning. Indeed, it is easy to find examples of bidding consistent with this behavior in the experiments.[4]

Our second empirical observation is that not all silent auctions operate using the ascending format. A small proportion operates on a "sealed bid" format in which bidders write bids on pieces of papers and place them in a container, one container for each item.[5] What we suggest here is that this alternative institution, the "sealed bid silent auction," might yield greater revenue than the ascending version. As one would expect with a sealed bid format, efficiencies might suffer, but charities are, after all, more interested in revenue that in economic efficiency. The purpose of this paper is to analyze the performance of the sealed bid silent auction in the same laboratory silent auction test bed used in Isaac and Schnier.

3. DESIGN OF THE CURRENT EXPERIMENTS

We replicated most aspects of the experimental design of Isaac and Schnier with the obvious exception of changing the form of the auction. In brief, there were 16 items for sale simultaneously and geographically dispersed around the room according to Fig. 1. There were eight potential bidders. For each item in each period, the number of active (non-zero value) bidders, between two and eight inclusive, was randomly chosen with a uniform distribution. Then, the subject IDs to receive the positive values were randomly chosen. Finally, each bidder with a positive value had a value randomly chosen in the interval (0.00, 20.00) using a uniform distribution. The subjects were informed of these random processes.

The new institutions tested were the first- and the second-price sealed bid auction. At each bidding station, we placed a "supersized" foam coffee mug with an opaque, slotted top. The letter of the associated item was clearly marked on each mug. Each bidder had a pad of bidding slips on which they

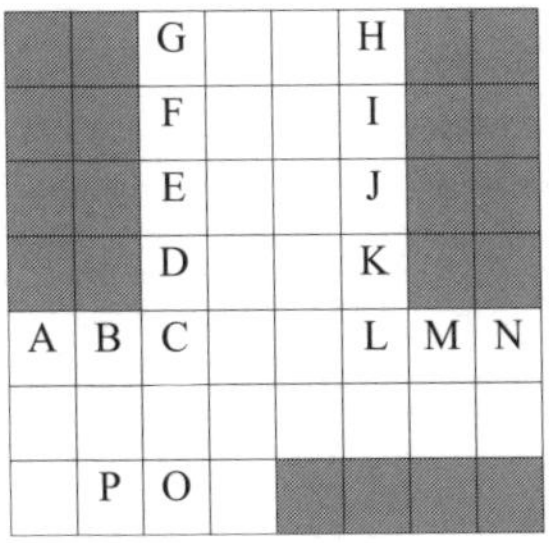

		G		H		
		F		I		
		E		J		
		D		K		
A	B	C		L	M	N
	P	O				

Fig. 1. Geographical Dispersion of Bidding Stations.

were required to write their bidder ID, the item being bid on, their bid, and the time remaining on the clock.[6] They then inserted the bidding slip into the mug.[7]

A design feature that we had some difficulty in standardizing was the clock time of the auctions. In Isaac and Schnier, periods lasted 12 min. One obvious possibility was keeping the clock time at 12 min. The problem with this approach is that while standardizing on clock time, the faster pace of the sealed bid auction had the potential to lengthen the "boredom" time of the subjects, an artifact that presumably would not be present in the field, given the embedded social environment of many silent auctions. Volunteer graduate students assisted us in calibrating this question, and agreed that 12 min would impose a substantial boredom factor on the subjects. We decided on 7 min clock time to approximate the same "pace" as the previous auctions.[8]

We decided to reproduce the structure and the value-draws of Isaac and Schnier. Specifically, each session consisted of five periods with the value assignments within each period being the same as Isaac and Schnier. Unlike the previous research, we elected to exclude the charitable bonus payments in periods 3 and 4. In other words, we are focusing solely on the effect of the institutional change itself without looking at the interactive effects of institutional change and the value-environment treatment used by Isaac and Schnier. With five periods in a session, we adopt a within-group sequence based upon the type of auction: three sessions of F,F,S,S,F and three sessions of S,S,F,F,S. Thus periods 1, 2, and 5 provide a cross-group, same-value comparison of the results from both the first-price, the second-price auction, and the ascending auctions of Isaac and Schnier. The switchover in periods 3 and 4 provides for a within-group comparison of the two types of sealed bid auction. A tabular roadmap is presented below in Table 1.

Table 1. Guide to sessions.

Institution	Minimum Increment	No. of Sessions	Period 1	Period 2	Period 3	Period 4	Period 5
Ascending	0.25	3	Ascending 25	Ascending 25	No data	No data	Ascending 25
Ascending	0.50	3	Ascending 50	Ascending 50	No data	No data	Ascending 50
FFSSF	NA	3	First price	First price	Second price	Second price	First price
SSFFS	NA	3	Second price	Second price	First price	First price	Second price

4. HYPOTHESES

A model of bidding in independent private value, sealed bid auctions with unknown number of rival bidders is presented by Krishna (2002). If we conjecture that the sealed bid auctions reduce the transactions cost of the geographically dispersed objects, then this model matches the framework of our silent auctions with one possible exception: bidders in silent auctions may not have correct expectations on the number of rival bidders. Nevertheless, this model is a most satisfactory reference point. Krishna presents the model at two levels: aggregate revenue results and individual bidding. The focus of this paper is on the aggregate revenue results of the two auctions. Because of the complexity of the first-price bid functions, we will examine the results of individual bidding decisions in a companion paper (Isaac, Pevnitskaya, & Schnier, 2005) in process. We will focus here upon the aggregate revenue and efficiency results, but our hypotheses will nevertheless depend upon a key result of the bidding theory.[9]

The key theoretical benchmark presented by Krishna is very simple: with risk-neutral bidders, revenue equivalence is maintained not only between the first- and second-price version of the sealed bid auctions with an unknown number or rival bidders, but also with regards to the predictions which arise from using the revenue predictions with known numbers of bidders, so long as bidders' expectations about the number of rivals are "correct." Thus, we can continue, as in our previous paper, to use the sum of the second highest values as a useful benchmark for expected valuation.[10] Of course, changing the assumption of risk neutrality leaves predicted bids, and hence revenue, in the second-price auction unchanged, but may change expected revenue in the first-price auctions.

The second important part of our model is, of course, the idea that revenue in the ascending sealed bid auctions suffered from the geographical dispersion of items and the resulting decisions of some bidders to withdraw from some auctions at prices that were still profitable. When combining this empirical model of revenue loss in the ascending with the results presented by Krishna, we can state a series of conjectures, as follows:

Conjecture 1. Revenue in both the first- and second-price sealed bid silent auctions will be greater than in the ascending silent auctions.

We can contrast the revenue equivalence hypothesis to the familiar tendency of single-unit first price auctions to generate revenues greater than the risk-neutral prediction (Kagel, 1995) to obtain a pair of alternative conjectures, as follows:

Conjecture 2 (revenue equivalence). The revenues from the first- and second-price sealed bid auctions will be the same.

Conjecture 3 (the so-called "risk-averse" bidding). The revenues from the first-price sealed bid silent auction will be greater than the revenues from the second-price sealed bid auction.

Finally, the theory for individual bidding behavior in the second-price silent auction predicts that bids equal value regardless of assumptions about risk preferences. On the other hand, the bids of risk-averse bidders in first-price auctions may depend upon risk attitudes, which raise the possibility that inefficient outcomes may result. This yields a final conjecture on efficiency, as follows:

Conjecture 4. Efficiencies in the first-price sealed bid silent auction will be no higher than in the second-price sealed bid silent auctions.

Because we already know that efficiencies in the ascending silent auctions are somewhat lower than 100%, there is no clear expected ranking between efficiencies in the first-price silent auctions and the ascending auctions. There is, however, a suggested relationship between second-price sealed bid efficiencies and efficiencies in the ascending auction.

Conjecture 5. Efficiencies in the second-price silent auctions will be higher than efficiencies in the ascending silent auctions.

Finally, we suspect from the prior data that if there is a change in revenue levels with the sealed bid auctions, this ought to reflect a difference in the distribution in revenue indices for the individual auctions, with the ascending auctions having a larger lower tail of low revenue auctions.

Conjecture 6. The distribution of revenue indices will differ between the sealed bid and the ascending silent auctions.

5. RESULTS

5.1. Descriptive Statistics

Table 2 presents both the efficiency and revenue indices, averaged across all periods and all sessions, of the two types of ascending auctions (increments

Table 2. [a]Mean Efficiency and Revenue Indices.

Auction Type	Ascending 0.25	Ascending 0.50	First Price	Second Price
Mean efficiency	0.9488	0.9687	0.9711	0.9785
Mean revenue index	0.8131	0.9271	1.0781	0.9548

[a]The mean is taken across all periods in all sessions. In the ascending auctions, there are three periods in each of three sessions for a total of nine data points for each type. In the sealed bid auctions, each type is represented by three periods in three auctions and two periods in three auctions for a total of 15 periods for each type.

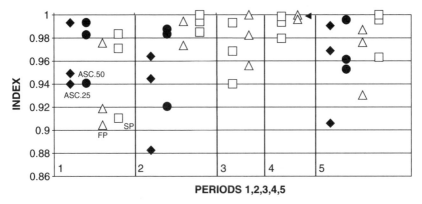

Fig. 2. Efficiency Indices by Session and by Period.

of 0.25 and 0.50) and the two types of sealed bid auctions (first and second price).

Notice that the average efficiencies in the sealed bid auctions are in the same ballpark as, although slightly higher than, the ascending auctions. The revenue indices, on the other hand, appear much higher with the sealed bid auctions, with the first-price auctions producing the most revenue.

Of course, these aggregate measures may mask variation both between sessions and also between periods. Figs. 2 and 3 present the disaggregated data on efficiencies and revenue, respectively. The data in these figures are presented as follows. Each icon is the efficiency or revenue index from one period to one experiment. The darkened icons represent the ascending auctions, and the open icons represent the sealed bid auctions (first price as triangles, second price as squares). A small arrow represents two observations at visually the same point.[11] The ordering of the FP, SP icons switches in periods 3 and 4 to be consistent with the sequence order in any given

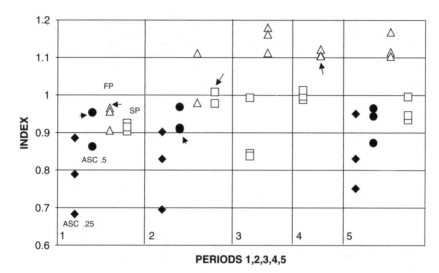

Fig. 3. Revenue Indices by Session and by Period.

experiment. That is, data from the F,F,S,S,F experiments are always pre-sented in the third column; that from the S,S,F,F,S, are always presented in the fourth column.

Consistent with the relatively close average efficiencies, there are no obvious patterns in the per-period efficiencies. The issue of revenue generation is the main interest of this paper and produced the more interesting results in the aggregate numbers, so we will discuss them in more detail. What stands out in the data is that there appear to be two categories of revenue outliers. First, there is a lagging "tail" of low revenues from several of the ascending auctions, most notably the "ascending 0.25" auctions. This effect can be illustrated at the level of individual auctions as displayed in Fig. 4. This is a "histogram" of individual auction results sorted by the revenue index. Notice that in the far left bin, (index <0.55) there is a spike of results from the ascending auctions with a 0.25 minimum bidding increment, and similar spikes dominate all the way through to 0.85. There is a weaker effect with the ascending 0.50 auctions. Second, there is a general upward bump in the revenue in the first-price sealed bid auctions. Likewise, referring to Fig. 4, there is an obvious spike for rev-enue indices > 1.35 for the first-price sealed bid auctions.[12]

The theories we have relied upon are static, and yet our bidders engage in five consecutive silent auctions. This raises the possibility of sequencing effects. The ascending auctions look fairly stable. There appears to be a

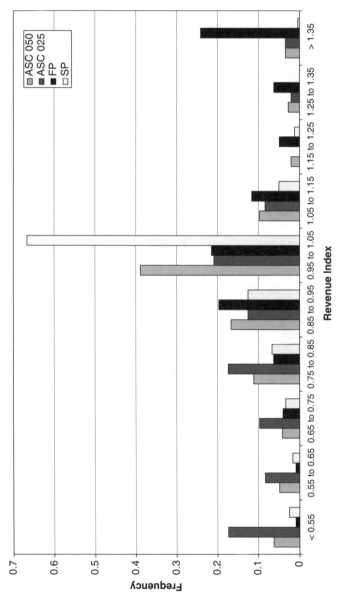

Fig. 4. Distribution of Revenue Indices by Individual Auction.

learning effect for the sealed bid auctions: after period 1 for both first- and second-price auctions, and after period 3 (the switchover) for second-price auctions. After the "initial contact periods," the second-price results appear stable and close to the (predicted) level of 1.0, while after the first period, the first-price auctions routinely yield more than the predicted-risk neutral amount of revenue to the seller. This implies that participants in these auctions within the field may require either some initial exposure to the auction institution or be informed of its comparative differences with the ascending auction before revenue differences are realized by the auctioneer. Within the parametric tests subsection that follows, we investigate this hypothesis using regression analysis.

5.2. Parametric Tests

We turn next to parametric tests of differences in aggregate efficiency and revenue. We do not have enough data to run credible parametric tests of all four treatments against each other in each of the relevant periods. Therefore, we present two alternate approaches. First, we compare each of the four treatments against one another, but we pool across all relevant periods. In Table 3, we list all six comparisons (in the previous tables we listed the levels, so for these comparisons, we report the differences). The efficiencies are compared by Wilcoxon rank tests (because of the upper bound problems), and we report only the difference and the Wilcoxon significance result. The revenues are compared by a t-test assuming unequal variances. We report the difference, the actual t-statistic, and whether or not it is significant at either of the usual levels.

These parametric tests suggest that the apparent differences in efficiencies in the treatments are not in general statistically significant, but the apparent differences in revenue are.

Table 3. Pooled Efficiency and Revenue Comparisons.

	Efficiency Difference	Revenue Difference
Ascending 0.25 vs. Ascending 0.50	−0.0199	−0.1139 (−3.42)**
Ascending 0.25 vs. first price	−0.0242	−0.2650 (−6.86)**
Ascending 0.25 vs. second price	−0.0297**	−0.1417 (−4.09)**
Ascending 0.50 vs. first price	−0.0043	−0.1510 (−5.62)**
Ascending 0.50 vs. second price	−0.0098	−0.0277 (−1.3)
First price vs. second price	−0.0055	+0.1233 (+4.5)**

Note: See Table 2 for the number of observations in each.
**Significant at 0.05.

Next, consider another aggregation of the data. This time, we will look at period-by-period comparisons, pooling across the two subtreatments. That is, for each period we compare all ascending data versus all sealed bid data. Because of the results of the previous test, we confine our attention to the revenue data. This test will provide evidence as to whether there is a sequencing pattern to the data as suggested by the data presentation in Figs. 3 and 4. The results are given in Table 4. Recall that these comparisons are possible in only three periods.

These results are consistent with our conclusions from informal observation of the data. The revenue difference in the institutions is subject to an experience effect. At the point of initial exposure to the institutions, the increase in revenue from the sealed bid auctions is not statistically significant. However, following the initial exposure to the institutions, there is a pronounced increase in revenue from the sealed bid institutions.

The patterns of the distributions of revenue indices (Fig. 4) suggest differences in the distributions are responsible for the differences in revenue, with spikes at the lower end for the ascending auctions, and spikes at the upper end for the first-price sealed bid auctions. We conducted K–S tests of each pair of distributions and found that each paired comparison yielded differences that were statistically significant at p-values of 0.0001.

Finally, we report regression results also based upon the individual auction results. We performed a Tobit estimation where an observation is the revenue index for a single auction.[13] To test the effects of the institution, we used the first-price periods as baseline, and included a dummy for "Ascending 0.50," "Ascending 0.25," and "Second Price" periods. To examine whether or not there was indeed the novelty effect we discussed above, we included a dummy "Initial Exposure" in the first period in which the subjects have experience with that particular institution, and then included additional dummies for "Initial First Price" exposure and "Initial Second Price" exposure.

Table 4. Pooled Comparisons: All Ascending versus All Sealed Bid by Period.

Period of Comparison	Revenue: Ascending–Sealed Bid
Period 1	−0.0738 (−1.68)
Period 2	−0.1536 (−3.38)**
Period 5	−0.1581 (−3.00)**

Note: In a given period, there will be six observations of ascending auctions and six observations of sealed bid auctions.
**Significant at 0.05.

The results of the regression are presented in Table 5. There are several things to notice. First, as the default variable, the tendency for revenues in the first-price auctions at the regression means is 1.1778 (i.e., $1.2608 + 0.0624 - 0.1462$) in the initial contact periods and 1.2608 in other periods. This is consistent (although more extreme) than the 1.08 simple mean from the aggregated data. Notice next that the dummy variables of institution are all highly significant and of the anticipated sign. Moreover, they yield exactly the same ranking as we saw previously: first-price sealed bid, second-price sealed bid, ascending 0.05, and ascending 0.25. Finally, the impact of initial exposure in the ascending auctions is given simply by the dummy "Initial Exposure." This coefficient is slightly positive and statistically insignificant, indicating that the novelty issue is not in operation in the ascending auctions. However, whether or not it was the initial first- or initial second-price auction did have an effect on the revenue index. Initial exposure had a negative and significant effect on the revenue index for both sealed bid auctions, with the initial exposure to the second-price sealed bid auction yielding a slightly smaller reduction in the revenue index.

In summary, looking across all of the data and the statistical tests and the Tobit estimation, we conclude the following about our research conjectures.

We accept Conjecture 1 that revenue is greater in the sealed bid silent auctions than in the ascending silent actions (see Tables 2–5, Figs. 2 and 3). However, it should be noted that when decoupled, the incremental effect is stronger when comparing the first-price auctions to the ascending auctions. This leads directly to our conclusion on Conjecture 2.

Table 5.   Regression Results.

Independent Variable	Coefficient/t-statistic
Constant	1.2608(36.55)**
Ascending 0.5	−0.3187(−6.36)**
Ascending 0.25	−0.4463(−8.91)**
Second price	−0.2913(−6.15)**
Initial exposure	0.0624(1.28)
Initial first price	−0.1462(−2.04)*
Initial second price	−0.1471(−2.08)*
Psuedo-R^2	0.1221
Number of observations	752

Note: Dependent variable = revenue index for each individual auction.
*Significant at 95% level;
**Significant at 99% level.

We reject Conjecture 2 of revenue neutrality between first- and second-price sealed silent auctions in favor of Conjecture 3, which postulates more revenue from the first-price auctions (see Tables 2–5, Figs. 2 and 3).

We accept Conjecture 4 that efficiencies are not higher in the first-price than in the second-price sealed bid silent auctions, and we partially accept (for second-price versus ascending with 0.25 minimum increment but not versus ascending with 0.50 minimum increment) Conjecture 5 that efficiencies are higher in the second-price auction than in the ascending auctions. There was no a priori conjecture, but it appears that efficiencies in the first-price sealed bid silent auctions are not statistically different than those from the ascending auctions (see Table 3).

We accept Conjecture 6 that the distribution of revenue indices differs for the ascending and sealed bid auctions. In addition, our statistical test indicates that there is a difference between the two ascending auctions (0.25 versus 0.50 minimum increment). Furthermore, our statistical test indicates that there is a difference between the first- and the second-price sealed bid silent auction (K–S tests).

Finally, although not drawn from an a priori hypothesis, we conclude the existence of a sequencing effect in which the revenue difference between the sealed bid and ascending auctions increases with experience (see Tables 4 and 5).

6. DISCUSSION AND CONCLUSIONS

In terms of our experimental environment, the conclusions we report are both straightforward and relatively unambiguous. Standardizing on the underlying economic environment, a silent auction generates more revenue when using sealed bid auctions (particularly first-price sealed bid auctions) than it does with the traditional open outcry-ascending auctions. This revenue enhancement occurs with no obvious corresponding loss of efficiency. This revenue enhancement appears to come from two distinct effects. First, both types of sealed bid auctions eliminate the "lower tails" of revenue that are present in the ascending auction with smaller bid increments. Second, the first-price sealed bid auction (as opposed to the second-price sealed bid auction) exhibits a distinct tendency to generate revenue greater than the risk-neutral Nash prediction.

Despite the clarity of these results, caution must be taken in extrapolating them to the field, for at least two reasons. First, the comparisons we report here assume exactly the same set of potential bidders. If sealed bid silent auctions were to be, for any reason, less successful in attracting visitors into the auction event, the revenue advantage reported here could disappear.[14] The policy recommendation for charity silent auctions organizers would perhaps include the following: (1) keep the other activities typically associated with these small scale silent auctions as attractive in either case as possible; or (2) experiment with using a mixture of ascending and silent auctions.

Likewise, neither our ascending auctions nor our sealed bid auctions made any provision for inducing either affiliated values of the standard type nor any "see and be seen" price preference valuations. These two conditions could conceivably affect the relative revenue generation properties of the two types of silent auctions, either for reasons that have been captured theoretically (Milgrom & Weber, 1982; Salmon & Isaac, 2005) or for reasons that have not yet been modeled formally. For an example of the latter, consider the following. Salmon and Isaac model see-and-be-seen preferences as a bidder having a price preference only when he is the winning bidder. What Salmon and Isaac do not consider is the possibility that the *intensity* of price preference might vary depending upon whether a silent auction was open-outcry (ascending) with bids continuously seen by participants versus sealed bid. It seems not out of the question that the open-outcry format of the ascending auction might generate a more rivalrous bidding environment than sealed bidding, especially on high-ticket items. Again, selective trials of the different auction types appear to be in order.

NOTES

1. Another proposed remedy is to stagger the closings of different parts of the auction, which is done in some field silent auctions. We do not explore that idea in this paper. Also, we do not investigate a comparison with non-auction institutions (see Morgan & Sefton, 2000; Davis, Razzolini, Reilly, & Wilson, 2005).

2. This is using "surplus achieved" measure of efficiency, namely, the ratio of the total market surplus actually achieved to maximum possible market surplus. We measure at the level of a market period, so when the bidders with the highest valuation for each object win the respective auction the efficiency index will be 1.00.

3. That is, when the total seller revenue equals the sum of each of the second highest valuations, the revenue index will be 1.00.

4. It should be noted that, standardizing on the number of rivals, items with higher induced value would be ex ante more profitable to a bidder. However, this need not be the case ex post, and it need not even be the case ex ante if one could take account of differences in the number of rival bidders on the items.

5. One of the authors attended such an auction over 30 years ago.

6. Only one winning bidding slip (out of 480) was invalidated due to absent information. In addition, there were six other bidding slips invalidated for various reasons of absent or incorrect information whose status cannot be determined (out of a total of 2205).

7. In order to keep bidders from wanting to pry open the slots in order to see if they were the only bidder, each mug always contained at least one yellow bid slip marked "blank." Subjects knew this, and in fact a volunteer monitor saw us put one in each mug.

8. In all other respects, these auctions are nominally the same as the ascending auctions. This includes a bankruptcy rule for bidders who repeatedly win items at above-value payments. However, the bankruptcy rule became a much greater concern here. We allowed bidders to bid over value and make losses, with the losses deducted from accumulated earnings and the small up-front capital, but not from the show-up fee. A bankrupt subject was reinitialized, and allowed to continue with an additional restriction that they did not bid in excess of value. We had one subject go bankrupt, but not from the usual strategic mistakes but rather from actually misunderstanding the rules of the experiment. After re-initialization, there were no further difficulties.

9. In neither the field nor the lab are silent auction bidders told their actual number of rivals. In our experiments they are told the random process. Whether their bidding indicates that they are able to discern that pattern is something that we will explore further in Isaac, Pevnitskaya, and Schnier (2005). In that paper, we also explore a broader literature on individual bidding behavior. In any event, the usual caveat applies: we are not claiming to test the Krishna model in an environment giving it its "best shot."

10. The benchmark is virtually indistinguishable whether we use the sum of the actual second highest values or the risk-neutral Vickrey bid function on the actual highest values.

11. We report only two of the three first-price observations for period 2. There was a self-reported and obvious error in understanding the rules by one of the participants that made that data incomparable. This bidder, in period 2, believed that actual redemption values were much higher than what was written on the record sheets. Because this subject was therefore bidding far over actual valuation, were this period to to be included it would make the first-price sealed bid revenue indices even larger than reported here. After helping the subject with the accounting worksheet for period 2, the misunderstanding was corrected and there were no similar problems in subsequent periods.

12. We conducted K–S tests on the possible difference between these distributions of revenue indices. Each of the tests showed a difference at $P = 0.0001$.

13. The Tobit was chosen because of two truncations: one was the natural truncation at below zero. The second was an imposed truncation at 3.00 (three times the predicted revenue). This was because in a small number of instances (13 out of 752), extremely large revenue indices were obtained. This is one of the reasons we calculate parametric tests already reported upon the aggregate revenue for the period – these spikes tend to get washed out when averaging across the period. In addition, we tried a formal panel estimation with fixed effects but the results added no interpretation to what is reported here and had some undesirable problems with calculated standard errors.

14. See Ivanova-Stenzel and Salmon (2004) for an example in which bidders can be shown to have preferences over auction types.

ACKNOWLEDGMENTS

We would like to thank the Florida State University and the University of Rhode Island for support of this research, an anonymous referee who provided many useful suggestions, and graduate students working at Florida State and Rhode Island for assistance in conducting the experiments and analyzing the data. All remaining errors are our own.

REFERENCES

Davis, D. D., Razzolini, L., Reilly R., & Wilson, B. J. (2005). Raising revenues for charity: Auctions versus lotteries (in this volume).

Isaac, R. M., Pevnitskaya, S., & Schnier, K. (2005). Bidder behavior in multiple-good sealed bid auctions where the number of bidders is unknown (work in process).

Isaac, R. M., & Schnier, K. (2005). Silent auctions in the field and in the laboratory. *Economic Inquiry, 43*, 715–733.

Ivanova-Stenzel, R., & Salmon, T. (2004). Bidder preferences among auction institutions. *Economic Inquiry, 42*, 223–236.

Kagel, J. H. (1995). Auctions: A survey of experimental results. In: J. Kagel & A. E. Roth (Eds), *The handbook of experimental economics.* Princeton, NJ: Princeton University Press.

Krishna, V. (2002). *Auction theory.* San Diego, CA: Academic Press.

Milgrom, P. R., & Weber, R. J. (1982). A theory of auctions and competitive bidding. *Econometrica, 50*, 1089–1122.

Morgan, J., & Sefton, M. (2000). Funding public goods with lotteries: Experimental evidence. *Review of Economic Studies, 67*, 785–810.

Salmon, T., & Isaac, R. M. (2005). Revenue from the saints, the show-offs, and the predators (in this volume).

RAISING REVENUES FOR CHARITY: AUCTIONS VERSUS LOTTERIES

Douglas D. Davis, Laura Razzolini, Robert J. Reilly and Bart J. Wilson

ABSTRACT

We report an experiment conducted to gain insight into factors that may affect revenues in English auctions and lotteries, two commonly used charity fund-raising formats. In particular, we examine how changes in the marginal per capita return (MPCR) from the public component of bidding, and how changes in the distribution of values affect the revenue properties of each format. Although we observe some predicted comparative static effects, the dominant result is that lottery revenues uniformly exceed English auction revenues. The similarity of lottery and English auction bids across sales formats appears to drive the excess lottery revenues.

1. INTRODUCTION

Auctions and lotteries are standard means of raising funds for local public goods. Members of schools, churches, local sports clubs and community arts

Experiments Investigating Fundraising and Charitable Contributors
Research in Experimental Economics, Volume 11, 47–91
Copyright © 2006 by Elsevier Ltd.
All rights of reproduction in any form reserved
ISSN: 0193-2306/doi:10.1016/S0193-2306(06)11003-0

groups gather with frequency at fund-raising dinners and receptions to recognize their common interest in the charitable cause and the generosity (and
in some cases the luck) of their fellows, some of whom win or purchase items
that they value highly.

Beyond the utility of participating in such events, charity lotteries and
auctions can also raise money effectively, and that aspect is the focus of this
paper. Morgan (2000) analyzes the use of a lottery as a fund-raising mechanism. Assuming homogeneous individual valuations for the prize, Morgan
shows that when lottery ticket purchases reflect a combination of private
values for the raffled item and some return from contributing to a charitable organization, a lottery may generate substantially higher revenues
than would fund-raising efforts through standard voluntary contributions.
Intuitively, the chance of winning the raffled item mitigates the free-rider
incentives that undermine fund-raising through private voluntary contributions. Using experimental methods, Morgan and Sefton (2000) generate empirical support for this prediction. Holding constant, the rate of
return that participants derive from public contributions (the marginal
per capita return ($MPCR$), Morgan and Sefton observe markedly higher
contributions in charity lotteries than in comparable voluntary contributions games, a difference that increases as participants become experienced
with the mechanisms.

This paper extends the analysis of Morgan (2000) and Morgan and Sefton
(2000) in two dimensions pertinent to many naturally occurring charity
fund-raising events. First, we allow for prize value heterogeneities. Significant value heterogeneities characterize many of the items typically offered
for sale at charity events. At a local school auction, for example, differences
in the perceived contribution of a particular son or daughter, sentimentality
and aesthetic preferences may create very heterogeneous values among bidding parents for a collective class art project.[1]

Second, we consider the effects of altering the fund-raising format. In
natural contexts, the most standard selling formats at charity events include
the lottery (or raffle) mentioned above as well as an ascending price English
auction. In the lottery, participants buy tickets, each potentially giving the
holder the right to win a prize. At a pre-announced closing time, one of the
tickets is drawn at random and the prize is awarded to the ticket holder. The
English auction sales format is sometimes conducted orally with an auctioneer, and sometimes conducted as a "silent auction." Oral auctions most
typically follow standard English auction rules, with an auctioneer soliciting
ascending bids until a single bidder remains, who purchases the item at his
or her final bid price. In the silent auction, bidders submit bids in writing for

an item up to a pre-announced closing time. During the silent auction, a recorder monitors bids privately as they are submitted, and displays continuously and publicly the highest bid. At the close of the auction, the highest bidder wins, and pays the bid price.[2]

The potential revenue consequences of a fund-raising sales format are not always the only factor driving the sales format decision. Some religious organizations proscribe the use of lotteries or raffles as a type of gambling.[3] Further, regulations regarding lotteries vary substantially across states and countries, and in many instances charity lotteries are effectively illegal.[4] However, in may instances the organizers or "hosts" of charity fund-raising events face no restrictions in their choice of selling format, and these hosts not only vary lottery and silent auction selling formats across fund-raising events, but they vary selling formats across items at a single event.[5] Participants may purchase lottery tickets for an automobile or a vacation package, for example, and then bid in a silent auction for other items. We suspect that the issues of value heterogeneity and selling formats are inter-related. In particular, fund-raisers may base their choice of selling format for an item on the kind of participants they expect may bid for the item as well as the likely distribution of values among bidders.

Some theoretical studies have examined the effects of changing the sales format in charity events. However, the existing literature focuses on the relationship between sealed-bid auctions and a variety of "all-pay" auctions where the high bidder wins the auction, but all bids are paid. Engers and McManus (2004) show that a first price all-pay auction generates higher revenues than a first price sealed bid auction. They further compare revenue predictions between the all-pay auction and the second-price sealed bid auctions. (Predictions of the latter auction format are typically used to derive price and revenue predictions for English auctions.)[6] Although Engers and McManus are unable to order unambiguously the revenue predictions for the two formats, they show that with enough bidders, the all-pay format generates higher revenues than the sealed bid auction. Goeree, Maashand, Onderstal, & Turner (2005) generalize the analysis of charitable all-pay auctions. They show that winner-pay auctions are poor revenue raisers, because the value of the highest-valued bidder sets an upper bound on revenues. All-pay auctions can generate much higher revenues. In particular, any $k+1$th price all-pay auction generates higher revenues than any kth price all-pay auction. Further, given a constant *MPCR* "h," kth price all-pay auction revenues become infinite whenever $k \leq 1/h$.

In addition to our focus on the lottery and English auction selling formats typical of naturally occurring charity fund-raising events, we depart from the existing literature in that we assume public knowledge of value realizations. We make this assumption primarily for the purpose of analytical simplicity. The publicity of value information simplifies particularly the analysis of the heterogeneous value lottery. However, we stress that such an assumption does not outrageously mischaracterize many local charity fundraisers. Although the "hosts" at local charity fund-raisers may not know the entire distribution of value draws for any auction the local charity may conduct, we doubt that the hosts view potential bidders as random draws from a distribution. In particular, they probably can distinguish the items likely to attract only one or only a very small number of high-value bidders from those items with much more homogeneous valuations, and may attempt to adjust the sales format correspondingly.[7]

Our lottery predictions follow from Hillman and Riley (1989) and Fang (2002), who use a rent-seeking context to motivate an analysis of lotteries in the case of heterogeneous, but publicly known values.[8] In this paper, we extend the analysis of heterogeneous, but publicly known values to the charity context and then we compare revenue predictions with the case of the known-values English auction. We find that revenue predictions are importantly affected by the $MPCR$ from the public good, and by the distribution of values among bidders. In particular, the English auction generates higher expected revenues than a lottery when the item for sale is sufficiently idiosyncratic (that is, only a very few bidders value the item highly), and when the return from the public good component is low (that is, the $MPCR$ is low).

We proceed as follows: Section 2 develops bid and revenue predictions for the silent auction and for lotteries in the case of known but heterogeneous values. Section 3 presents the experimental design, Section 4 discusses the experimental results and a short Section 5 concludes.

2. A SIMPLE MODEL CHARITY AUCTIONS AND LOTTERIES

In what follows, we first develop bid and revenue predictions for the English auction, and then we consider equilibrium bid and revenue predictions for the lottery.[9] We close with bid and revenue comparisons under the two institutions.

Consider a situation where n agents, $i = 1, \ldots, n$ compete for an indivisible object or prize. Each agent is endowed with a heterogeneous value for the item, $V_i > 0$, which is common knowledge. Without loss of generality, we rank order the values so that $V_1 \geq V_2 \ldots \geq V_n > 0$. The proceeds from either sales format go toward a public good that benefits all agents equally. For simplicity assume that the marginal benefit from the public good, or the *MPCR*, is a constant equal to h, $0 \leq h < 1$.

2.1. The English Auction with Known Values and Charitable Intentions

Assume that each bidder optimizes a simple quasi-linear utility function commonly encountered in the literature on public good auctions (see Morgan, 2000)

$$U_i = \begin{cases} V_i - b_i + hb_i & \text{if bidder } i \text{ wins the auction with bid } b_i \\ hb_j & \text{if some bidder } j \neq i \text{ wins with bid } b_j \end{cases}$$

where $0 \leq h < 1$. The equilibrium outcome is dichotomous, the winning bid depending on whether h is zero or positive. An informal derivation of the equilibrium follows. The case where $h = 0$ is the standard English auction of a private good for which the winning bid is well known to be $b_1 = V_2$. For the case where $h > 0$, any bidder will remain in the bidding as long as the utility from doing so exceeds the utility of dropping out. Consider the maximal potential bid for the high-value bidder 1. If forced by the other bidders, bidder 1 will raise the bid to V_1. Dropping out at $b_1 = V_1 - \varepsilon$ leaves bidder 1 without winning the auction and with a utility $U_1 = hb_j = h(V_1 - \varepsilon) < hV_1$ from the contribution to the public good by auction winner j. Winning the auction with an above-value bid $b_1 = V_1 + \varepsilon$ results in utility $U_1 = hV_1 + \varepsilon(h - 1) < hV_1$ since $0 < h < 1$. If bidder 1 is able to win the auction with a bid $b_1 = V_1$, the resulting utility is $U_1 = V_1 - V_1 + hV_1 = hV_1$, dominating either of the above scenarios.

Now consider the bid strategy for any bidder j other than high-value bidder 1. Knowing that bidder 1 will remain in the auction until the bid equals V_1 but no higher, bidder j maximizes his or her return by staying in the auction until b_j is arbitrarily close to V_1, earning utility $U_j = hV_1$. Thus, the equilibrium winning bid and equilibrium revenue are V_1.[10]

The static feature of this game bears emphasis. In a repeated context, the highest-valued bidder 1 could impose losses on low value bidders who are submitting bids above their private values. Nevertheless, the effect of the charitable component on the equilibrium bid strategy in the English auction context merits emphasis. Given public values, a positive *MPCR* $(0 < h < 1)$ increases the equilibrium bid from V_2 to V_1. The prediction is independent of the magnitude of h, provided that $0 < h < 1$. Further, additional increases in the marginal public return (h) affect neither bids nor revenues. We summarize these results in the form of a first conjecture about the behavior we expect to observe in our experiments.

Conjecture 1. Any positive $MPCR = h$, $0 < h < 1$ shifts the bids and revenues for the public information English auction from V_2 to V_1. Any further increase to an $MPCR = h'$ $h < h' < 1$, affects neither bids nor revenues.

2.2. Lottery with Known Heterogeneous Values and Charitable Intentions

Unlike the English auction, lottery participants pay their bids regardless of whether they win the prize. Given heterogeneous but common knowledge values for the prize, a subset of the n potential bidders in a lottery may find non-participation optimal. Consider the bids of the m bidders, $m < n$, who do find participation optimal. Each participant i bids b_i (makes lottery ticket purchases of b_i) to maximize expected utility given by

$$E(U_i) = \frac{b_i}{B(m)} V_i - b_i + hB(m), \quad b_i \geq 0 \tag{1}$$

where $B(m)$ represents the sum of bids by all m participating agents and $\frac{b_i}{B(m)}$ is the probability of winning the lottery. Optimizing Eq. (1) with respect to b_i and taking as given the bids of all the other agents yields the first order condition

$$\frac{V_i(B(m) - b_i)}{B(m)^2} + h = 1, \quad i = 1, \ldots, m. \tag{2}$$

Solving for the optimal bid,

$$b_i = B(m) - B(m)^2 \left(\frac{1 - h}{V_i} \right), \quad i = 1, \ldots, m. \tag{3}$$

Summing over the m bidders, Eq. (3) yields an expression for the sum of bids or the total contributions to the charity.

$$B(m) = \frac{m - 1}{(1 - h)\Sigma_{i=1}^{m} \frac{1}{V_i}} \tag{4}$$

Hillman and Riley (1989) characterize the Nash equilibrium for a lottery game with n players in terms of the largest subset n^* of bidders, $2 \leq n^* \leq n$, each of whom submit strictly positive bids, and the remaining $n - n^*$ bidders who submit zero bids.[11] This result extends in a straightforward way to the present case, since the addition of a linear public return from the lottery changes both individual values and $B(m)$ by a factor $1/(1-h)$. Formally, define

$$k = \min\{m : v_{m+1} \leq (1-h)B(m), \quad m = 2,\ldots,n-1\}$$
$$n^* = \min\{k, n\} \tag{5}$$

Then Nash equilibrium bids in this extension of Hillman and Riley are

$$b_i^* = \begin{cases} b_i(n^*), & \text{for } i = 1,\ldots,n^* \\ 0, & \text{for } i = n^*+1,\ldots,n \end{cases} \tag{5a}$$

where $b_i(n^*)$ is defined in Eq. (3) with substitution from Eq. (4) using $B(m) = B(n^*)$ in Eq. (4). Lottery revenues are given by $B(n^*)$.

Prior to comparing predicted revenues across different fund-raising formats, one feature of the lottery with a public return component merits comment. Observe from Eq. (4) that the equilibrium revenue increases with h, the *MPCR*. We state this implication as a second conjecture about the behavior we expect to observe in our experiments.

Conjecture 2. Lottery revenues move directly with the *MPCR*.

2.3. Revenue Comparisons

The English auction yields higher equilibrium revenues than the lottery if $V_1 > B(n^*)$ or

$$V_1 > \frac{n^* - 1}{(1-h)\Sigma_{i=1}^{n^*} \dfrac{1}{V_i}} \tag{6}$$

Rearranging terms yields

$$(1-h)V_1 < \frac{n^*-1}{\sum_{i=2}^{n^*} \frac{1}{V_i} + \frac{1}{V_1}} \quad \text{or,}$$

$$1 - h < \frac{n^*-1}{\sum_{i=2}^{n^*} \frac{V_1}{V_i} + 1} \tag{7}$$

Notice that inequality Eq. (7) holds (and the English auction generates relatively more revenues than the lottery) (i) as h, the *MPCR*, becomes small, and (ii) as V_1 becomes large relative to the other value draws. We summarize these revenue comparison results as two final conjectures about the behavior we expect to observe in our experiments.

Conjecture 3. Given a positive *MPCR*, the ratio of lottery revenues to English auction revenues moves directly with the *MPCR*.

Conjecture 4. Given a positive *MPCR*, the ratio of lottery revenues to English auction revenues moves inversely with the high-value draw, V_1.

As a final comment prior to presenting the experimental design, observe that the revenue effects articulated in Conjectures 1–4 can be sizable if sellers play static Nash equilibrium strategies. Table 1 illustrates English auction and lottery revenue predictions in the case of four agents with $h = \{0, 1/3, 2/3\}$, and for three mean preserving value realizations, $L = \{500, 500, 500, 500\}$, $M = \{650, 500, 425, 425\}$ and $H = \{800, 500, 350, 350\}$. Looking at the English auction revenue predictions shown in the left portion of Table 1, observe that raising h above zero raises revenue predictions from V_2 to V_1, as stated in Conjecture 1. Under the H set of value realizations, English auction revenues increase by 60% (from 500 to 800) as h increases from 0 to 1/3. However, the effect is confined to the first deviation of h above zero. Doubling h from 1/3 to 2/3 does not further affect English auction revenues.

The grid in the left panel of Table 1 lists lottery revenue predictions. As stated in Conjecture 2, lottery revenues move continuously with changes in h. Holding constant the value sets, lottery revenues increase roughly 50% as h increases from 0 to 1/3, and then roughly double as h increases from 1/3 to 2/3.

Consider finally, the comparative revenue effects summarized in Conjectures 3 and 4. Starting at the upper right corners of the English auction and lottery grids in Table 1 observe that with the L value set and $h = 2/3$, predicted lottery revenues more than double the predicted silent auction revenues (1125 cents vs. 500 cents). Moving down and to the left observe that these differences fall and then reverse. With the H value set, and $h = 0$, silent auction revenue predictions exceed lottery revenues by roughly 50% (500 cents vs. 335 cents).

Table 1. Predicted Revenue Comparisons: English Auction and Lottery (in cents).

Value Set	English Auction			Lottery		
	$h = 0$	$h = 1/3$	$h = 2/3$	$h = 0$	$h = 1/3$	$h = 2/3$
L: {500, 500, 500, 500}	500	500	500	375	563	1125
M: {650, 500, 425, 425}	500	650	650	364	546	1092
H: {800, 500, 350, 350}	500	800	800	335	502	1004

Examining predicted bids and earnings for the two sales formats lends insight into the factors driving the revenue predictions shown in Table 1. Consider the first bid and earning predictions for the English auction, summarized in Table 2(a). For the M and H value sets, notice that raising h above zero raises the bid from the second highest value (V_2) to the highest value (V_1). Notice also that as h increases, predicted earnings shift from zero for all bidders (for the L value set) or zero for all bidders but the high-value bidder (for the M and H value sets) to positive and equal earnings for all bidders. Finally, given $h > 0$, notice that increases in the *MPCR* do not alter English auction bid predictions, but equilibrium payoffs for all bidders increase continuously.[12]

Table 2(b) summarizes bid and expected earnings predictions for the lotteries. Lottery bids are notably more heterogeneous than those predicted in the English auction. Lottery participants submit identical bids only with the L (homogeneous) value set, and the high-value bidder (V_1) bids increasingly more relative to his or her rivals as the value heterogeneity increases. Interestingly, however, in the lottery, higher bids do not necessarily translate into higher expected earnings. Notice, for example, that with the H and M value sets and $h = 2/3$, the two low value bidders (V_3) actually enjoy higher expected earnings than the high value (V_1) and medium value (V_2) bidders.[13]

Table 2(a).   Bid and Earning Predictions: English Auction (in cents)[a].

Value Set	$h = 0$		$h = 1/3$		$h = 2/3$	
	Bid	Earnings	Bid	Earnings	Bid	Earnings
L						
$V_1 = 500$	500	0	500	167	500	333
$V_1 = 500$	500	0	500	167	500	333
$V_1 = 500$	500	0	500	167	500	333
$V_1 = 500$	500	0	500	167	500	333
M						
$V_1 = 650$	500	150	650	217	650	433
$V_2 = 500$	499	0	649	217	649	433
$V_3 = 425$	499	0	649	217	649	433
$V_3 = 425$	499	0	649	217	649	433
H						
$V_1 = 800$	500	300	800	267	800	533
$V_2 = 500$	499	0	799	267	799	533
$V_3 = 350$	499	0	799	267	799	533
$V_3 = 350$	499	0	799	267	799	533

[a]Entries presume a minimum bid increment of 1 cent. Our theoretical development presumes a continuous bid grid and that the minimum bid increment, $\varepsilon > 0$.

Table 2(b).   Bid and Expected Earnings Predictions: Lotteries (in cents).

Value Set	$h = 0$		$h = 1/3$		$h = 2/3$	
	Bid	Expected Earnings	Bid	Expected Earnings	Bid	Expected Earnings
L						
$V_1 = 500$	94	31	141	172	282	594
$V_1 = 500$	94	31	141	172	282	594
$V_1 = 500$	94	31	141	172	282	594
$V_1 = 500$	94	31	141	172	282	594
M						
$V_1 = 650$	160	126	240	228	481	533
$V_2 = 500$	99	37	149	169	297	567
$V_3 = 425$	52	9	78	165	157	632
$V_3 = 425$	52	9	78	165	157	632
H						
$V_1 = 800$	195	271	292	341	584	551
$V_2 = 500$	111	55	166	167	332	503
$V_3 = 350$	15	1	22	161	44	641
$V_3 = 350$	15	1	22	161	44	641

3. EXPERIMENTAL DESIGN AND PROCEDURES

To evaluate the behavioral relevance of Conjectures 1–4, we conduct the following experiment. The experiment consists of a series of thirty 24-period lottery and auction sessions. Our parameterization follows from the *MPCR* values {0, 1/3, 2/3} and the value sets {*H, M* and *L*} used to generate the predictions in Table 1. In each session, a constant group of four bidders places lottery or auction bids under each of the value set combinations listed in Table 1. To facilitate procedures and to give participants some familiarity with both the auction institution and the public return from bidding, we hold both the *MPCR* and the auction institution constant within sessions. Thus, given two auction institutions and three *MPCR* values, the experiment consists of six treatment cells.

Our primary interest is in the explanatory power of static Nash equilibrium predictions, when value realizations are not repeated extensively. To this end, we rotate both value sets, and the assignment of values to participants across periods within each session. Given four bidders and three value sets, we can, in a 12-period rotation, induce the high-value draw (and the second high-value draw) on each bidder once for each value set. Our

24-period auction or lottery sequence consists of two realizations of this 12-period rotation. To facilitate across-session comparisons, we repeat the same sequence of value set and value assignments each session. Table A1 in Appendix 1 enumerates the sequence of value assignments.

3.1. Experimental Procedures

At the outset of each session, we randomly seat volunteers at visually isolated PCs, and an experiment monitor reads instructions aloud as participants follow along on a copy of their own. The instructions explain English auction- or lottery-bidding procedures, including how to submit and modify bids on their computer, the effects of the group investment and the way earnings are calculated. To assist ticket purchase decisions in the lottery, participants are given a ticket calculator. With the calculator, participants can calculate expected earnings per period given differing assumptions about their own ticket purchases and the sum of purchases by the other participants.[14] After answering any questions the session begins.

At the outset of each period, each participant is endowed with 800 laboratory cents, and the monitor announces and writes on a white board the value set for the period (the value assignments and individual bidders, however, are not linked). In the English auctions, participants have 40 s to submit a bid. To avoid deadline effects, we implement a "soft-stop" termination rule. Any bid submitted in the final 5 s of an auction period automatically extends the period by an additional 10 s. In the lotteries, participants have 90 s to purchase tickets.[15] In either sales format, participants could submit bids or make ticket purchases in amounts up to and including their initial 800 cent endowment for the period. At the close of each period, a winner is identified, and each bidder's endowment for the period is incremented by the private and public returns from the auction to determine period earnings. The computer program also maintains for each participant a running total of his or her cumulative earnings.

This process is repeated 24 times, using the value schedule in Table A1 (this table is not distributed to the participants). After period 24 the session ends, a monitor privately pays each participant the sum of his or her salient earnings, plus a $5 appearance fee, and then dismisses them. We convert lab dollars into cash at the pre-announced rate of 2000 lab cents for US$1.[16] The participants were 120 student volunteers, primarily undergraduates, from George Mason University during the Spring Semester, 2003. Earnings for 45–60 min sessions ranged from $11.50 to $29.75, and averaged $18.75 (including the $5 appearance fee).

4. EXPERIMENTAL RESULTS

4.1. Overview

The mean revenue paths shown in Fig. 1 illustrate some of the primary experimental results.[17] Most prominently, observe that independent of the *MPCR* condition, lottery revenues (thin gray lines) exceed persistently both the English auction revenue (thin black lines) and static Nash predicted lottery revenues (thick broken gray lines). In contrast to the comparatively stable and near-Nash revenue outcomes in the English auctions, lottery revenue outcomes persistently exceed static Nash lottery predictions, often spectacularly, by margins of 200–300%. Lottery revenues approach English auction revenues only in the latter periods of the $h = 0$ treatments (when English auctions are predicted to raise substantially higher revenues). Lottery revenues in excess of Nash predictions have been observed previously in a charity lottery context ($h > 0$) with symmetrical bidders by Morgan and Sefton (2000), and in asymmetric rent-seeking contexts (with $h = 0$) by Davis and Reilly (1998, 2000). However, to the best of our knowledge, the immense surplus of lottery revenues over static Nash predictions observed here is unique. Apparently, the simultaneous presence of asymmetric bidders and a positive *MPCR* generates a strong interactive effect.

Although the scale of excess lottery revenues dominates other effects, notice also that in the latter portion of the sessions, some predicted comparative static effects emerge. Consider in particular the predicted and observed mean revenues for the English auctions, shown in the upper panels of Fig. 2. Observed revenues fail to follow predictions in the first session half. Nevertheless, revenues for the H ('•'), L (' × ') and particularly the M ('∘') value sets spread at least weakly in the predicted rank order in the second session half. Mean predicted and observed lottery revenues, shown in the lower panels of Fig. 2, illustrate the predicted *MPCR* effect. A weak relationship between lottery revenues and the *MPCR* in the first half gathers considerable strength in the second half.[18]

4.2. Revenue Effects

To evaluate quantitatively these observations, as well to evaluate formally Conjectures 1–4, we use a linear mixed-effects model to estimate revenues in the different sales format, value dispersion and *MPCR* conditions.

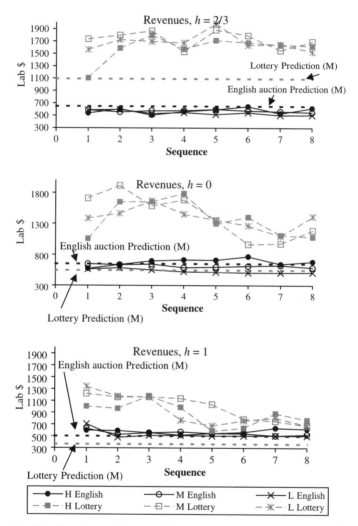

Fig. 1. English Auction and Lottery Revenues. *Key*: Each panel illustrates mean revenues for the five sessions in each *MPCR* condition ($h = 0$, $1/3$, $2/3$). English auction and lottery observations are separated into sets of eight sequences conducted under the *H*, *M* and *L* value dispersions. For clarity, English auction and lottery predictions are printed for only the *M* value set.

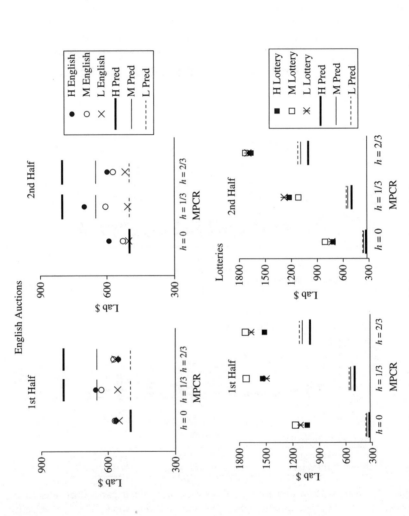

Fig 2. Observed and Predicted Revenues by Session Half. *Key*: Each panel plots mean revenues for the first- or second half of sessions in a treatment against static Nash prediction. Within panels, markers identify revenues by *MPCR* ($h = 0$, $1/3$, $2/3$) and by value dispersion (H, M or L).

Specifically, we estimate revenues in period t of session i (R_{it}) as

$$R_{it} = \beta_0 + \left[\beta_{ev} v_t + \beta_{ev^H} v_t^H + \beta_{eh} h_i + \beta_{eh^{2/3}} h_i^{2/3} \right.$$
$$\left. + \beta_{ehv} h_i v_t + \beta_{ehv^H} h_i v_t^H + \beta_{eh^{2/3}v} h_i^{2/3} v_t + \beta_{eh^{2/3}v^H} h_i^{2/3} v_t^H \right] e_i$$
$$+ \left[\beta_\ell + \beta_{\ell v} v_t + \beta_{\ell v^H} v_t^H + \beta_{\ell h} h_i + \beta_{\ell h^{2/3}} h_i^{2/3} \right.$$
$$\left. + \beta_{\ell hv} h_i v_t + \beta_{\ell hv^H} h_i v_t^H + \beta_{\ell h^{67}v} h_i^{2/3} v_t + \beta_{\ell h^{2/3}v^H} h_i^{2/3} v_t^H \right] \ell_i$$
$$+ \xi_i + \varepsilon_{it}$$
$$i = 1, \ldots, 30, \quad t = 1, \ldots, 12, \tag{8}$$

where the fixed effects are defined as follows: $e_i = 1$ if session i was an English auction, $\ell_i = 1$ if session i was a lottery, $h_i = 1$ if session i used $h = 1/3$ or $2/3$, $h_i^{2/3} = 1$ if session i used $h = 2/3$, $v_t = 1$ if period t used the M or H value sets and $v_t^H = 1$ if period t used the H value set.

To control for interdependencies within sessions we define sessions as panels, and then assume a random effects error structure within panels. Also, to control for serial correlation we assume a first order autoregressive process. Thus, the sessions in Eq. (8) are modeled as random effects $\xi_i \sim N(0, \sigma_\xi^2)$. We also accommodate non-spherical disturbances by $\varepsilon_{it} + \rho silon_{it-hrm1} + \eta_{it}$, $|\eta_{it}| < hrm1$ and $\eta_{it} \sim N(hrm0, gma^{hrm2}\eta_t)$. Finally, to gain insight into temporal effects, we divide the data into two 12-period halves, and conduct separate regressions on each half.[19]

Despite its length, Eq. (8) is easy to follow. We model value set heterogeneity and *MPCR* interactions as marginal changes to a cumulative total, starting with $h = 0$ and the L value set in the English auction as the baseline revenue, β_0. The coefficients for each of the other 17 terms estimate the marginal revenue effects of treatment changes that deviate in progressive increments from the baseline condition. The first two rows consist of *MPCR* and value-set interactions for the English auctions. The second two rows list a parallel set of interactions for the lotteries as well as a lottery intercept term (when $h = 0$ with the L value set). Modeling interactions as in Eq. (8) generates non-arbitrary estimates of each of the 18 treatment cells as a unique set of parameters. Table 3 summarizes these parameters. Notice in particular the bold entries in Table 3. These entries highlight the marginal effects that distinguish each treatment cell. Column (d) of Table 4 lists the predicted magnitude of these marginal effects given static Nash behavior.

Table 3. Parameter Combinations Yielding Revenue Estimates.

	English Auction		
	$\sim h \; (h = 0)$	$h \; (h = 1/3)$	$h^{2/3} \; (h = 2/3)$
$\sim v \; (L)$	$\boldsymbol{\beta_0}$	$\beta_0 + \boldsymbol{eh}$	$\beta_0 + eh + \boldsymbol{eh^{2/3}}$
$v \; (M)$	$\beta_0 + \boldsymbol{ev}$	$\beta_0 + eh + ev + \boldsymbol{ehv}$	$\beta_0 + eh + ev + ehv + \boldsymbol{eh^{2/3}} + \boldsymbol{eh^{2/3}v}$
$v^H \; (H)$	$\beta_0 + ev + \boldsymbol{ev^H}$	$\beta_0 + eh + ev + ev^H + ehv + \boldsymbol{ehv^H}$	$\beta_0 + eh + ev + ehv + ev^H + eh^{2/3} + eh^{2/3}v + ehv^H$ $\quad + \boldsymbol{eh^{2/3}v^H}$

	Lotteries		
	$\sim h \; (h = 0)$	$h \; (h = 1/3)$	$h^{2/3} \; (h = 2/3)$
$\sim v \; (L)$	$\beta_0 + \ell$	$\beta_0 + \ell + \boldsymbol{\ell h}$	$\beta_0 + \ell + \ell h + \ell h^{2/3}$
$v \; (M)$	$\beta_0 + \ell + \boldsymbol{\ell v}$	$\beta_0 + \ell + \ell h + \ell v + \boldsymbol{\ell h v}$	$\beta_0 + \ell + \ell h + \ell v + \ell h v + \ell h^{67} + \ell h^{67} v$
$v^H \; (H)$	$\beta_0 + \ell + \ell v + \boldsymbol{\ell v^H}$	$\beta_0 + \ell + \ell h + \ell v + \ell v^H$ $\quad + \ell h v + \boldsymbol{\ell h v^H}$	$\beta_0 + \ell + \ell h + \ell v + \ell h v + \ell v^H + \ell h^{67}$ $\quad + \ell h^{67} v + \ell h v^H + \ell h^{67} v^H$

Columns (b) and (c) of Table 4 report the estimates. In Table 4, as well as in the tables that follow, we evaluate both comparative static effects (e.g., coefficients that deviate from zero in the theoretically predicted direction) and conformance with equilibrium predictions. The entries in parenthesis below each parameter report the probability that an estimate deviates significantly from zero in the direction predicted by static Nash behavior. Boldfaced italicized and bold upright entries highlight, respectively, instances where estimates deviate from zero at 90 and 95% confidence levels. Single and double asterisks in printed aside entries indicate, respectively, 90 and 95% confidence levels that an estimate deviates from the predicted effect.[20]

The results in Table 4 reflect clearly some of the observations made previously. Notice in particular the large and significant ℓ estimates, highlighted with a gray box in row (1.1). These estimates are not boldfaced, as they deviate above, rather than below zero as predicted. However, as indicated by the asterisks, both the first-half estimate of 784.1 and the second-half estimate of 316.76 significantly and substantially exceed the static Nash prediction of -125. Notice also the ℓh and $\ell h^{2/3}$ coefficients, shown in rows (1.4) and (1.5) of Table 4. These coefficients estimate the marginal effects of *MPCR* increases in lotteries. In the first session half, ℓh and $\ell h^{2/3}$ are relatively small and differ insignificantly from zero. However, in the second session half, $\ell h = 480.35$ and $\ell h^{2/3} = 408.93$, and both significantly exceed zero, as predicted, suggesting that with some repetition lottery revenues become sensitive to the *MPCR*.

Table 4. Revenue Estimates.

	(a) Parameters	(b) First Half	(c) Second Half	(d) Predicted
0.1	β_0	**547.04**	**503.31**	500
		(0.00)	**(0.00)**	
0.2	ev	22.93	27.20	0
		(0.37)	(0.36)	
0.3	ev^H	−3.92	59.74	0
		(0.48)	(0.40)	
0.4	eh	10.13	4.41	0
		(0.48)	(0.49)	
0.5	$eh^{2/3}$	7.48	13.54	0
		(0.48)	(0.47)	
0.6	ehv	46.22	69.61	150
		(0.23)	(0.26)	
0.7	ehv^H	29.94	37.55	150
		(0.16)	(0.18)	
0.8	$eh^{2/3}v$	−55.77	−46.81	0
		(0.29)	(0.33)	
0.9	$eh^{2/3}v^H$	−55.70	−68.74	0
		(0.30)	(0.26)	
1.1	ℓ	784.10**	316.76**	−125
		(100.00)	(0.98)	
1.2	ℓv	54.96*	110.60*	−11
		(0.22)	(0.93)	
1.3	ℓv^H	**−144.59**	**−160.38***	−29
		(0.03)	**(0.02)**	
1.4	ℓh	161.46	**480.35***	188
		(0.19)	**(0.00)**	
1.5	$\ell h^{2/3}$	178.70**	408.93	562
		(0.17)	**(0.01)**	
1.6	ℓhv	147.81	**−287.68****	−6
		(0.93)	**(0.00)**	
1.7	ℓhv^H	**−149.75***	252.34**	−15
		(0.02)	(0.99)	
1.8	$\ell h^{2/3}v$	−177.36	203.06	−16
		(0.04)	(0.93)	
1.9	$\ell h^{2/3}v^H$	−28.59	**−172.18**	−44
		(0.40)	**(0.05)**	
	$\chi^2(18)$	**108.40**	**118.34**	
	ρ	0.24	0.14	
	N	360	359	

Notes: Numbers in parentheses are *p* values giving the probability that the estimates could be that far from zero in the predicted direction when the true parameter value is zero. **Bold** entries highlight instances where $p < 0.05$.

*Indicates deviation from predicted value at a minimum 90% confidence level.

**Indicates deviation from predicted value at a minimum 95% confidence level.

The marginal results in Table 4, however, reflect other observations incompletely. Notice in particular the ehv and ehv^H parameters reported in rows (0.6) and (0.7) of Table 4. These parameters estimate the marginal effects of increases in V_1, the maximal value draw, on English auction revenues. In contrast to predictions, the ehv and ehv^H parameter estimates not only fall below their predicted values of 150, but also the estimates do not differ significantly from zero in either the first or the second session halves. The insignificance of the these estimates stands in apparent contrast to the mean revenue results for the second session half shown in the upper right portion of Fig. 2, particularly when $h = 1/3$. Unanticipated interaction effects disguise the effects illustrated in Fig. 2. The ehv and ehv^H coefficients estimate only the cumulative marginal effects of increasing *both* value set heterogeneity *and* the *MPCR* (from $h = 0$ to $h = 1/3$). Estimating the effect of value heterogeneity increases when $h = 0.33$ requires evaluation of the sums $ev+ehv$ and ev^H+ehv^H. As is evident from the ev and ev^H estimates shown in rows (0.2) and (0.3) of Table 4, these latter terms, which reflect some tendency for subjects to bid above Nash predictions when $h = 0$, become relatively large quantitatively (albeit insignificant individually) in the second session half.

In fact, unanticipated interaction effects generally undermine a comprehensive evaluation of treatment effects from results reported in Table 4. The lottery estimates contain some particularly notable examples. Consider the parameters ℓhv and ℓhv^H, shown in rows (1.6) and (1.7) of Table 4. In the second session half, these parameters take on values of -287.68 and 252.35, respectively, far different from their predicted levels of -6 and -15. To evaluate the robustness of sales format, value set and *MPCR* treatment effects, we must account for the impacts of these unpredicted interaction effects. Below, we draw formal conclusions about experimental results that account for interaction effects by evaluating observed outcomes in light of predicted changes in the parameter combinations shown in Table 3.[21]

Consider first the effects of switching the sales format from an English auction to a lottery. Establishing the robustness of the tendency for lottery revenues to exceed English auction revenues requires comparison of each lottery parameter combination shown in the lower portion of Table 3 with its English auction counterpart, shown in the upper portion of Table 3. Table 5(a) summarizes the predicted effects. The left panel of Table 5(a) lists the resulting parameter differences, and the right panel of Table 5(a) prints the predicted values of these combinations, given static Nash equilibrium bidding. Notice in the right panel of Table 5(a) that lottery revenues are certainly not predicted to exceed consistently English auction revenues. Indeed, five of the

Table 5(a). Parameter Combinations that Evaluate the Difference between Lottery Revenues and English Auction Revenues. and Predicted Values.

	Parameter Combinations				Predicted Values		
	$\sim h\ (h=0)$	$h\ (h=1/3)$	$h^{67}\ (h=2/3)$		$\sim h\ (0)$	$h\ (1/3)$	$h^{67}\ (2/3)$
$\sim v\ (L)$	ℓ	$\ell + \ell h - eh$	$\ell + \ell h + \ell h^{2/3} - eh - eh^{67}$	$\sim v\ (L)$	-125	63	625
$v\ (M)$	$\ell + \ell v - ev$	$\ell + \ell h + \ell v + \ell hv$ $-eh - ev - ehv$	$\ell + \ell h + \ell v + \ell hv + \ell h^{2/3} v - eh - ev - ehv$ $-eh^{2/3} - eh^{2/3} v$	$v\ (M)$	-136	-104	442
$v^H(H)$	$\ell + \ell v + \ell v^H$ $- ev - ev^H$	$\ell + \ell h + \ell v + \ell v^H$ $+ \ell hv + \ell hv^H - eh$ $- ev - ev^H$ $- ehv - ehv^H$	$\ell + \ell h + \ell v + \ell hv + \ell h^{2/3} v$ $+ \ell h^{2/3} v + \ell hv^H + \ell h^{2/3}$ $v^H - eh - ev - ehv - eh^{2/3}$ $- eh^{2/3} v - ehv^H - eh^{2/3} v^H$	$v^H(H)$	-165	-298	204

Table 5(b). Observed Differences in Lottery and English Auction Revenues.

	First Half				Second Half		
	$\sim h(0)$	$h\ (h=1/3)$	$h^{2/3}\ (h=2/3)$		$\sim h\ (0)$	$h\ (1/3)$	$h^{2/3}\ (2/3)$
$\sim v\ (L)$	784.1**	**938.1****	**1106.7****	$\sim v\ (L)$	316.7**	**792.7****	**1181.1****
	(1.00)	**(0.00)**	**(0.00)**		(0.98)	**(0.00)**	**(0.00)**
$v\ (M)$	816.1**	1071.7**	**1118.7****	$v\ (M)$	400.2**	518.8**	**1164.7****
	(1.00)	(1.00)	**(0.00)**		(1.00)	(1.00)	**(0.00)**
$v^H(H)$	675.5**	895.9**	**1027.2****	$v^H(H)$	108.0**	513.5**	**1055.9****
	(1.00)	(1.00)	**(0.00)**		(0.87)	(1.00)	**(0.00)**

Notes: Numbers in parentheses are p values giving the probability that the estimates could be that far from zero in the predicted direction when the true parameter value is zero. **Bold** entries highlight instances where $p < 0.05$.
**Indicates deviation from predicted value at a minimum 95% confidence level.

nine predicted differences are negative, and some of the differences are quantitatively quite large (the hv^H prediction, for example, is -298 cents).

In an analysis comprised entirely of indicator variables, we can evaluate the significance of parameter restrictions by constructing new indicator variables as the sum of the indicator values for each of the combined parameters. The estimated parameter value for the combined variable recovers an estimate of the sum of the predicted parameter combinations shown in the left hand side of Table 5(a). Table 5(b), which uses the same reporting format used in Table 4, summarizes the relevant estimates.[22] As is evident from the double asterisks in each entry, the difference between lottery and English auction revenues uniformly exceeds the predicted differences both in the first and in the second session halves. Further, notice that lottery revenues uniformly exceed English auction revenues, often by quantitatively very large amounts. The dominance of lotteries over English auctions as a revenue-raising mechanism represents our first finding.

Finding 1. Lottery revenues persistently exceed English auction revenues. This result is robust to repetition, the *MPCR* level and the value set used.

We turn now to the theoretical revenue predictions stated as Conjectures 1–4. Conjecture 1 is a comparative static claim about English auctions. Specifically, given a positive *MPCR*, Conjecture 1 posits that English auction revenues increase with V_1, the highest induced value. To evaluate this conjecture we restrict attention to the six English auctions treatment cells, where $h > 0$ (e.g., the columns $h = 1/3$ and $h = 2/3$ in the upper portion of Table 3). To calculate the predicted equilibrium differences associated with changing the value set, difference the entries within each column (*MPCR* level) across rows (value sets). The left and right panels of Table 6(a) illustrate, respectively, the resulting relevant parameter combinations, and the predicted combination values. Notice the predicted value of 150 in each cell in the right panel of Table 6(a). These predictions reflect the predicted effects on total revenue of increasing V_1 (from 500 to 650, or from 650 to 800) when $h = 1/3$ (the left-hand column) and when $h = 2/3$ (the right-hand column).

Table 6(b) summarizes estimates of value set changes on English auction revenues. In the first session half, summarized in the left panel of Table 6(b), observe that value set changes do not affect English auction revenues significantly. However, turning to the panel on the right hand side, notice that with repetition bids spread consistently in the predicted direction, and that the differences are significant (at a 90% confidence level) when $h = 1/3$.

Table 6(a). Parameter Combinations to Evaluate the Effects of Value Set Heterogeneity on English Auction Revenues, and Predicted Values.

	Parameter Combinations				Predicted Values	
	$\sim h$ (0)	h (1/3)	$h^{2/3}$ (2/3)		$\sim h$ (0)	h (1/3)	$h^{2/3}$ (2/3)
v less $\sim v$ (M less L)		$ev + ehv$	$ev + ehv + eh^{2/3}v$	v less $\sim v$ (M less L)		150	150
v^H less v (H less M)		$ev^H + ehv^H$	$eh^{2/3} + eh^{2/3}v + eh^{2/3}v^H$	v^H less v (H less M)		150	150

Table 6(b). Observed Effects of Value Set Changes on English Auction Revenues.

	First Half				Second Half		
	$\sim h$ (0)	h (1/3)	$h^{2/3}$ (2/3)		$\sim h$ (0)	h (1/3)	$h^{2/3}$ (2/3)
v less $\sim v$ (M less L)		69.15	13.38	v less $\sim v$ (M less L)		**96.81**	50.00
		(0.18)	(0.43)			**(0.10)**	(0.25)
v^H less v (H less M)		26.02	−29.68**	v^H less v (H less M)		**97.29**	28.55
		(0.35)	(0.37)			**(0.10)**	(0.35)

Notes: Numbers in parentheses are p values giving the probability that the estimates could be that far from zero in the predicted direction when the true parameter value is zero. **Bold Italicized** entries highlight instances where $p < 0.10$.
**Indicates deviation from predicted value at a minimum 95% confidence level.

Importantly, the way that V_1 increments affect English auction revenues is not entirely consistent with the underlying theory. As mentioned in the introduction to this analysis, participants show some tendency to bid above the predicted second highest value when $h = 0$. Notice further, in the right panel of Table 6(b) that value set changes fail to increase English auction revenues significantly when $h = 2/3$. We have no definitive explanation as to why the effects of V_1 increases appear to diminish as the $MPCR$ increases from $h = 1/3$ to $h = 2/3$, and offer this result as a curiosity for further investigation.[23] In any case, the limited effects of value set increases on English auction revenues form a second finding.

Finding 2. With repetition, and with $h = 1/3$ revenues in full-information English auctions move directly with the highest induced value. However, the effect is weaker than predicted, and in any case revenue-enhancing effects of increasing the highest induced value no longer remains significant when $h = 2/3$.

Consider next the lotteries. Conjecture 2 posits that lottery revenues move directly with the $MPCR$. To evaluate this conjecture, we find, for each value set, the lottery parameter combinations in Table 3 that survive changes in the $MPCR$ (e.g., difference the row entries in the lower portion of Table 3 across columns). The left and right panels of Table 7(a) illustrate, respectively, parameter combinations and their predicted values. Notice in the right panel of Table 7(a) that $MPCR$ increases affect predicted revenues convexly: for each value set, the effect of increasing h from 1/3 to 2/3 more than doubles the effects of increasing h from 0 to 1/3.

Table 7(a). Parameter Combinations that Evaluate the Effects of Increasing the $MPCR$ (h) on Lottery Revenues and Predicted Values.

	Parameter Combinations			Predicted Values	
	h from $\sim h$ (1/3 from 0)	$h^{2/3}$ from h (2/3 from 1/3)		h from $\sim h$ (1/3 from 0)	$h^{2/3}$ from h (2/3 from 1/3)
$\sim v$ (L)	ℓh	$\ell h^{2/3}$	$\sim v$ (L)	188	562
v (M)	$\ell h + \ell h v$	$\ell h^{2/3} + \ell h^{2/3} v$	v (M)	182	546
v^H(H)	$\ell h + \ell h v + \ell h v^H$	$\ell h^{2/3} + \ell h^{2/3} v + \ell h^{2/3} v^H$	v^H(H)	167	502

Table 7(b). Observed Effects of $MPCR$ Changes on Lottery Revenues.

	First Half			Second Half	
	h from $\sim h$ (1/3 from 0)	$h^{2/3}$ from h (2/3 from 1/3)		h from $\sim h$ (1/3 from 0)	$h^{2/3}$ from h (2/3 from 1/3)
$\sim v$ (L)	161.46	178.7**	$\sim v$ (L)	480.35*	408.93
	(0.39)	(0.18)		(0.00)	(0.00)
v (M)	**309.27**	1.34**	v (M)	192.67	612.59
	(0.05)	(0.50)		(0.12)	(0.00)
v^H (H)	**304.11**	29.93	v^H (H)	445.01*	440.41
	(0.05)	(0.44)		(0.00)	(0.05)

Notes: Numbers in parentheses are p values giving the probability that the estimates could be that far from zero in the predicted direction when the true parameter value is zero. **Bold** entries highlight instances where $p < 0.05$.
*Indicates deviation from predicted value at a minimum 90% confidence level.
**Indicates deviation from predicted value at a minimum 95% confidence level.

The observed effects of $MPCR$ increases in lotteries, printed in Table 7(b) suggest that lottery participants respond to $MPCR$ increases, and that the effect becomes more pronounced with repetition. As seen in the left panel of Table 7(b), in the first session half, the relationship between $MPCR$ changes and lottery revenues follows predictions imprecisely: increasing h from 0 to 1/3 raises revenues in all value sets, and significantly so for the M and H sets. However, further increasing h from 1/3 to 2/3 exerts no significant additional effect for inexperienced participants, despite a considerably larger predicted effect. In the second session half, summarized on the right hand side of Table 7(b) lottery revenues still increase by more than the predicted amount for the increase in h from 0 to 1/3. However, with repetition, the lotteries exhibit an increased sensitivity to the adjustment in h from 1/3 to 2/3. Further, all the lottery revenue adjustments in the second half significantly exceed zero, except for increasing h from 0 to 1/3 with the M value set. In this case, the observed revenue increase of 192.67 nearly matches the predicted increase of 182. However, sampling variability renders this difference insignificant. We summarize these observations as a third finding.

Finding 3. Lottery revenues tend to move directly with the *MPCR*. The effects of *MPCR* changes on revenues increase with repetition.

Conjectures 3 and 4 evaluate the relative revenue effects of *MPCR* and value set changes in lotteries and English auctions. Conjecture 3 posits that given a positive *MPCR*, the ratio of lottery revenues to English auction revenues moves directly with the *MPCR*. Lottery and English auction revenue changes associated with the *MPCR* increases provide relevant evidence to evaluate this conjecture: Conjecture 3 receives support to the extent that lottery revenues increase more with a change in the *MPCR* than English auction revenues over the relevant range. In terms of the parameter combinations listed in Table 3, we evaluate whether the lottery parameter combinations that survive subtracting row entries across the columns $h = 1/3$ and $h = 2/3$ significantly exceed the comparable English auction parameter combinations. The left and right panels of Table 8(a) summarize, respectively, the relevant combinations as well as the differences predicted from equilibrium behavior.[24]

The observed relative effects of *MPCR* increases, as summarized in Table 8(b), suggest that the predicted effects of increasing the *MPCR* emerge, but only with repetition. In the first session half, *MPCR* increases stimulated only relatively small and insignificant increases in lottery revenues over English auction revenues. But with repetition, *MPCR* increases stimulated both substantially and significantly more lottery revenues than English auction revenues. In each value set, lottery revenues increased at least 395 cents more than English auction revenues, and the differences all exceed zero at a minimum 90% confidence level. These observations form our fourth finding.

Table 8(a). Parameter Combinations that Evaluate the Effects of *MPCR* increases on Lottery Revenues Relative to English Auction Revenues and Predicted Differences.

	Parameter Combinations		Predicted Difference
	$h^{2/3}$ from h (2/3 from 1/3)		$h^{2/3}$ from h (2/3 from 1/3)
$\sim v$ (L)	$\ell h^{2/3} - eh^{2/3}$	$\sim v$ (L)	562
v (M)	$\ell h^{2/3} + \ell h^{2/3} v - eh^{2/3} - eh^{2/3} v$	v (M)	546
v^H (H)	$\ell h^{2/3} + \ell h^{2/3} v + \ell h^{2/3} v^H - eh^{2/3} - eh^{2/3} v + eh^{2/3} v^H$	v^H (H)	502

Table 8(b). Observed Effects of *MPCR* Increases on Lottery Revenues Relative to English Auction Revenues.

	First Half		Second Half
	$h^{2/3}$ from h (2/3 from 1/3)		$h^{2/3}$ from h (2/3 from 1/3)
$\sim v(L)$	168.57	$\sim v(L)$	**395.39**
	(0.51)		**(0.08)**
$v\,(M)$	46.98*	$v\,(M)$	**645.86**
	(0.85)		**(0.00)**
$v^H(H)$	131.27*	$v^H(H)$	**542.42**
	(0.37)		**(0.02)**

Notes: Numbers in parentheses are *p* values giving the probability that the estimates could be that far from zero in the predicted direction when the true parameter value is zero. **Bold** entries highlight instances where $p < 0.05$.
*Indicates deviation from predicted value at a minimum 90% confidence level.

Finding 4. With $h > 0$, the ratio of lottery revenues relative to English auction revenues moves directly with the *MPCR*.

Conjecture 4 evaluates the relative effects of value heterogeneity changes on the two sales formats. Specifically, the conjecture posits that given $h > 0$, the ratio of lottery revenues to English auction revenues moves inversely with value dispersion. Evidence supports Conjecture 4 to the extent that English auction revenues increase more (or decrease less) than comparable lottery revenues when the high value, V_1, increases. In terms of the parameter combinations shown in Table 3, we evaluate whether the English auction parameter combinations that survive differing relevant column entries ($h = 1/3$ and $h^{2/3} = 2/3$) across rows (e.g., v less $\sim v$, and v^H less v) significantly exceed the comparable parameter combinations in lotteries. As was the case for the other conjectures, Table 9(a) summarizes relevant parameter combinations and the predicted differences.

Observed differences, summarized in Table 9(b) provide equivocal support for Conjecture 4. Notice that for the first session half, shown in the left panel of Table 9(b), lottery revenues actually respond more than English auction revenues to the change from the *L* value set to the *M* value set (as indicated by the negative entries in the upper row). However, for the change from the *M* to the *H* value set English auction revenues increase significantly more than lottery revenues, as predicted, and the effect is significantly different from zero at a 95% confidence level when $h = 1/3$. The effects of increasing V_1 do not clearly extend with repetition. The relative effects of changing from the *L* to the *M* value set become positive in the second

Table 9(a). Parameter Combinations that Evaluate the Effects of Increases in Value Set Heterogeneity on English Auction Revenues Relative to Lottery Revenues and Predicted Differences.

	Parameter Combinations			Predicted Differences		
$\sim h$ (0)	h (1/3)	$h^{2/3}$ (2/3)		$\sim h$ (0)	h (1/3)	$h^{2/3}$ (2/3)
v less $\sim v$ (*M* less *L*)	$ev + ehv$ $-\ell v - \ell hv$	$ev^H + ehv^H + eh^{2/3}v^H - \ell v^H$ $-\ell hv^H - \ell h^{2/3}v^H$	v less $\sim v$ (*M* less *L*)		167	183
v^H less v (*H* less *M*)	$ev^H + ehv^H$ $-\ell v^H - hv^H$	$ev^H + ehv^H + eh^{2/3}v^H - \ell v^H$ $-\ell hv^H - \ell h^{2/3}v^H$	v^H less v (*H* less *M*)		194	238

Table 9(b). Observed Marginal Differences between English Auction Revenues and Lottery Revenues as Value Set Heterogeneity Increases t.

	First Half				Second Half		
	$\sim h$ (0)	h (1/3)	$h^{2/3}$ (2/3)		$\sim h$ (0)	h (1/3)	$h^{2/3}$ (2/3)
v less $\sim v$ (*M* less *L*)	−133.62** (0.91)	−12.03 (0.98)		v less $\sim v$ (*M* less *L*)	**273.89 (0.00)**	23.42 (0.15)	
v^H less v (*H* less *M*)	**175.77 (0.05)**	91.48 (0.42)		v^H less v (*H* less *M*)	5.33* (0.48)	***108.77** (0.10)***	

Notes: Numbers in parentheses are p values giving the probability that the estimates could be that far from zero in the predicted direction when the true parameter value is zero. **Bold** entries highlight instances where $p < 0.05$. ***Bold Italicized*** entries highlight instances where $p < 0.10$. *Indicates deviation from predicted value at a minimum 90% confidence level. **Indicates deviation from predicted value at a minimum 95% confidence level.

session half (and significantly so when $h = 1/3$). Repetition also appears to diminish the effects of changing from the *M* to the *H* value set. These inconclusive results form a fifth finding.

Finding 5. The ratio of lottery revenues to English auction revenues does not consistently move inversely with increases in V_1.

4.3. Bidding

Although we framed our theoretical analysis largely in terms of revenue effects, a consideration of bidding behavior provides some insight into the experimental results. The predicted and observed mean closing English auction bids and mean lottery bids, shown in Fig. 3, suggest two features of bidding that drive much of the results summarized in Findings 1–5.[25] First,

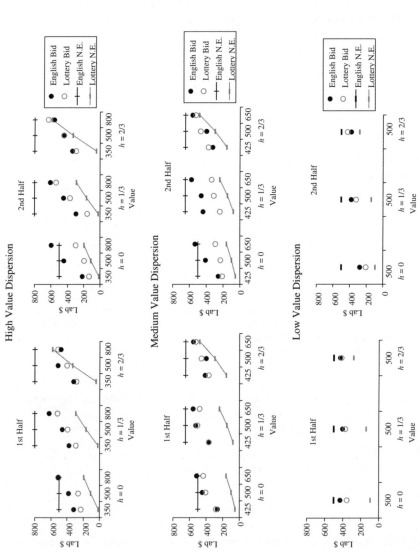

Fig. 3. Observed and Predicted Bids by Session Half. *Key*: Each panel plots mean closing English auction and lottery bids for the first or second half of sessions in a value dispersion condition. Within panels, markers identify bids by *MPCR* ($h = 0$, 1/3, 2/3) and by auction type (English auction or lottery).

neither closing English auction bids ('•') nor lottery bids ('∘') track underlying English auction predictions ('-+-') or lottery predictions ('---') particularly well. In the English auctions, bids tend to move with underlying values, contrary to the predicted behavior in this full information game, and the effect does not appear to dissipate with repetition. In the lotteries, all bidders persistently exceed static Nash lottery predictions. Comparing lottery bids across the left and right columns of Fig. 3, notice that unlike the English auctions, lottery bids show some tendency to decay in the direction of Nash predictions with repetition, as can be seen from comparing lottery bids across the left and right columns of the figure. Nevertheless, even with repetition, overbidding persists in the lotteries.

Second, notice the similarity of closing English auction and lottery bids, particularly in the first session half, summarized in the left panels. With repetition, the difference between closing English auction and lottery bids increases, as lottery participants adjust their bids downward. However, the similarity of bids across sales formats in the first portion of sessions suggests why lottery revenues so spectacularly exceed English auction revenues. At least in this four-bidder context, bids are similar across sales formats. The similarity of lottery and English auction bids results in increased lottery revenues, because unlike the English auction, all lottery bids are paid.

To provide the quantitative support for the above observations regarding bidding behavior, we again use a linear mixed effects model to estimate differences in closing English auction and lottery bids. Following the convention for identifying bid predictions used in Tables 2(a) and (b), label the high, medium and low induced values as V_1, V_2 and V_3, respectively. Then, for each *MPCR* level ($h = 0, 1/3, 2/3$) we estimate the bid by participant i in period t (Bid_{it}) as

$$Bid_{it} = \beta_0 + \beta_{v^2\ell}v_t^2\ell_i + \left(\beta_{v^1} + \beta_{v^1\ell}\ell_i\right)v_t^1$$
$$+ \left(\beta_{v^3} + \beta_{v^3\ell}\ell_i\right)v_t^3 + \xi_i + \varepsilon_{it}$$
$$i = 1, \ldots, 40 \quad t = 1, \ldots, 4 \quad \text{or} \quad 5, \ldots, 8 \tag{9}$$

where $\ell_i = 1$ if participant i was in a lottery session, $v_t^1 = 1$ if participant i's value draw in period t was 800 in the H set, or 650 in the M set, $v_t^2 = 1$ if participant i's value draw in period t was 500 and $v_t^3 = 1$ if participant i's value draw in period t was 350 in the H value set or 425 in the M value set. We estimate bids in the H, M and L value sets separately.[26] Also, as with Eq. (8) we control for interdependencies within sessions, this time by defining individuals as panels, and then assume a random effects error structure within panels. Also, to control for serial correlation we assume a first-order autoregressive process. Thus, in Eq. (9) $\xi_i \sim N(0, \sigma_\xi^2)$, $\varepsilon_{it} + \rho_{e_{it-1}} + \eta_{it}$, $|\eta_{it}| < 1$ and $\eta_{it} \sim N(0, \sigma^2 \eta_t)$. Finally, to allow for insight into temporal effects, we divide the data into two twelve period halves, and conduct separate regressions on each half.

The structure of Eq. (9) merits comment. Using closing English auction bids for the bidder(s) with a value of 500 as the intercept, we estimate the marginal effects of each of the other realizations in the value set as well as the incremental effects of switching the sales format to a lottery at each value set. To the extent that bids move with underlying values, the V_1 parameters (800 or 650) will be positive and the V_3 parameters (350 or 425) will be negative. To the extent lottery and English auction bids track each other, lottery bid estimates (e.g., those appended with an ℓ) will parallel comparable English auction estimates.

Regression results, printed in Tables 10(a–c), illustrate both the persistent tendency for closing bids to follow values in the English auctions, and for English auction and lottery bids to track each other. Consider first the correlation between closing bids and values in the English auctions. The shaded portions of Tables 10(a) and (b) highlight the relevant evidence. Where bids

Table 10(a).   Bid Estimates – High Value Dispersion.

Parameter (p)	First Half			Second Half		
	$h = 0$	$h = 1/3$	$h = 2/3$	$h = 0$	$h = 1/3$	$h = 2/3$
β_0	380.97 (0.00)	**461.33** **(0.00)**	**516.76** **(0.00)**	**443.90** **(0.00)**	**448.40** **(0.00)**	**435.54** **(0.00)**
v^3 (350)	−63.31 (0.14)	*−85.09* *(0.09)*	**−196.57** **(0.00)**	**−226.75** **(0.00)**	**−151.88** **(0.01)**	**−95.71** **(0.05)**
v^1 (800)	**132.89** **(0.02)**	**164.31** **(0.01)**	−36.36 (0.28)	**153.33** **(0.01)**	**159.09** **(0.00)**	**121.66** **(0.03)**
$v^2\ell$	*−117.31* *(0.07)*	−67.33 (0.19)	**−113.56** **(0.05)**	**−249.98** **(0.00)**	−77.81 (0.15)	6.85 (0.46)
$v^3\ell$	*−87.26* *(0.08)*	−85.09 (0.11)	−36.18 (0.24)	−84.80 (0.06)	**−139.40** **(0.01)**	−43.20 (0.25)
$v^1\ell$	−5.37 (0.47)	*−103.72* *(0.09)*	61.99 (0.18)	**−297.88** **(0.00)**	−69.48 (0.17)	72.57 (0.17)
$\chi^2(6)$	**40.75**	**32.42**	**41.16**	**80.06**	**87.57**	**52.91**
ρ	0.09	0.08	−0.01	0.25	0.11	0.13
N	160	160	160	160	160	160

Notes: Numbers in parentheses are p values giving the probability that the estimates could be that far from zero in the predicted direction when the true parameter value is zero. **Bold** entries highlight instances where $p < 0.05$. ***Bold Italicized*** entries highlight instances where $p < 0.10$.

Table 10(b). Bid Estimates – Medium Value Dispersion.

Parameter (p)	First Half			Second Half		
	$h = 0$	$h = 1/3$	$h = 2/3$	$h = 0$	$h = 1/3$	$h = 2/3$
β_0	**446.10**	**526.56**	**401.29**	**408.39**	**460.73**	**397.16**
	(0.00)	**(0.00)**	**(0.00)**	**(0.00)**	**(0.00)**	**(0.00)**
v^3 (425)	**−182.55**	**−164.40**	14.09	**−151.03**	−20.87	*−72.85*
	(0.00)	**(0.00)**	(0.38)	**(0.00)**	(0.21)	*(0.10)*
v^1 (650)	69.40	31.32	**156.86**	**125.04**	**114.92**	**167.69**
	(0.12)	(0.32)	**(0.00)**	**(0.01)**	**(0.02)**	**(0.01)**
$v^2\ell$	−39.20	−20.16	59.21	**−177.70**	**−149.85**	70.35
	(0.29)	(0.39)	(0.18)	**(0.00)**	**(0.01)**	(0.18)
$v^3\ell$	18.27	6.35	−43.61	−47.29	**−200.55**	50.93
	(0.38)	(0.45)	(0.20)	(0.17)	**(0.00)**	(0.20)
$v^1\ell$	−80.65	−78.12	−31.32	**−241.21**	**−239.29**	−40.53
	(0.13)	(0.12)	(0.31)	**(0.00)**	**(0.00)**	(0.27)
$\chi^2(6)$	37.11	22.90	26.05	52.02	32.05	26.05
ρ	0.13	0.04	0.04	0.04	0.08	0.04
N	160	160	160	160	160	160

Notes: Numbers in parentheses are p values giving the probability that the estimates could be that far from zero in the predicted direction when the true parameter value is zero. **Bold** entries highlight instances where $p < 0.05$. ***Bold Italicized*** entries highlight instances where $p < 0.10$.

Table 10(c). Bid Estimates – Low Value Dispersion.

	First Half			Second Half		
	$h = 0$	$h = 1/3$	$h = 2/3$	$h = 0$	$h = 1/3$	$h = 2/3$
β_0	**430.23**	**402.96**	**430.52**	**276.75**	**380.68**	**381.00**
	(0.00)	**(0.00)**	**(0.00)**	**(0.00)**	**(0.00)**	**(0.00)**
$v500\ell$	*−74.08*	−30.47	14.84	*−72.18*	−58.54	44.15
	(0.06)	(0.24)	(0.36)	*(0.09)*	(0.11)	(0.21)
$\chi^2(2)$	2.60	0.49	0.09	1.81	1.55	0.60
ρ	0.18	0.05	0.11	0.05	−0.07	0.04
N	160	160	160	160	160	160

Notes: Numbers in parentheses are p values giving the probability that the estimates could be that far from zero in the predicted direction when the true parameter value is zero. **Bold** entries highlight instances where $p < 0.05$. ***Bold Italicized*** entries highlight instances where $p < 0.10$.

and underlying values are uncorrelated (as predicted in the English auction), the coefficients on value deviations from 500 would differ insignificantly from zero. Scanning down the shaded portion in left column of Tables 10(a) and (b), notice that in the first session half, the null hypothesis is rejected at a minimum 90% confidence level in seven of the 12 comparisons. Nor does the tendency for English auction bids to track underlying values diminish with repetition. To the contrary, as shown in the shaded boxes on the right-hand side of Tables 10(a) and (b), the null hypothesis that bids are insensitive to value deviations is rejected in 10 of the 12 comparisons.

The hollow boxes in Tables 10(a–c) provide evidence pertinent to the correlation between closing English auction and lottery bids. If sellers follow static Nash bidding strategies, for every combination of *MPCR* and values, lottery bids should be much lower than closing English auction bids. However, scanning down the hollow boxes on left-hand side of Tables 10(a–c), observe that in the session halves, closing English auction bids and lottery bids are more similar than different. We can reject the null hypothesis that lottery bids are not less than English auction bids at a minimum of 90% confidence level in only five of the 21 combinations of *MPCR* and value. With repetition, lottery and English auction bids separate to some extent. Nevertheless, separation remains incomplete. As summarized in the hollow boxes shown in the right-hand side of Tables 10(a–c), lottery bids are significantly below English auction bids in 10 of the 21 combinations of *MPCR* and value. We summarize these observations as a final, sixth finding.

Finding 6. The similarity of bids across sales formats drives the observed excessive lottery revenues. Contrary to predictions, closing bids in our full information English auctions move with underlying values. Lottery bids track closing English auction bids closely, despite the fact that lottery bids are paid whether or not the bidder wins the auction.

5. CLOSING COMMENTS

Given the choice between lottery and English auction sales formats to raise charitable funds, our experimental results suggest that lotteries are clearly the preferred sales format. Lottery revenues uniformly dominate English auction revenues. Further, an analysis of bids indicates that a failure of participants to adjust their bids for changes in the sales format drives the excess lottery revenues.

Viewed in light of our results, the persistence of the English auction as a preferred fund-raising sales format prompts some reflection on the relationship between our experimental environment and naturally occurring charity events. Two potentially important differences come to mind. First, naturally occurring charity raffles often have a large number of participants. As the number of bidders becomes large, participants may come to adjust their bid for the sales format.[27] Second, in a fund-raising context, bidders in oral English auctions may derive some considerable utility from demonstrating publicly their largess, and their determination to do whatever necessary to take home an item coveted by group members.[28] In future research, we plan to evaluate these and other related issues.[29]

Issues other than the bidding environment may also explain the persistence of English auctions as a fund-raising sales format. As mentioned in the introduction, religious and legal restrictions proscribe the use of lotteries in many circumstances. But even aside from these restrictions, evidence from the fund-raising trade literature suggests that the silent auction variant of the English auction is widely viewed as a pleasant, non-threatening event that provides the "social-glue" that allows fund-raising effects to occur in the first place. The silent auction format creates a social context that draws in participants, and creates an audience for the high-revenue items, which may be raffled off, or sold at live auction. To the extent that this latter explanation drives the survival of auctions as a sales format, our comparative static results suggest when the silent auctions may be least costly: lottery revenues are highly sensitive to the *MPCR*, and at least guarded evidence suggests that English auction revenues increase with value heterogeneity. Thus, fund-raisers may do well to use the silent auction format for items valued highly by particular individuals, perhaps at the beginning of an evening, when the case for the charity has yet to be made. To the extent charitable intentions increase (and sobriety falls) as an event progresses, our results suggest that fund-raisers may then find it wise to raffle off big-ticket items toward the end of the evening.

NOTES

1. Value heterogeneities are not limited to local fund-raising events. For example, Engers and McManus (2004) discuss several charity auctions, such as the wine auctions hosted by Hospices de Beaune, the Napa Valley wine auctions and an auction of guitars conducted in 1999 by musician Eric Clapton. More generally, items sold in charity fund-raisers tend to be unique, non-standard items for which a retail price is not well established. Other frequently auctioned items include dancers' shoes, the products of local artists and sporting memorabilia (see e.g., Wyman, 1990, pp. 77–79). The possibility of a robust aftermarket may reduce the scope of value of heterogeneities. However, except for very big ticket items, transactions costs and financial constraints likely undermine the scope of aftermarkets frequently.

2. As Isaac and Schnier (2005) observe, silent auctions also often involve the simultaneous sale of a variety of goods. These authors report that the simultaneous closing of bids for multiple items in silent auctions generates sizable revenue losses relative to auctions conducted one at a time. A tendency for participants to "guard" or monitor most closely the items that they value most highly dampens the bidding activity.

3. The Baptist and United Methodist Churches appear to be the most uniform in their opposition to lotteries. For explicit statements, see, for example, *the United Methodist News Service Backgrounder on Gambling* (2002) or Prichart (1991).

4. For example, attorney Jed R. Mandel, advises fund-raisers that most states proscribe as illegal gambling lotteries that are not run by the state. Certain states and localities allow exceptions for not-for-profit organizations, and in other instances charitable organizations can often circumvent state restrictions by structuring their lottery appropriately. However, Mr. Mandel advises charitable organizations to get legal counsel prior to conducting a charity lottery. See Mandel (2003).

5. Indeed charity fund-raisers do not limit themselves to the auction and lottery formats described here. Interesting institutional fund-raising variants include "Tumbola," a lottery where each ticket entitles the holder to a randomly selected prize, an "R-auction" where the auctioneer auctions off portions of a lottery wheel and a "cent lottery" where participants purchase multiple ticket packets, which they split and place into jars aside from multiple items that are raffled simultaneously. For a description of different fund-raising sales formats, see Nash (2000) or Wyman (1990).

6. Engers and McManus are careful to observe that second price auction bid and revenue predictions match those of an English auction only for a special "button auction" a variant of the English auction. In the button auction, bidders indicate initial interest in an item by depressing a button. Bidders release their buttons as an ascending bid clock raises bids above their reservation prices. The bid clock stops and the auction ends when only one bidder remains. In a context where bids have no charitable component, Isaac, Salmon and Zillante (2006) show that "jump-bidding" or the possibility of increasing bids by more than the minimum increment may cause divergence in revenue predictions between second price and English auctions.

7. One of the author's personal experiences with a private school fund-raising event supports this observation. In a private school in a small University town, auction organizers base the sales format decision for collective class projects at least partly on whether or not one of the students' parents in a class is a doctor.

8. Fang shows that in the known but private value case, lotteries may have advantages over the all-pay auction formats. In particular, he shows that given sufficient value heterogeneity, the lottery can raise higher revenues (e.g., cause more complete dissipation) than an all-pay auction. Fang also shows that the "exclusion principle" shown to apply to all-pay auctions by Baye, Kovenock and de Vries (1994) does not extend to the lottery. These results are interesting in that they differ somewhat from some conjectures by Goeree et al. (2005) about the relationship between lotteries and all-pay auctions in the case where values are not known. Goeree and Turner argue that an all-pay auction is essentially an efficient variant of a lottery and that removing the uncertainty about the winner will increase bids.

9. Pooling the analysis of silent and oral versions of ascending bid auctions, abstracts from some complications peculiar to the silent auction format. As noted by Isaac and Schnier (2005), multiple silent auctions tend to be conducted simultaneously.

Also silent auctions typically have a fixed closing time, which may encourage deadline effects, such as pulling high bids at the last minute, or waiting until the last minute to submit bids. In our experimental implementation of the English auction we abstract from these problems by auctioning off only one item at a time, and by injecting a "soft" closing rule where we extend bidding with the submission of late bids.

10. This result may be viewed as a special case of revenue predictions for the private value English auction. Goeree et al. (2005) show that in the case of private values and a positive *MPCR*, English auction revenues are bound by the expected value of the first and second order statistics from the value distribution, given n draws, $E(V_2^n)$ and $E(V_1^n)$. Engers and McManus (2004) also anticipate our result. "Note how different strategies in the button auction would be if all valuations were common knowledge. In this full information situation all bidders other than the one with the highest valuation would want to remain in the auction for as long as possible to inflate the payment that the winner makes to the charity" (p. 12).

11. In his Theorem 1, Hemming Fang (2002) establishes uniqueness of the equilibrium characterized by Hillman and Riley (1989).

12. In the public-value English auction with $h > 0$, the winning bidder realizes no surplus from winning the item, and thus the equilibrium earnings reflect the social welfare of the winning bid. This welfare would be reduced if the auctioned item came at a cost to the charity.

13. With $h = 2/3$, lottery participants uniformly enjoy 2/3 of the sum of bids. Expected earnings for the V_1 and V_2 value bidders are lower because the expected value of the prize is less than their optimal bid. Despite relatively low expected earnings, the predictions shown in Table 2(b) represent an equilibrium. Bid reductions for the V_1 or V_2 value bidders would reduce expected earnings for these bidders.

14. A calculator is unnecessary in the English auction, since participants see their potential public and private returns updated in real time, as they submit bids.

15. The 90 s lottery period roughly equated the temporal length of the English auction and lottery periods.

16. The conversion factor allows closer approximation of equilibrium bid predictions than would be possible with a penny grid in US currency.

17. In the panels of Fig. 1, the sequence of realizations of each value set in a session comprises the horizontal scale. As Table A1 illustrates, our design rotates the different value sets in a roughly even order throughout the sessions. Thus, in each session participants face each value set eight times.

18. Comparing the upper and lower panels of Fig. 2, notice that we double the vertical scale of the lotteries relative to the English auctions. The doubling of the scale facilitates our highlighting both the comparatively subtle effects of increasing value dispersion in the English auctions, and the much more pronounced relationship between lottery revenues and the *MPCR*. Notice also in the lower panel of Fig. 2 that even in the latter session halves, lottery revenues fail to consistently move inversely to value heterogeneity, as predicted.

19. The xtregar procedure in the STATA statistical package generates the estimates reported in Table 4.

20. Thus, the probabilities reported below the estimates reflect results of one-tailed tests, while the asterisks reporting the significance of deviations from Nash predictions reflect results of two-tailed tests.

21. The problem of accounting for interaction effects arises frequently in the analysis of experimental data. We offer the rather lengthy analysis of the problem here as a suggested general approach.

22. The standard errors of estimates for the combined parameters provide the basis for the statistical comparisons made in Table 5(b).

23. One possibility is that participants attend more closely to the *relative* earnings effects of a bidding decision than to the *absolute* earnings effects. Although the absolute earnings consequences of raising a bid are independent of the *MPCR*, the percentage earnings increments fall with *MPCR* increases. To see this, consider the earnings consequences of a bid of 600 for the high-value bidder when $V_1 = 800$. When $h = 1/3$, the V_1 bidder earns $(800-600)+0.33(600) = 400$ from winning the auction, and $0.33(600) = 200$ from losing. When $h = 2/3$, the V_1 bidder earns $(800-600)+0.67(600) = 600$ from winning the auction and $0.67(600) = 400$ from losing. Although the earnings difference between winning and losing is 200 in either condition, the change represents a 50% increase over the return from losing when $h = 1/3$, but only a 33% increase in earnings when $h = 2/3$. Indeed, the very high relative increase in earnings may explain why high-value bidders respond to bids above 500, despite the fact that such bids leave lower valued rivals exposed to losses. When $h = 0$, the V_1 bidder earns $(800-600)+200 = 400$ from winning the auction, and 0.200 from losing, there is a 100% increase.

24. Notice in the right side of Table 8(a) that the predicted differences equal the marginal effect of increasing h on lottery revenues, shown for example, in the right side of Table 7(a). Recall that given $h>0$, additional h increases do not affect predicted English auction revenues.

25. "Closing bids" in the English auctions are the final bids submitted in a period by participants with a particular value draw. Mean closing bids are closing bids averaged across period segments, and bidders with the value draw.

26. Since values are homogenous, the regression for the L value set estimates only the first two parameters in Eq. (9).

27. Casual observation suggests that some adjustment must take place. Churches and school raffles for big ticket items, such as automobiles often include revenue caps, whereby total ticket sales are limited to a pre-announced fixed number. Presumably such commitments would be unnecessary if bidders did not adjust ticket purchases for lottery sales format. On the other hand, if overbidding in lotteries persists when the number of bidders is small, a charity sales format that sharply restricted the number of bidders might actually result in increased revenues.

28. In their analysis of some naturally occurring charity auctions, Isaac and Schnier (2005) report some evidence of what they call "see and be seen" preferences as an explainer of jump-bidding activity in silent charity auctions. Curiously, such preferences appear to be sensitive to the charity. More aggressive bidding was observed in an auction held for a private preparatory school than was observed in a pair of church auctions.

29. Relaxing our assumption that bidders have full information about the value draws represents an additional dimension of our experimental design that merits further investigation. However, although suppressing information about value draws may reduce English auction bids somewhat, we are skeptical that information about value draws drives the excessive lottery revenues. Looking at the mean revenues

shown in Fig. 2, for example, notice that lottery revenues do not appear to be importantly affected by value set changes.

ACKNOWLEDGMENTS

We thank, without implicating, David Harless, Dan Houser, Mark Isaac and Kevin McCabe for their comments as well as the participants in an ICES Seminar at George Mason University and sessions at the 2002 Southern Economics Association Meetings in New Orleans, LA and the 2003 Economic Science Association Meetings in Pittsburgh. Financial support from the National Science Foundation, the Virginia Commonwealth University Faculty Excellence Fund and the Robert M. Hearin Support Foundation are gratefully acknowledged. We also thank Jeffrey Kirchner for writing the software.

REFERENCES

Baye, M., Kovenock, D., & De Vries, C. G. (1994). The solution to the Tullock rent-seeking game when $R > 2$: Mixed strategy equilibria and mean dissipation rates. *Public Choice*, *81*, 363–380.

Davis, D. D., & Reilly, R. J. (1998). Do too many cooks always spoil the stew? An experimental analysis of rent-seeking and the role of a strategic buyer. *Public Choice*, *95*, 89–115.

Davis, D. D., & Reilly, R. J. (2000). Multiple buyers, rent-defending and the observed social costs of monopoly. *Pacific Economic Review*, *5*, 389–410.

Engers, M., & McManus, B. (2004). *Charity auctions*. St. Louis: Manuscript, Washington University.

Fang, H. (2002). Lottery versus all-pay auction models of lobbying. *Public Choice*, *112*, 351–371.

Goeree, J., Maashand, E., Onderstal, S., & Turner, J. L. (2005). How (not) to raise money. *Journal of Political Economy*, *113*, 897–918.

Hillman, A., & Riley, J. G. (1989). Politically contestable rents and transfers. *Economics and Politics*, *1*, 17–39.

Isaac, R. M., Salmon, T. C., & Zillante, A. (2006). *A theory of jump bidding in ascending auctions*. Journal of Economic Behaviour and Organization (Forthcoming).

Isaac, R. M., & Schnier, K. (2005). Silent auctions in the field and in the laboratory. *Economic Inquiry*, *43*, 715–733.

Mandel, J. (2003). Primedia business magazines and media association meetings. www.MeetingsNet.com

Morgan, J. (2000). Financing public goods by means of lotteries. *Review of Economics Studies*, *67*, 761–784.

Morgan, J., & Sefton, M. (2000). Funding public goods with lotteries: Experimental evidence. *Review of Economic Studies*, *67*, 785–810.

Nash, D. (2000). www.fetesandfestivals.com.au/contactus.htm

Prichart, R. (1991). Gambling and the christian faith. *Keep Believing Ministries*, http://
    www.cmcop.org/sermons/htm/issues/910725.htm
United Methodist News Service Backgrounder on Gambling. (2002). http://umns.umc.org/
    backgrounders/gambling.html
Wyman, K. (1990). *Guide to special events fundraising. Voluntary action program of Canadian
    heritage* (2nd ed.), www.pch.gc.ca/cp-pc/ComPartnE/pub_list.htm

APPENDIX 1

Table A1. Value Assignments (in Lab Dollars).

Period	Value set	Bidder			
		1	2	3	4
1	H	350	350	500	800
2	L	500	500	500	500
3	M	425	650	500	425
4	L	500	500	500	500
5	H	800	500	350	350
6	M	425	425	650	500
7	L	500	500	500	500
8	M	650	425	500	425
9	H	350	500	800	350
10	M	500	425	425	650
11	L	500	500	500	500
12	H	350	800	350	500
13	M	425	500	425	650
14	H	800	350	500	350
15	L	500	500	500	500
16	H	500	350	800	350
17	M	500	650	425	425
18	L	500	500	500	500
19	M	425	425	650	500
20	L	500	500	500	500
21	H	500	350	350	800
22	L	500	500	500	500
23	H	350	800	350	500
24	M	650	500	425	425

APPENDIX 2. EXPERIMENT INSTRUCTIONS

This appendix contains instructions for the English auction and the lottery sessions. These instructions presume that the $MPCR = 1/3$. Screen displays and illustrative examples were changed appropriately when the $MPCR = 2/3$. Also, these instructions omit arrows included in the instructions used, which connect the text with the pertinent illustrative figures.

[Read to all.] This is an experiment (Appendix 2) in the economics of decision making. Various research foundations have provided funds for this research. The instructions are simple, and if you understand them, you may earn a considerable amount of money that will be paid to you in *cash* at the end of the experiment. Your earnings will be determined partly by your decisions and partly by the decisions of others. If you have questions at any time while reading the instructions, please raise your hand and a laboratory monitor will assist you.

[English auctions.] This is what your screen will look like in the experiment (see Fig. A1). In each period of the experiment you will be matched with three other people, your counterparts. You and your counterparts will be bidding in an auction to purchase a fictitious product. If you purchase the product, you will receive as part of your earnings the value of the item. Please note that you and your counterparts may have different values for this item. The monitor will write the values for all participants on the Board at the front of the room at the beginning of the auction.

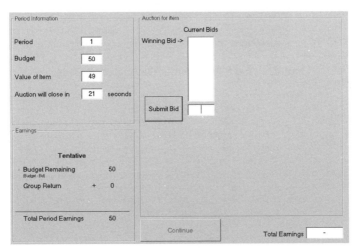

Fig. A1. English Auction Screen Display.

How do you participate in the auction and purchase this fictitious product? On the right-hand side of your screen, you and your counterparts will submit a *bid* to purchase the item in the auction (see Fig. A2). A *bid* is the amount that you are willing to pay for the item. To submit a bid, simply type the amount you are willing to pay in the white box and click on the 'submit bid' button. You will then be asked to confirm that bid as shown below.

You may submit any bid you like, in unit increments, up to your budget for the period. No bids with decimals will be accepted. Each bid that you submit must be greater than the current highest bid. The current highest (or winning) bid is displayed at the top of the list, and your bids are denoted by an asterisk. In Fig. A3, you currently have the highest winning bid of 31. If the auction is to end at this point, you will pay 31 to purchase the fictitious item.

When does the auction end? A clock is displayed on the left-hand side of your screen in the 'period information' frame. The auction will open with 90 s on the clock. If there is a new winning bid in the last 5 s of the auction,

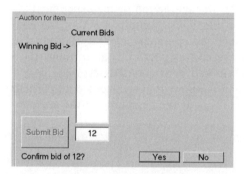

Fig. A2. Bid Submission in the English Auction.

Fig. A3. The English Auction Bid Queue.

another 10 s will be added to the clock. The auction will end when there are no new winning bids for the last 5 s on the clock (see Fig. A4).

Each period, you will be given a budget with which to bid in the auction. This budget is the most with which you can bid in the auction. Any amount unspent in the budget will be added to your earnings for that period.

Your earnings for a period are summarized in the bottom left portion of your screen. In addition to the value of the item and any unspent amount of the budget, each person also receives earnings based upon the final winning bid, regardless if they win the auction or not. Specifically, each person earns 1/3 of the winning bid. We will call this amount the 'group return.'

Suppose that the winning bid was 31 and your budget is 50. Example 1 summarizes your earnings if you submitted the winning bid of 31 (see Fig. A5). Your remaining budget is $50 - 31 = 19$. Your earnings from the 'group return' are $31 \times 1/3 = 10.33$. Total period earnings are the sum of the remaining budget, the group return and the item value.

Example 2 summarizes your earnings if you did not win the auction (see Fig. A6). Your remaining budget is 50 because you did not spend it in the auction, and your earnings from the 'group return' are still $31 \times 1/3 = 10.33$. In this case, total period earnings are the sum of your budget and the group return.

In each period there will be one auction. When the auction concludes, click the 'continue' button at the bottom of the screen to go onto the next period for a new auction. At the end of the experiment, your experimental dollars will be converted into cash at the rate of 1000 experimental dollars for *US\$ 1*.

[Lotteries.] This is what your screen will look like in the experiment (see Fig. A7). In each period of the experiment you will be matched with three other people, your counterparts. You and your counterparts will be

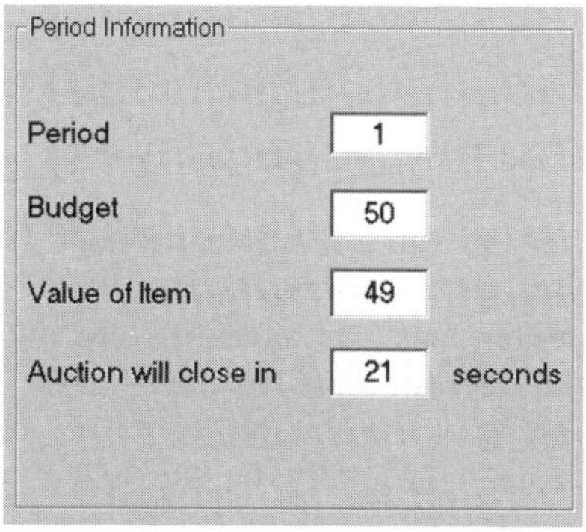

Fig. A4.   English Auction Period Information.

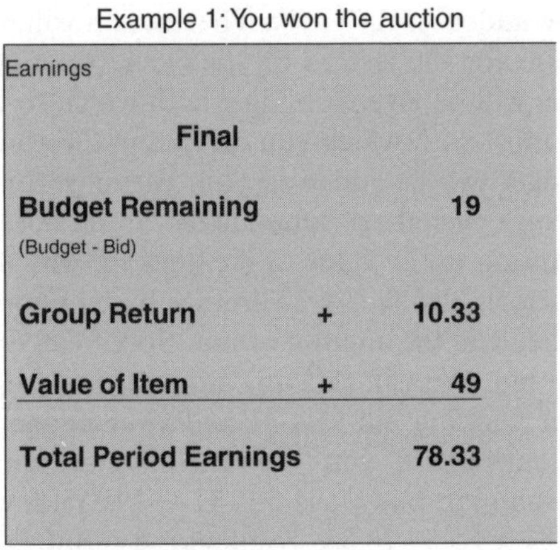

Example 1: You won the auction

Earnings		
Final		
Budget Remaining		**19**
(Budget - Bid)		
Group Return	**+**	**10.33**
Value of Item	**+**	**49**
Total Period Earnings		**78.33**

Fig. A5.   Period Earnings for the English Auction Winner.

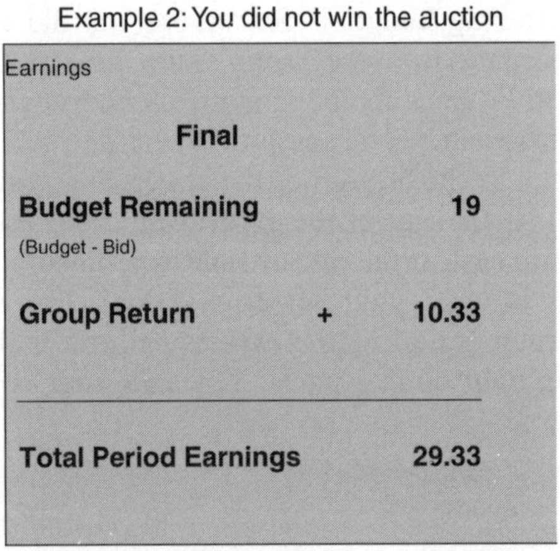

Example 2: You did not win the auction

Earnings		
Final		
Budget Remaining		**19**
(Budget - Bid)		
Group Return	**+**	**10.33**
Total Period Earnings		**29.33**

Fig. A6.   Period Earnings for English Auction Non-winners.

participating in a lottery to win a fictitious product. If you win the lottery, you will receive as part of your earnings the value of the item. Please note that you and your counterparts may have different values for this item. The monitor will write the values for all participants on the Board at the front of the room at the beginning of the auction.

How do you participate in the lottery? On the right-hand side of your screen, you and your counterparts will submit your lottery purchases. To submit the amount of your lottery purchase, simply type the amount you are willing to

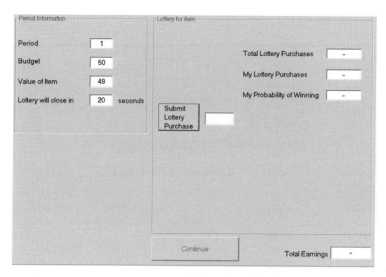

Fig. A7. Lottery Screen Display.

spend in the white box and click on the 'submit lottery purchase' button. You will then be asked to confirm that amount as shown here (see Fig. A8).

How does the lottery work? The period will open with 90 s on the clock in the 'period information' frame on the left-hand side of your screen (see Fig. A9). You and your counterparts will then have 90 s to submit your lottery purchases. If you do not submit *and* confirm an amount before the clock expires, then you are not entered in the lottery to win the item.

Once the clock expires, the total amount spent on the lottery will be displayed on the right-hand side of the screen. Your probability of winning the auction depends on how much you spent in the lottery and the total amount spent by you and your counterparts. Specifically, your probability of winning the lottery is the ratio of your lottery purchases to the total amount of lottery purchases. In the example on the right, you spent 15 in the lottery and total amount spent was 45. Hence, your probability of winning the lottery is 15/45 or 33% (see Fig. A10).

This probability of winning is represented in Fig. A10. The black line represents the total amount spent on lottery purchases and the width of orange box on top of the black line indicates your portion of the lottery purchases. After the clock expires, the computer will randomly determine which experimental dollar *along* that black line is the winner. In this case, the red pointer indicates that somebody else won the lottery. If the red triangle points at your orange portion of the line, then you have won the item.

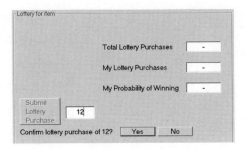

Fig. A8. Lottery Ticket Purchases.

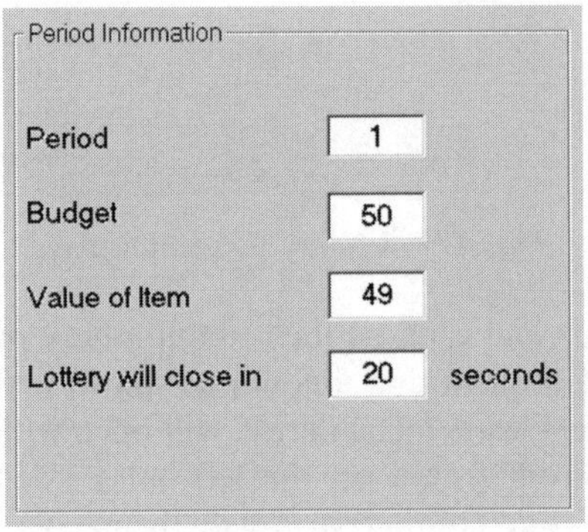

Fig. A9. Lottery Period Information.

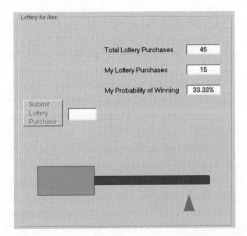

Fig. A10. Lottery Probabilities and Winner Determination.

In each period, you will be given a budget with which to spend in the lottery. This budget is the most with which you can spend in the lottery. You may spend any amount you like in a period, in unit increments, up to your period budget for the period. No bids with decimals will be accepted. Any amount unspent in the budget will be added to your earnings for that period.

Your earnings for a period are summarized in the bottom left portion of your screen. In addition to the value of the item and any unspent amount of the budget, each person also receives earnings based upon the total amount spent in the lottery, regardless if they win the lottery or not. Specifically, each person earns 1/3 of the total amount spent. We will call this amount the 'group return' because everyone earns an equal portion of the total amount spent.

Suppose that you spent 15 on the lottery and your budget is 50. Example 1 summarizes your earnings if you won the lottery (see Fig. A11). Your remaining budget is $50-15 = 35$. Also suppose that everyone else spent a total of 36 on the lottery, so the total lottery expenditures are $36 + 15 = 51$. Your earnings from the 'group return' are $51 \times 1/3 = 17$. The value from winning the item is 49. In this case, the total period earnings of 101 are the sum of the remaining budget, the group return and the item value.

Example 2 summarizes your earnings if you did not win the lottery (see Fig. A12). The only difference is that you did not win the lottery and so you do not receive the value of the item as part of your earnings. Thus, total period earnings are the sum of your remaining budget and the group return.

In each period there will be one lottery. When the lottery concludes, click the 'continue' button at the bottom of the screen to go onto the next period

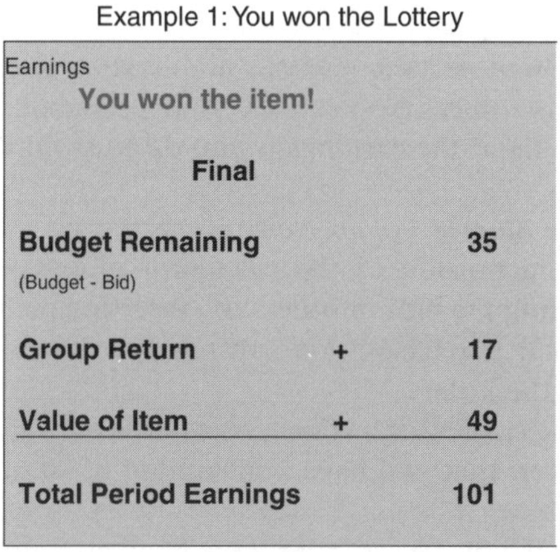

Example 1: You won the Lottery

Earnings		
You won the item!		
Final		
Budget Remaining		35
(Budget - Bid)		
Group Return	+	17
Value of Item	+	49
Total Period Earnings		101

Fig. A11. Period Earnings for the Lottery Winner.

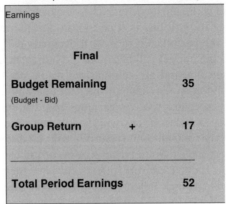

Fig. A12. Period Earnings for Lottery Non-Winners.

for a new lottery. At the end of the experiment, your experimental dollars will be converted into cash at the rate of 1000 experimental dollars for *US$ 1*.

Calculator

To assist you in making your lottery purchase decisions, we provide you with a calculator that appears vertically on the left portion of your screen. The calculator consists of three parts. The upper part contains information about the parameters in your session (see Fig. A13).

The second portion is a *purchase calculator*. By inserting your item value for the period as well as your guesses about your lottery purchases and lottery purchases by others, you can see your probability of winning, your earnings if you win and the earnings if you do not win the lottery.

Please Enter Some Sample Values Now

Finally, the bottom portion of the calculator allows you to check your assumption regarding the bids of others. By inserting period results for your purchases, and total purchases, you can see how much everyone else collectively spent on the lottery.

You may use the calculator as much or as little as you like in the session. Remember, however, that you have a maximum of 90 s to make a decision each period.

Any questions? If not, please raise your hand to indicate that you have finished reading the instructions.

Parameters

Group Return Rate	
	0.33
Your Budget	
	80

Purchase Calculator

Item Value
0
Your Lottery Purchases
0
Lottery Purchases by Others
0
Probability of Winning the Lottery
0.0
Earnings if you win the Lottery
0.0
Earnings if you do NOT win the Lottery
0.00

Assessing Results

Your Lottery Purchases
0
Total Lottery Purchases
0
Lottery Purchases by Others
0

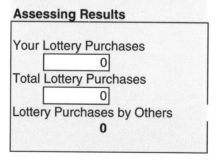

Fig. A13. Lottery Calculator.

THE OPTIMAL DESIGN OF CHARITABLE LOTTERIES: THEORY AND EXPERIMENTAL EVIDENCE

Andreas Lange, John A. List, Michael K. Price and Shannon M. Price

ABSTRACT

Charitable lotteries represent one of today's most popular fund-raising schemes. This study begins by developing theory examining the optimal design of a charitable lottery. We show that any prize distribution is only optimal for a group of n symmetric agents with given risk preference. However, there exist multiple prize distributions that generate contributions approaching the optimal level over a range of individual risk posture. We test our theory using a battery of experimental treatments. Our results suggest that lotteries dominate the voluntary contribution mechanism (VCM) in terms of total dollars raised. Moreover, the performance of lotteries weakly depends on individual risk preference.

1. INTRODUCTION

Charitable lotteries represent an interesting fund-raising tool. The basic premise of the charitable lottery is that competition for a private prize

Experiments Investigating Fundraising and Charitable Contributors
Research in Experimental Economics, Volume 11, 93–119
Copyright © 2006 by Elsevier Ltd.
ISSN: 0193-2306/doi:10.1016/S0193-2306(06)11004-2

introduces a compensating externality that attenuates the free-rider problem (see e.g., Morgan, 2000). Intuitively, the possibility of winning a prize serves to reduce the gap between private and social marginal benefit, which may stimulate contributions to the public account. Prior experimental work (Morgan & Sefton, 2000; Lange, List, & Price, 2005; Dale, 2004) lends support to this theoretical prediction: relative to the standard VCM, lotteries with exogenously determined prize values increase the provision of a public good.[1]

Lange et al. (2005) extend the model of Morgan (2000) to consider the effects of risk aversion and preference heterogeneity on charitable contributions. The Lange et al. model introduces a variant of the Morgan lottery mechanism that provides multiple prizes. Lange et al. show that when agents are sufficiently risk averse or have heterogeneous valuations for the public good, total contribution levels may be increased by splitting one large prize into several smaller prizes. We extend this analysis by exploring the optimal design of charitable lotteries. Specifically, we examine how changes in the total number of participants, the total available prize budget, and individual risk postures affect the optimal prize distribution. We show that any specific prize distribution is only optimal for a fixed group of n symmetric agents with a specific level of risk aversion. However, using mathematical simulations, we show that multiple potential prize distributions can generate contribution levels which approach this optimum over a wide range of individual risk postures.[2]

A second portion of the paper reports a laboratory experiment designed to evaluate the behavioral interactions between the distribution of lottery prizes and risk posture. The laboratory experiment consists of two parts. The first part of the experiment employs a series of experimental treatments to examine the contribution decisions of agents in a public good setting. These treatments compare the outcomes of the VCM, the single fixed-prize lottery (SPL) and the n-prize lottery (NPL) for agents who have symmetric valuations for the public good, but who may differ in revealed risk preference. The second part of the experiment was designed to lend insights into subjects' risk postures using the Holt and Laury (2002) paired lottery-choice design and link those preferences to behavior in the public goods game.

By way of preview, the experimental results provide mixed support for the theoretical predictions. First, we find that charitable lotteries raise more revenue than a similar VCM. The dominance of the lottery as a fund-raising mechanism, however, is weakened when one considers revenues net of the prize values. Second, we find guarded support for the conjecture that individual risk postures affect the performance of the SPL and NPL.

We organize our paper as follows: Section 2 presents our theoretical model, Section 3 summarizes the experimental design, Section 4 discusses the results, and Section 5 concludes.

2. THE NPL AND RISK AVERSION

This section explores the impact of risk preference on the design of charitable lotteries. We concentrate on an economy with n potentially risk-averse agents each with identical valuations for a public good. The payoff of a representative agent is given by

$$u_i = y_i + hG$$

where y_i is a numeraire commodity (income) and G denotes the total provision level of a linear public good. Agents' initial income is denoted by w. Throughout, we assume that provision of the public good is socially desirable (e.g., $nh > 1$) but that no rational agent would elect to voluntarily contribute to the charity as individual valuations for the public good are such that $0 < h < 1$.

Our model follows the basic framework of Morgan (2000), Morgan and Sefton (2000), and Lange et al. (2005) in introducing a charitable lottery as a mechanism designed to alleviate free-riding incentives in the provision of the public good. Assume that the charitable fundraiser has a prize budget of P, which may be divided into n different prizes. We restrict attention to a variant of the NPL in which each agent can only win a single prize ($P_s \geq 0$) and consider the optimal distribution of prizes in such a lottery for a fundraiser with a given fixed prize budget: $\sum_{s=1}^{n} P_s = P$.

We denote the probability that agent i wins a given prize s by π_{si}. For all prizes s and for any agent i, these probabilities depend on both the agent's contribution level b_i and the contribution levels of all other agents in the economy. Assuming that the other (symmetric) agents each contribute b_{-i}, these probabilities are given by

$$\pi_{1i} = \frac{b_i}{b_i + (n-1)b_{-i}}$$

$$\pi_{2i} = \frac{(n-1)b_{-i}}{b_i + (n-1)b_{-i}} \frac{b_i}{b_i + (n-2)b_{-i}}$$

$$\cdots$$

$$\pi_{si} = \frac{(n-1)b_{-i}}{b_i + (n-1)b_{-i}} \frac{(n-2)b_{-i}}{b_i + (n-2)b_{-i}} \cdots \frac{b_i}{b_i + (n-s)b_{-i}}$$

Intuitively, each probability π_{si} represents agent i's probability of winning prize s conditioned on having failed to win prizes 1 through $s-1$. Each agent influences the probability π_{si} by their choice of b_i. For any respective probability, π_{si}, the marginal effect of an increase in agent i's contribution level is given by

$$\frac{\partial \pi_{si}}{\partial b_i} = \frac{\pi_{si}}{b_i} - \sum_{j=1}^{s} \frac{\pi_{si}}{b_i + (n-j)b_{-i}}$$

As agents are assumed symmetric, we restrict attention to symmetric equilibrium ($b_i = b_{-i} = b$) and therefore obtain

$$\pi_{si} = \frac{1}{n}$$

$$\frac{\partial \pi_{si}}{\partial b_i} = \frac{1}{nb} H(s), \quad \text{where} \quad H(s) = 1 - \sum_{j=0}^{s-1} \frac{1}{n-j} \tag{1}$$

Finally, assume that agents' utilities are characterized by constant absolute risk aversion (CARA). Under this assumption, the Bernoulli utility function for an agent is given by $\rho(z) = -\frac{1}{\sigma}\exp(-\sigma z)$. Then, the expected utility of agent i is defined as

$$EU_i = \sum_{s=1}^{n} \pi_{si}\rho(P_s - b_i + hB)$$

where $B = \sum_{i=1}^{n} b_i$. Thus,

$$EU_i = \sum_{s=1}^{n} \pi_{si}\rho(P_s - b_i + hB) = -\frac{1}{\sigma}\sum_{s=1}^{n} \pi_{si}\exp[-\sigma(P_s - b_i + hB)]$$

$$= -\frac{1}{\sigma}\exp[\sigma(b_i - hB)]\sum_{s=1}^{n} \pi_{si}\exp[-\sigma P_s]$$

Consider now the optimal contribution level of agent i. Agent i will select a contribution level ($0 \leq b_i \leq w$) that maximizes her expected utility taking as given the equilibrium contribution decisions of all other agents. The first order condition for this maximization problem is given by

$$
-\frac{1}{\sigma}\exp[\sigma(b_i - hB)]\sum_{s=1}^{n}\left(\sigma(1-h)\pi_{si} + \frac{\partial\pi_{si}}{\partial b_i}\right)\exp[-\sigma P_s]\begin{Bmatrix} \leq \\ = \\ \geq \end{Bmatrix}0,
$$

$$
\text{if}\begin{cases} b_i = 0 \\ 0 < b_i < w \\ b_i = w \end{cases}
$$

$$
\rightleftharpoons \sum_{s=1}^{n}\left(\sigma(1-h)\pi_{si} + \frac{\partial\pi_{si}}{\partial b_i}\right)\exp[-\sigma P_s]\begin{Bmatrix} \geq \\ = \\ \leq \end{Bmatrix}0, \quad \text{if}\begin{cases} b_i = 0 \\ 0 < b_i < w \\ b_i = w \end{cases} \quad (2)
$$

As agents are assumed symmetric we focus on symmetric equilibria. It should be noted that zero contributions ($b_i = b = 0$) cannot represent an equilibrium as an agent could secure the first prize by contributing an arbitrary small amount ($\partial\pi_{1i}/\partial b_i = \infty$). Furthermore, if the other corner solution where agents contribute all their wealth and the first order condition holds with inequality the fund-raiser can reduce the total prize budget without affecting overall provision of the public good – agents will still contribute all of their wealth. As we are interested in the optimal lottery design, we therefore concentrate on the case of an interior solution to Eq. (2).

We can therefore use Eq. (1) to rewrite the first-order condition in Eq. (2) as

$$
0 = \sum_{s=1}^{n}(\sigma(1-h)b + H(s))\exp[-\sigma P_s]
$$

$$
b = \frac{1}{\sigma(1-h)}\frac{-\sum_{s=1}^{n}H(s)\exp[-\sigma P_s]}{\sum_{s=1}^{n}\exp[-\sigma P_s]}
$$

$$
= \frac{1}{\sigma(1-h)}\frac{\sum_{s=1}^{n-1}H(s)(1 - \exp[-\sigma(P_s - P_n)])}{1 + \sum_{s=1}^{n-1}\exp[-\sigma(P_s - P_n)]} \quad (3)
$$

where the last equality follows from the fact that $H(n) + \sum_{s=1}^{n-1} H(s) = nb\sum_{s=1}^{n} \partial \pi_{si}/\partial b_i = 0$. If the goal is to maximize total contributions given a fixed budget $P = \sum_s P_s$, a charitable fundraiser has to select that distribution of prizes which maximizes the right hand side in the Eq. (3).[3] Eq. (3) immediately implies two initial criteria for any such optimal prize distribution. First, the ranking of prizes should obey $P_1 \geq \cdots \geq P_n$ – i.e., prizes should be awarded in decreasing order of magnitude. To see this result, note that since $H(r)$ is decreasing in r, we therefore have that for all $r < t$ and for all $X > Y$, $-H(r)\exp[-\sigma X] - H(t)\exp[-\sigma Y] > -H(r)\exp[-\sigma Y] - H(t)\exp[-\sigma X]$. Second, it should be noted that only the difference from the smallest prize P_n matters in determining contributions. Hence, it is always optimal to choose $P_n = 0$.

The optimal prize distribution is obtained by maximizing b with respect to P_r ($r < n$) such that $P = \sum_s P_s$, $P_n = 0$, which yields

$$\frac{\partial b}{\partial P_r} \begin{Bmatrix} = \\ \leq \end{Bmatrix} \lambda \quad \text{for } P_r \begin{Bmatrix} > \\ = \end{Bmatrix} 0 \quad (\lambda \geq 0)$$

where

$$\frac{\frac{\partial b}{\partial P_r}}{\frac{\partial b}{\partial P_t}} = \exp[-\sigma(P_r - P_t)] \frac{H(r)\left(1 + \sum_{s=1}^{n-1} \exp[-\sigma P_s]\right) + \sum_{s=1}^{n-1} H(s)(1 - \exp[-\sigma P_s])}{H(t)\left(1 + \sum_{s=1}^{n-1} \exp[-\sigma P_s]\right) + \sum_{s=1}^{n-1} H(s)(1 - \exp[-\sigma P_s])}$$

$$(4)$$

For the risk-neutral case $\sigma = 0$, Eq. (4) implies $(\partial b/\partial P_r)/(\partial b/\partial P_t) = H(r)/H(t) > 1$ for $r < t$ and therefore that in an optimum only one prize $P_1 = P$ is provided.[4]

However, for risk-averse agents, the SPL may not represent the optimal fundraising mechanism. Given an economy with risk-averse agents, splitting a single prize of value P into multiple prizes of lesser value may lead to an increase in total contributions. Intuitively, if only one prize is provided agents have only a $1/n$ chance to receive a prize. However, with the introduction of lower ordered prizes, the chances that the agent wins at least a single prize (albeit of lesser value) increase. The overall incentives to contribute therefore depend on the risk aversion of agents and the agent's associated willingness to sacrifice a lower expected payoff for a reduced variation in expected winnings.

Consider the relationship between risk aversion and the optimal number of prizes. Assuming that $P_r > P_t > 0$ ($r < t$) are fixed, Eq. (4) implies that

$(\partial b/\partial P_r)/(\partial b/\partial P_t) > 1$ for small σ, and $(\partial b/\partial P_r)/(\partial b/\partial P_t) < 1$ for large σ. In the former (as in the risk-neutral) case, it is optimal to shift weight to the larger prize. However, in the latter case, the difference between prizes should be reduced. Therefore, it immediately follows that the greater the level of individual risk aversion, the larger should be the number of prizes provided by the charitable fundraiser. In fact, a charitable fundraiser should provide $n-1$ prizes whenever agents demonstrate high levels of risk aversion.

The optimality of introducing a certain number of prizes therefore depends on the risk posture of agents, i.e., on how risk-averse agents are and on how much risk they face. For a given CARA-level, the number of agents and the total prize money are the decisive factors determining the risk faced by an agent that participates in a given lottery.[5] For example, the more agents that participate in a lottery, the smaller are the chances of any given agent winning a prize. However, this risk can only be attenuated by splitting the prize budget into multiple prizes of lesser value, which increases the probability of receiving a positive financial payout. Alternately, a charitable fund-raiser may wish to introduce additional prizes whenever there is an increase in the total prize budget P as agents base contributions on the difference between P_1 and P_n.

To examine in greater detail the optimal prize distributions, consider the following example that is used later in our experimental setting. Assume that there are $n = 4$ symmetric agents each with a constant MPCR = 0.75 for contributions to a public good. Suppose that a charitable fundraiser links contributions to the public good with a charitable lottery of prize budget of $P = \$4.00$. From Eq. (1), we have that $H(1) = 3/4$, $H(2) = 5/12$, and $H(3) = -1/12$ for this lottery. Using Eqs. (3) and (4) to calculate the optimal prizes, we obtain Fig. 1 which illustrates the optimal prize distribution as a function of the level of individual risk aversion.[6]

From the figure, we observe that it is optimal to provide a single prize whenever $\sigma < 0.14$. However, if the CARA risk posture of agents lies in the interval $0.14 < \sigma < 0.64$, then two prizes should be provided with the difference between these two prizes diminishing in individual risk preference. Finally, if the CARA-level of agents exceeds $\sigma > 0.64$, then the optimal lottery awards three prizes.

While our theoretical model provides a direct link between risk preference and the optimal distribution of any fixed prize budget, adjusting lottery prizes to specific individual risk preferences is problematic. Charitable fundraisers typically do not observe the risk posture of potential donors. Thus, it would be beneficial to derive some rule of thumb and specify a certain distribution of prizes, which should outperform the SPL.

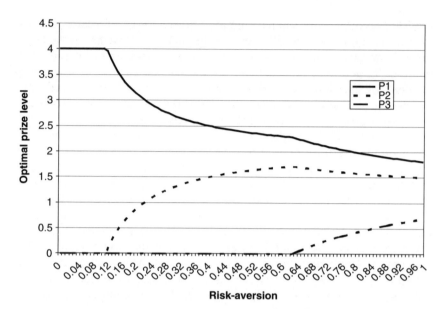

Fig. 1. Optimal Prize Distribution as a Function of Risk Aversion σ.

Consider one such distribution (which is used in our NPL treatment), with a lottery that pays three prizes: $P_1 = \$2.50$, $P_2 = \$1.00$, and $P_3 = \$0.50$. Using Eq. (3), we can directly compare the contributions levels in this lottery with those of an SPL with prize $P = \$4.00$. Based on such comparison, we find that the three-prize lottery should outperform the SPL whenever the CARA risk posture of agents is represented by $\sigma > 0.30$ – i.e., agents demonstrate intermediate levels of risk aversion.[7] Fig. 2 plots individual contributions in this three-prize lottery relative to those generated in the SPL as a percentage of the optimal lottery – the lottery depicted in Fig. 1.

We can see that a three-prize lottery with prize set (\$2.50, \$1.00, \$0.50) performs relatively well compared to the optimal lottery. Over a wide range of risk-aversion levels it yields more than 90% of the contributions realized in the optimal lottery. However, the SPL yields substantially smaller contributions as risk aversion increases. For example, for agents with risk-aversion level given by $\sigma = 1.0$, contributions in the SPL are only 50% of the level that could be obtained from the optimal lottery.

As Fig. 2 suggests, charitable institutions need not know the exact risk preference of potential donors. The lottery design used in the experiment (and many such similar prize distributions) should come close to the optimal

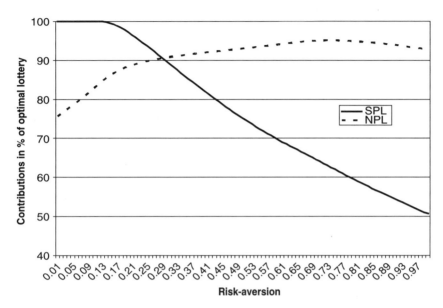

Fig. 2. Lottery Contributions as a Percent of Optimal Lottery.

design over a wide range of risk aversion. In fact, our NPL predicts lower contributions than the SPL only for agents demonstrating rather small levels of risk aversion $-\sigma \leq 0.30$. For agents with CARA risk preference above this threshold, our NPL should generate greater contributions than both our baseline VCM treatment and our SPL treatment.

In summary, the above analysis provides three testable hypotheses regarding performance of charitable lotteries and their optimal design: (i) charitable lotteries generate greater contributions than a VCM; (ii) when agents are risk neutral (risk loving) and have symmetric MPCRs for the public good, contributions in the SPL are greater than those in an equivalent-valued NPL; and (iii) when agents have symmetric MPCRs, there exists a level of risk aversion, $\sigma > 0.30$, above which contributions in the NPL are greater than those generated in an equivalent valued SPL.

3. EXPERIMENTAL DESIGN

We design an experiment that is closely linked with the above analysis to examine these three conjectures – Table 1 provides a design summary. We

Table 1. Experimental Design.

Treatment	Experimental Parameters
VCM	24 Subjects 15 Rounds Random rematching MPCR = 0.75 Bonus = 8 tokens in group account
SPL	24 Subjects 15 Rounds Random rematching MPCR = 0.75 Bonus = {8, 0, 0, 0} in private account
NPL	24 Subjects 15 Rounds Random rematching MPCR = 0.75 Bonus = {5, 2, 1, 0} in private account

Note: Cell entries provide the experimental design and parameters for each treatment. In each of the 15 rounds the subjects were endowed with 10 tokens and randomly assigned to 4 person groups. The bonus for individual subjects depends on the lottery prize won. For example, in the NPL, in each group there was one subject winning 5 tokens, one subject winning 2 tokens, one subject winning 1 token, and one subject winning 0 tokens.

begin with the traditional control treatment that induces symmetric MPCRs across agents in a VCM. We cross this treatment with comparable SPL and NPL treatments, leading to a total of three treatments.

All treatments were conducted at the University of Maryland – College Park. The experiment consisted of three sessions (one session for each mechanism) held on separate days with different subjects. Each session consisted of two parts, the first to gather information on individual contribution decisions across the various treatments. The second part was included to gather information on individual risk postures. We describe, in turn, each part of the session.

3.1. Part 1

The first part of the experiment was designed to compare contribution levels across the SPL, the NPL, and the VCM. The VCM treatment and the SPL treatment followed the instructions from Morgan and Sefton (2000) to enable direct comparison. Table 1 summarizes the key features of our experimental design and the number of participants in each treatment. Subjects were recruited on campus using posters and emails that advertised subjects could "earn extra cash by participating in an experiment in economic decision-making." The message stated that students would be paid in cash at the end of the session and that sessions generally take less than an hour and a half. The same protocol was used to ensure that each session was run identically.

Each subject was seated at linked computer terminals that were used to transmit all decision and payoff information. All sessions were programmed using the software toolkit *z-Tree* developed by Fischbacher (1999). The sessions each consisted of 17 rounds, the first two being practice. The subjects were instructed that the practice rounds would not affect earnings. Once the individuals were seated and logged into the terminals, a set of instructions and a record sheet were handed out. The subjects were asked to follow along as the instructions (included in Appendix A) were read aloud. After the instructions were read and the subjects' questions were answered the first practice round began.

At the beginning of each round subjects were randomly assigned to groups of four. The subjects were not aware of whom they were grouped with, but they did know that the groups changed every round. Each round the subjects were endowed with 10 tokens. Their task was simple: decide how many tokens to place in the group account and how many to keep in their private account. The decision was entered in the computer and also recorded on the record sheet. When all subjects had made their choice, the computer would inform them of the total number of tokens placed in their group account, the number of points from the group account and the private account, as well as any bonus points that were earned. The payoff for the round was determined by summing the points from the group account, points from the private account, and any bonus points received. Once each of the subjects had recorded all of this information on their record sheets, the next round would begin.

The points for each round were determined as follows. For all sessions, subjects received 100 points for each token placed in their private account. They were awarded 75 points for each token placed in the group account by themselves and the other members of their group. Additionally, each session had a different method for earning bonus points.

We follow Morgan and Sefton (2000) by adding the value of the prize (8 tokens) to the group account in the VCM, which makes the VCM treatment comparable to the SPL and NPL treatments. Therefore, in the VCM session, all subjects, regardless of their contributions to the group account, earned 600 bonus points, which represent the value of 8 tokens placed in the group accounts. In the SPL sessions, group members competed for a lottery prize of 800 points, which represents the value of 8 tokens placed in the private account. Each subject's chance of winning the prize was based on his or her contribution to the group account compared to the aggregate number of tokens placed in the group account by all group members. For the NPL sessions, group members competed for three lottery prizes of values 500, 200, and 100 points, which respectively represent the value of 5, 2, and 1 token placed in the private account. As in the SPL sessions, subjects' chance of winning the first prize was based on his or her share of group contributions. The three prizes were awarded in order of value, and without replacement, meaning that in each round, three of the four group members would receive some bonus points.

At the end of the last round, one of the nonpractice rounds was chosen at random as the one that would determine earnings. Subjects were paid 50 cents for every 100 points earned. They recorded their earnings for *Part 1* of the session and prepared for *Part 2*.

3.2. Part 2

The second part of the experiment was designed to lend insights into subjects' risk postures and link those preferences to behavior in the public goods game described above. One technique for examining the effects of risk posture on observed behavior is to use binary lottery procedures to induce a specific risk preference (Roth & Malouf, 1979; Berg, Daley, Dickhaut, & O'Brien, 1986). The crux of the binary lottery procedure is that payments to subjects are made using an artificial medium that maps into the probability of winning a prize. Provided that the behavior of subjects is consistent with expected utility maximization, the experimenter can induce any predetermined risk preference by altering the mapping of the medium into the probability of winning the prize. While conceptually appealing, previous experimental work provides mixed evidence in support of the binary lottery procedure as a method to induce individual risk posture (see e.g., Rietz, 1993; Cox & Oaxaca, 1995; Selten, Sadrieh, & Abbink, 1999; Berg, Dickhaut, & Rietz, 2003).[8]

Here, rather than trying to induce specific risk postures, we use measures of individual risk postures gathered from one experimental game as controls to analyze differences in behavior across agents in the public goods game. Measuring risk postures in one game and then using these measures to more closely explore behavior in another is not novel to this study (see e.g., Eckel

& Wilson, 2004). However, we recognize that this procedure is not devoid of criticism. Even if risk measures meaningfully assess risk preference in one context, we must assume that these preferences remain stable across games and over time. Yet to our eyes the main assumption in this approach is that no individual level unobservables are systematically correlated with behavior in the public goods game. Because risk posture is not exogenously imposed on players, an important caveat must be placed on the results from such an exercise.[9]

In this part of the session, we replicate the low-payoff treatment of an experiment reported by Holt and Laury (2002; see Appendix B for instructions). In each of the three sessions this part was conducted in an identical manner. The treatment is based on 10 choices between paired lotteries where the probability of obtaining a given payoff possibility is varied across choices. The paired choices are included in the appendix. The payoff possibilities for Option A, $2.00 or $1.60, are much less variable than those for Option B, $3.85 or $0.10, which was considered the risky option. The odds of winning the higher payoff for each of the options increase with each decision. In the first decision, there is only a 1/10 chance of winning the higher payoff, so only the most risk-loving individuals should choose Option B. The expected payoff difference for choosing Option A is $1.17. As the probabilities of winning the higher payoff increase, individuals should cross over to Option B. The paired choices are designed so that a risk-neutral individual should choose Option A for the first four decisions and then switch to Option B for the remaining six decisions. The paired choices are also designed to determine degrees of risk aversion. For example, an agent who selects Option A for the first six decisions and then switches to Option B for the remaining four choices has an implied level of CARA risk preference of $\sigma \geq 0.30$.

Upon completion of Part 1 of the session, instructions and a decision sheet were handed out. After the directions were read and questions were answered, the subjects were asked to complete their decision sheets by choosing either A or B for each of the 10 decisions. The subjects were instructed that one of the decisions would be randomly selected ex post and used to determine their payoffs. Part of a deck of cards was used to determine payoffs, cards 2–10 and Aces to represent "1 s." After each subject completed his or her decision sheet, a monitor would approach the desk and randomly draw a card twice, once to select which of the 10 decisions to use, and a second time to determine the payoff for the option chosen, A or B, for the particular decision selected. After the first card was selected, it was placed back in the pile, the deck was reshuffled, and the second card was drawn. For example, if the first draw was an Ace, then the first decision choice would be used, and the subject's decision, A or B would be circled. A second draw then determines the subject's payment. For example, given that the first decision is binding, the draw of an Ace would yield $2.00 to the subject. If cards 2–10 were drawn the subject would earn $1.60. The subjects were aware that each decision had an equal chance of being selected.

Following determination of all payoffs for part 2, subjects computed their final earnings as the sum of their earnings for each part of the experiment. The final payoffs were then verified against the computer records, and subjects were paid privately in cash for their earnings. Each of the sessions took approximately 75 min and subjects earned $14.29 on average with a standard deviation of $2.52.

4. EXPERIMENTAL RESULTS

Our experimental design enables us to test a number of theoretical predictions regarding contribution levels across treatments. While the primary purpose of this article is to compare the performance of the SPL and NPL under various individual risk postures, we first examine the relative revenue-generating capacities of the lotteries and the VCM. A first testable hypothesis is that for any constant MPCR and exogenously determined prize value, mean contribution levels in both the NPL and SPL are greater than mean contributions in the VCM.[10] Both the NPL and the SPL introduce a compensating externality that serves to attenuate the tendency for agents to "free-ride." This hypothesis is directly testable using our experimental data and implies that

H1. Contributions to the public good are greater under any lottery than under a VCM.

Table 2 summarizes average contribution decisions for our experimental treatments across all periods combined and for the final five periods. As shown in the table, mean contribution levels in the NPL session were 5.68 with a standard deviation of 3.18 tokens. In the SPL session, mean contributions were 5.36 tokens with a standard deviation of 3.39 tokens. In the VCM treatment, mean contributions were 4.01 tokens with an associated standard deviation of 3.40 tokens.

While our data suggest a superiority of lotteries as a gross fund-raising mechanism, our results are much more guarded when comparing the net revenues raised by the various mechanisms. Comparing contribution levels net of the total prize value (an average of 2 tokens per person), our results

Table 2. Mean Contribution Levels by Risk Posture.

		All agents	CARA ($\sigma < 0.10$)	CARA ($0.10 \leq \sigma < 0.30$)	CARA ($\sigma \geq 0.30$)
VCM	Overall	4.01	3.64	4.93	4.03
		(3.40)	(3.15)	(2.86)	(3.62)
	Final 5 periods	4.05	3.70	4.6	4.14
		(3.46)	(3.20)	(3.56)	(3.62)
	No. of agents	24	8	3	13
SPL	Overall	5.36	7.00	4.53	5.30
		(3.39)	(3.86)	(3.43)	(3.04)
	Final 5 periods	5.81	8.75	5.43	5.11
		(3.51)	(2.29)	(3.77)	(3.24)
	No. of agents	24	4	7	13
NPL	Overall	5.68	6.59	5.92	5.23
		(3.18)	(3.42)	(3.03)	(3.08)
	Final 5 periods	5.88	6.16	6.87	5.31
		(3.21)	(3.59)	(2.74)	(3.18)
	No. of agents	24	4	7	13

Note: Figures in the table represent the average contribution levels (tokens) for each of the three treatments for all agents pooled and across three different risk postures. Summary statistics by period are provided for individual contribution levels along with respective standard errors (in parentheses). Risk posture is calculated using the midpoint of an indifference range. For example, in the VCM treatment there were eight agents with CARA preferences represented by $\sigma < 0.10$ who contributed an average of 3.64 tokens to the public account.

suggest that the VCM may be the preferred fund-raising instrument. Individual contributions (net of the prize value) are approximately 0.7 tokens (0.3 tokens) less per person in the SPL (NPL) treatment than in the VCM treatment. Perusal of the data reported in Table 2 generates our first result.

Result 1. Charitable lotteries generate greater gross contributions than a VCM. However, there is no statistical difference in net contributions (contributions net of the prize value) between a charitable lottery and a VCM.

Statistical support for the first part of Result 1 is provided by comparing mean contribution levels across our experimental treatments. There is an approximate 1.7 token difference in average individual contributions in the NPL relative to the VCM with this difference statistically significant at the $p < 0.05$ level using a one-tailed Mann–Whitney test.[11] Mean contribution levels in the SPL treatment are approximately 1.3 tokens greater than mean contributions in the VCM treatment with this difference statistically significant at the $p < 0.10$ level using a one-tailed Mann–Whitney test. However, comparing net contributions to the group account, our results suggest there is no difference in the provision of the public good between a charitable lottery and a VCM. The 0.7 token (0.3 token) difference in individual net contributions to the public good between the VCM and the SPL (NPL) treatments respectively is not statistically significant at any meaningful level.

4.1. Individual Risk Preference and Lottery Contributions

The analysis in Section 2 results in a number of testable hypotheses regarding the performance of the SPL-versus-the NPL conditioned on the underlying risk preference of agents. For risk-neutral agents, contributions in a lottery that provides a single prize should dominate those garnered from an equivalently valued NPL. Under our experimental design, however, any agent with a CARA risk parameter $\sigma > 0.30$ should contribute more in the NPL than they would in the SPL. This leads to our second testable hypothesis.

H2. For risk-neutral (risk-loving) agents – i.e., those agents with CARA preferences given by $\sigma < 0.10$ – contributions in the SPL treatment are greater than those in the NPL treatment. For agents with CARA risk preference given by $\sigma \geq 0.30$, contributions in the NPL are greater than those in the SPL.

Table 2 summarizes average contribution levels for agents across three distinct categorizations of risk preference: agents with CARA preferences represented by $\sigma < 0.10$; agents with CARA preferences represented by a σ that lies in the interval $0.10 \leq \sigma < 0.30$; and agents with CARA preferences represented by ($\sigma \geq 0.30$). The table summarizes contribution levels for these three types of agents across our experimental treatments averaged over all periods of the experiment and the final five periods of the experiment.

Comparing overall average contribution levels provides directional (but only mixed statistical) support for the first part of H2. Average contribution levels from risk-neutral (risk-loving) agents in the SPL are about 6.2% (0.41 tokens) greater than the average contribution levels of agents with similar risk preference in the NPL. However, if one restricts analysis to the final five periods of the experiment and compares average contribution levels for risk-neutral (risk-loving) agents the 2.59 token difference (8.75 tokens in the SPL treatment compared to 6.16 tokens in the NPL treatment) in average contributions between the SPL and NPL is marginally significant at the $p < 0.10$ level using a one-tailed Mann–Whitney test.

Examining the average contribution levels of agents classified as risk averse ($\sigma \geq 0.30$) across the SPL and NPL provides evidence at odds with the second part of H2. The overall average contribution levels of risk-averse agents in the SPL treatment are approximately one-tenth of a token greater than the average contribution levels for agents with similar risk preference in the NPL. Restricting attention to the final five periods this outcome is reversed – the average contributions of agents classified as risk averse in the NPL treatment are approximately two-tenths of a token greater than those classified as risk averse in treatment SPL. However, neither of these differences is statistically significant at any meaningful level.

Table 2 highlights the evolution of contribution levels for agents categorized as risk neutral ($\sigma < 0.10$)and those categorized as risk averse ($\sigma \geq 0.30$) across our two lottery treatments. The tables reveals two patterns of behavior consistent with the second part of H2: (i) a divergence of average contributions in the SPL between agents classified as risk neutral and those agents classified as risk averse; and (ii) a convergence of average contributions in the NPL for agents classified as risk neutral and those classified as risk averse.

In the SPL, agents classified as risk neutral contribute on average 1.70 tokens more (7.00 versus 5.30) then do agents with CARA measures of $\sigma \geq 0.30$. However, over the final five periods, the difference in average contributions for risk-neutral agents and those classified by $\sigma \geq 0.30$ increases to 3.64 tokens. While sample sizes are too small to allow us to draw statistically significant inference, the observed pattern of divergence is consistent with our conjecture that contributions in the SPL decline in the level of individual risk aversion.

In the NPL, we see an opposite result – convergence of contributions for risk-neutral agents and those with $\sigma \geq 0.30$ over time. In our NPL treatment, the difference in average contributions for risk-neutral agents and those with CARA parameter $\sigma \geq 0.30$ is 1.36 tokens (6.19 tokens versus 5.23 tokens). However, over the final five periods, this difference falls to 0.85 tokens (6.16 for risk-neutral agents and 5.31 for agents with $\sigma \geq 0.30$) – a result again consistent with our conjectures.

Combined, these comparisons lead to our second result.

Result 2. The performances of the SPL and NPLs as a fund-raising mechanism are weakly dependent on individual risk preference. Risk-neutral (risk-loving) participants are more sensitive to changes in the lottery prize structure.

To complement the unconditional insights and provide statistical support for Result 2, we estimate a series of regression models examining the contribution decisions of agents in our experimental treatments that explicitly controls for observable and unobservable differences across agents.

A problem in estimating such models is that the data are censored by design at the zero and 10 token contribution levels. To handle this censoring, we estimate a random-effects Tobit model with censoring from below (at the zero token level) and above (at the 10 token level).

In estimating individual contribution levels, the primary relationship of interest is the underlying latent structure.

$$C_{it}^* = X_{it}\beta + e_{it} \tag{5}$$

However, this latent structure is not directly observed since the data are censored from above (at 10 tokens) and below (at zero tokens). Rather, the relationship observed is given by

$$C_{it} = 0, \qquad \text{if } C_{it}^* \leq 0$$
$$C_{it} = C_{it}^*, \quad \text{if } 0 < C_{it}^* < 10$$
$$C_{it} = 10, \qquad \text{if } C_{it}^* \geq 10$$

for all individuals $i = 1, 2, \ldots, N$ and all periods $t = 1, 2, \ldots, T$. In estimating Eq. (5), it is assumed that $e_{it} = u_{it} + \alpha_i$ where the two components are individually and normally distributed with mean zero. It follows that the variance of the disturbance term e_{it} is $\text{Var}(e_{it}) = \sigma_u^2 + \sigma_\alpha^2$. By construction, the individual random effects, α_i, capture unobserved heterogeneities across individuals that would be left uncontrolled in standard cross-sectional analysis. The vector X_{it} includes indicators for our treatment effects, the interaction of treatment dummies and an indicator for risk-averse agents – those agents with $\sigma \geq 0.10$, and an interaction of one-period lagged contribution levels with the treatment indicators.

Empirical estimates from our model are presented in Columns 1–2 of Table 3. Cell entries include coefficient estimates and their associated standard errors. Column 1 provides insights consistent with Result 2: contribution levels in the both lottery treatments are lower for risk-averse agents than for risk-neutral (risk-loving) counterparts. As indicated in column 1, contribution levels for agents classified as risk averse in both the SPL and NPLs are lower than those received from a risk-neutral counterpart with these differences statistically significant at the $p < 0.05$ level. Restricting the analysis to the final five periods (column 2), we find that the contributions from risk-averse agents in the NPL are not statistically different than those recorded by risk-neutral counterparts. However, the contributions of risk-averse agents in the SPL over this same period are significantly lower than those of a risk-neutral counterpart.[12]

Table 3. Estimated Contribution Levels.

	Model A Midpoint All Periods	Model B Midpoint Final 5 Periods
Constant	2.77**	0.48
	(0.58)	(0.77)
SPL treatment	3.89**	2.64*
	(0.87)	(1.55)
NPL treatment	3.99**	4.51**
	(0.89)	(1.26)
Risk-averse agent in SPL	−1.75**	−2.37**
	(0.70)	(1.12)
Risk-averse agent in NPL	−2.15**	−1.28
	(0.76)	(0.91)
Risk-averse agent in VCM	0.30	0.46
	(0.77)	(0.79)
1 Period lag donation in SPL	0.25**	0.91**
	(0.07)	(0.12)
1 Period lag donation in NPL	0.05	0.38**
	(0.07)	(0.11)
1 Period lag donation in VCM	0.21**	0.69**
	(0.08)	(0.11)
Agent Random Effects	Yes	Yes
No. of agents	72	72
No. of observations	1,008	360
No. of left censored observations	139	49
No. of right censored observations	140	59
Log likelihood	−2178.73	−785.79

Note: Cell entries are parameter estimates from a random effects Tobit regression of contribution levels on indicated model covariates. The columns differ in how the individual measures of risk aversion are calculated using the simple Holt–Laury count for those agents that switch between Options A and B only once and the midpoint of the implied indifference region to determine the risk posture for those agents that switch more than once.
*Denotes statistical significance at the $p < 0.10$ Level.
**Denotes statistical significance at the $p < 0.05$ level.

5. CONCLUSIONS

This paper presents a theoretical and empirical inquiry into the use of lotteries as a means to fund public goods. Our theory provides a framework outlining the optimal structure of a fundraising drive. For risk-neutral (risk-loving) agents, this optimal structure links charitable contributions with a lottery that provides a single, fixed prize to the winner. However, for any fixed prize amount, there exists a threshold level of risk aversion where it becomes optimal to split a single, fixed prize into multiple prizes of lesser value. Furthermore, charitable institutions need not know the exact risk preference of potential donors as there exist many prize distributions that should elicit contributions that approximate those that would be elicited from the optimal lottery over a wide range of risk aversion. We test some of the predictions from our theoretical model and find that the performances of the SPL and NPLs as a fund-raising mechanism weakly depend on individual risk preference.

Overall, our paper highlights that there is much potentially useful behavioral economic research to be done in the area of charitable fundraising. Yet before we can begin to make reasonable arguments that behavior observed in the lab is a good indicator of behavior in the field, we must focus on the representativeness of experimental samples and the representativeness of the environment. In this spirit, this paper represents a necessary step in the discovery process. In other work we explore dimensions associated with more fully understanding the institutions (e.g., Lange et al., 2004, 2005) and taking the design to the field (e.g., Rondeau & List, 2004; Landry, Lange, List, Price, & Rupp, 2006).

NOTES

1. Dale (2004), however, reports that revenues raised by charitable lotteries net of the prize do not tend to exceed the revenues raised via a standard VCM.

2. There are a number of reasons why one would be interested in risk-aversion when examining charitable lotteries. First, lotteries are a widely used mechanism for charitable fund-raising. For example, as reported in Morgan (2000), approximately $6 billion was raised by private charities in the United States using lotteries in 1992. Given the prevalence of charitable lotteries as a fund-raising mechanism, it is difficult to imagine that such mechanisms induce participation only by risk-preferring individuals. Second, in our model, lottery contributions are linked to the provision of a public good. Hence, an agent purchasing a lottery ticket is purchasing not only a gamble in the lottery but also providing for greater provision of a public good. Provided that the returns to the public good are nonzero, the charitable lottery may serve to induce participation by risk-averse agents that would avoid an equivalent valued lottery whose proceeds were de-linked from the public good.

3. As a practical matter, one should note that the design of the optimal lottery is independent from the public good as a change in the MPCR leads only to a proportional change in the equilibrium contribution level for all agents.

4. From condition of Eq. (4) it follows that the single-prize lottery is also optimal if agents are assumed risk loving.

5. See Lange et al. (2005) for a more formal treatment of this problem.

6. In calculating the optimal prize distribution, we have converted the token values of the prize distribution used in the experiment into equivalent dollar amounts. The conversion rate is that 1 token won in the lottery is equal to $0.50. Thus a prize of 8 tokens is equivalent to a monetary prize of $4.00.

7. Based on the existing literature, we would expect that a large portion of agents in any population would demonstrate such levels of risk aversion. For example, Holt and Laury (2002) find estimates of relative risk aversion centered around the 0.3–0.5 range. Binswanger (1980) finds levels of relative risk aversion above 0.32 for farmers in rural India. Estimates of relative risk aversion range from 0.52 to 0.67 (Cox & Oaxaca, 1995; Goeree, Holt, & Palfrey, 2002) for first-price auctions using laboratory data and 0.56 using field data from timber auctions (Campo, Perrigne, & Vuong, 2000).

8. This literature highlights an important consideration when using the binary lottery procedure – the ability to induce preferences is sensitive to factors such as the level of interaction between subjects, the complexity of the choice environment, and the magnitude of the final payoffs.

9. There is however limited experimental evidence suggesting the stability of risk preference across games. For example, Goeree, Holt, and Palfrey (2003) find that estimates of risk posture implied from observed behavior in a matching pennies game are consistent with estimates of risk posture for the same subject pool using the Holt/Laury paired lottery design.

10. Dale (2004) provides a comparison of a single-prize lottery with endogenously determined prize value with that of a VCM and shows the importance of the theoretical assumption that prize values in a charitable lottery are ex ante fixed independently of contribution levels.

11. The unit of observation for all Mann–Whitney test results is the average contribution levels for an agent. The test statistic is thus based upon a comparison of the mean contribution levels for 24 independent observations (agents) across our three experimental treatments.

12. The empirical results presented in Table 3 are robust to the use of alternate classification schemes for individual risk preference. Results from these models are available in an unpublished appendix.

ACKNOWLEDGMENTS

We thank Doug Davis for very insightful and thorough comments that considerably improved this study. An anonymous reviewer provided sharp comments that improved the paper as well. Glenn Harrison, John Horowitz, and Ted McConnell also provided excellent comments during the discovery process. Any errors remain our own.

REFERENCES

Berg, J., Daley, L., Dickhaut, J., & O'Brien, J. (1986). Controlling preferences for lotteries on units of experimental exchange. *Quarterly Journal of Economics, 101*, 281–306.

Berg, J., Dickhaut, J., & Rietz, T. (2003). Preference reversals and induced risk preferences: Evidence for noisy maximization. *Journal of Risk and Uncertainty*, *27*, 139–170.

Binswanger, H. (1980). Attitude toward risk: Experimental measurement in rural India. *American Journal of Agricultural Economics*, *62*, 395–407.

Campo, S., Perrigne, I., & Vuong, Q. (2000). *Semi-parametric estimation of first-price auctions with risk aversion*. Working paper, University of Southern California.

Cox, J., & Oaxaca, R. (1995). Inducing risk-neutral preferences: Further analysis of the data. *Journal of Risk and Uncertainty*, *11*, 65–79.

Dale, D. (2004). Charitable lottery structure and fund raising: Theory and evidence. *Experimental Economics*, *7*, 217–234.

Eckel, C., & Wilson, R. (2004). Is trust a risky decision? *Journal of Economic Behavior and Organization*, *55*, 447–465.

Fischbacher, U. (1999). *Z-tree: Zurich toolbox for readymade economic experiments – experimenter's manual*. Working Paper no. 21, Institute for Empirical Research in Economics, University of Zurich.

Goeree, J., Holt, C., & Palfrey, T. (2002). Quantal response equilibrium and overbidding in private-value auctions. *Journal of Economic Theory*, *104*(1), 247–272.

Goeree, J., Holt, C., & Palfrey, T. (2003). Risk averse behavior in generalize matching pennies games. *Games and Economic Behavior*, *45*, 97–113.

Holt, C. A., & Laury, S. K. (2002). Risk aversion and incentive effects. *The American Economic Review*, *92*, 1644–1655.

Landry, C., Lange, A., List, J., Price, M., & Rupp, N. (2006). *Toward an understanding of the economics of charity: Evidence from a field experiment. Quarterly Journal of Economics (Forthcoming)*.

Lange, A., List, J., & Price, M. (2004). *Using tontines to finance public goods: Back to the future?* NBER Working Paper no. 10958.

Lange, A., List, J., & Price, M. (2005). *Using lotteries to finance public goods: Theory and experimental evidence*. Working paper, University of Maryland.

Morgan, J. (2000). Financing public goods by means of lotteries. *Review of Economic Studies*, *67*, 761–784.

Morgan, J., & Sefton, M. (2000). Funding public goods with lotteries: Experimental evidence. *Review of Economic Studies*, *67*, 785–810.

Rietz, T. (1993). Implementing and testing risk preference induction mechanisms in experimental sealed bid auction. *Journal of Risk and Uncertainty*, *7*, 199–213.

Rondeau, D., & List, J. (2004). *How to raise money: Evidence from laboratory and field experiments*. Working paper, University of Maryland.

Roth, A., & Malouf, M. (1979). Game-theoretic models and the role of bargaining. *Psychological Review*, *86*, 574–594.

Selten, R., Sadrieh, A., & Abbink, K. (1999). Money does not induce risk neutral behavior, but binary lotteries do even worse. *Theory and Decision*, *46*, 213–249.

APPENDIX A. INSTRUCTIONS – PART 1 – CONTRIBUTIONS DECISIONS

A.1. General Rules

This is an experiment in economic decision-making. If you follow the instructions carefully and make good decisions you can earn a considerable amount of money. You will be paid in private and in cash at the end of the session.

It is important that you do not talk, or in any way try to communicate, with other people during the session. If you have a question, raise your hand and a monitor will come over to where you are sitting and answer your question in private.

The experiment will consist of 17 rounds. The first 2 rounds will be practice. In each round, you will be randomly assigned to a group of four people. These groups will change each round. You will not know which of the other people in the room are in your group and the other people in the session will not know with whom they are grouped, in any round.

In each round, you will have the opportunity to earn points. At the end of the session, one of the nonpractice rounds will be randomly selected and you will be paid in cash an amount that will be determined by the number of points you earn during the randomly selected round.

A.2. Description of each Round

At the beginning of the first trial a subject number will be given on your terminal. Record that number on your record sheet. Each round you will be given an endowment of 10 tokens. At the beginning of each round, the computer will prompt you to enter the number of tokens you want to contribute to the group account. Enter a whole number between 0 and 10, record the number in column (B) on your record sheet, and click continue. Any tokens you do not place in your group account are placed in your private account. Once your decision is recorded, it cannot be changed. After everyone in your group has recorded their decisions, a screen will appear informing you of the number of tokens contributed to the group account by all group members, whether any bonus points have been earned, and your profit for the round. Record the information from that screen onto your record sheet as follows:

Tokens in Private Account	Column A
Your Contribution to Group Account	Column B
Total Tokens in Group Account	Column C
Private Account Points	Column D
Group Account Points	Column E
Bonus Points	Column F
Profit for Round	Column G

Once everyone has recorded his or her information, the next round will begin.

A.3. How Earnings are Determined

VCM
The number of points you earn in the round will be determined as follows. For each token placed in your private account you will earn 100 points. This amount is recorded in column (D) on your record sheet. You will receive 75 points for each token placed in your group account by you and the other people in your group. The group account points are recorded in column (E) on your record sheet. In addition, in each round you will also receive 600 bonus points regardless of how you and the other people in your group place your tokens. This amount is recorded in column (F). Your profit for the round is computed by summing the private account points, the group account points and the bonus points. This total is recorded in column (G) on the record sheet.

SPL
The number of points you earn in the round will be determined as follows. For each token placed in your private account you will earn 100 points. This amount is recorded in column (D) on your record sheet. You will receive 75 points for each token placed in your group account by you and the other people in your group. The group account points are recorded in column (E) of the record sheet.

In addition, in each round you have the chance to win 800 bonus points. At the end of each round a lottery will be drawn. Your odds of winning the lottery are determined by how much you contributed to the group account in that round. Specifically, your chances of winning the bonus points will be equal to the number of tokens you place in the group account, divided by the total number of tokens placed in the group account by you and the other people in your group. For example, if the group account contains 12 tokens of which 3 were placed by you, you will have a 3 in 12 chance of winning the bonus. If no tokens are placed in the group account, each member of the group will have an equal chance of winning the bonus. Record any bonus points earned in column (F) on your record sheet. Your profit for the round is computed by summing the private account points, the group account points and the bonus points. This total is recorded in column (G) on the record sheet.

NPL

The number of points you earn in the round will be determined as follows. For each token placed in your private account you will earn 100 points. This amount is recorded in column (D) on your record sheet. You will receive 75 points for each token placed in your group account by you and the other people in your group. The group account points are recorded in column (E) of the record sheet.

In addition, in each round you have the chance to win one of three bonus prizes. First prize is 500 points, second prize is 200 points, and third prize is 100 points. After all group members enter their contribution, a lottery will be drawn and bonus points will be awarded. Your odds of winning first prize are determined by how much you contributed to the group account in that round. Specifically, your chances of winning the 500 points will be equal to the number of tokens you place in the group account, divided by the total number of tokens placed in the group account by you and the other people in your group. This process is repeated for the two remaining prizes without replacement. For example, if each of the four players contributes the same number of tokens to the group account, each player will have a 1 in 4 chance of winning first prize. After first prize is drawn, the remaining three players will then each have a 1 in 3 chance of winning second prize. The last two players will then have a 1 in 2 chance of winning third prize. If no tokens are placed in the group account, each member of the group will have an equal chance of winning first prize. Bonus points are recorded in column (F) on your record sheet. Your profit for the round is computed by summing the private account points, the group account points and the bonus points. This total is recorded in column (G) on the record sheet.

At the end of the session we will draw a ticket from the box. In the box there is a numbered ticket for each round played (1–15). The number on the ticket that is drawn will determine the round for which you will be paid. Record the selected round and then your profit for that round in the space provided at the bottom of the record sheet. You will receive 50 cents in cash at the end of the session for every 100 points you earn in that round. This amount is recorded in the space titled earnings.

APPENDIX B. – INSTRUCTIONS – PART 2 – RISK AVERSION

Record your subject number from the previous part on your decision sheet. Your decision sheet shows 10 decisions listed on the left. Each decision is a paired choice between Options A and B. You will make 10 choices and record these in the final column, but only one of them will be used in the end to determine your earnings. Before you start making your 10 choices, please let me explain how these choices will affect your earnings for this part of the experiment.

We will use part of a deck of cards to determine payoffs; cards 2–10 and the Ace will represent "1." After you have made all of your choices, we will randomly select a card twice, once to select one of the 10 decisions to be used, and a second time to determine what your payoff is for the option you chose, A or B, for the particular decision selected. (After the first card is selected, it will be put back in the pile, the deck will be reshuffled, and the second card will be drawn.) Even though you will make 10 decisions, only one of these will end up affecting your earnings, but you will not know in advance which decision will be used. Obviously, each decision has an equal chance of being used in the end.

Now, please look at Decision 1 at the top. Option A pays $2.00 if the Ace is selected, and it pays $1.60 if the card selected is 2–10. Option B yields $3.85 if the Ace is selected, and it pays $0.10 if the card selected is 2–10. The other decisions are similar, except that as you move down the table, the chances of the higher payoff for each option increase. In fact, for Decision 10 in the bottom row, the cards will not be needed since each option pays the highest payoff for sure, so your choice here is between $2.00 or $3.85.

To summarize, you will make 10 choices: for each decision row you will have to choose between Options A and B. You may choose Option A for some decision rows and Option B for other rows, and you may change your decisions and make them in any order. When you are finished, we will come to your desk and pick a card to determine which of the 10 decisions will be used. Then we will put the card back in the deck, shuffle, and select a card again to determine your money earnings for the option you chose for that decision. Earnings for this choice will be added to your previous earnings, and you will be paid all earnings in cash when we finish.

So now please look at the empty boxes on the right side of the record sheet. You will have to write a decision, Option A or B in each of these boxes, and then the card selection will determine which one is going to count. We will look at the decision that you made for the choice that counts, and circle it, before selecting a card again to determine your earnings for this part. Then you will write your earnings in the blank at the bottom of the page.

Are there any questions? Now you may begin making your choices. Please do not talk with anyone else while we are doing this; raise your hand if you have a question.

Option A	Option B	Decision
1/10 of $2.00, 9/10 of $1.60	1/10 of $3.85, 9/10 of $0.10	
2/10 of $2.00, 8/10 of $1.60	2/10 of $3.85, 8/10 of $0.10	
3/10 of $2.00, 7/10 of $1.60	3/10 of $3.85, 7/10 of $0.10	
4/10 of $2.00, 6/10 of $1.60	4/10 of $3.85, 6/10 of $0.10	
5/10 of $2.00, 5/10 of $1.60	5/10 of $3.85, 5/10 of $0.10	
6/10 of $2.00, 4/10 of $1.60	6/10 of $3.85, 4/10 of $0.10	
7/10 of $2.00, 3/10 of $1.60	7/10 of $3.85, 3/10 of $0.10	
8/10 of $2.00, 2/10 of $1.60	8/10 of $3.85, 2/10 of $0.10	
9/10 of $2.00, 1/10 of $1.60	9/10 of $3.85, 1/10 of $0.10	
10/10 of $2.00, 0/10 of $1.60	10/10 of $3.85, 0/10 of $0.10	

MULTIPLE PUBLIC GOODS AND LOTTERY FUND RAISING

Robert Moir

ABSTRACT

Using analytical and experimental methods, this paper examines the extent to which targeted self-funding lotteries described by Morgan ((2000). Review of Economic Studies, 67(234), 761–784) improve social welfare in an environment with multiple public goods. Social welfare improves relative to the Nash prediction, when a single lottery is used to support provision of any socially desirable public good. However, social welfare is maximized if the lottery funds only the most socially desirable public good. Experimental results show that a lottery can fund a less socially desirable public good, but that efficiency declines as lottery ticket purchases crowd out voluntary contributions made in the absence of lotteries.

1. INTRODUCTION

It is a well-known economic theory that incentives to free ride off the contributions of others undermine the optimal provision of the public good through voluntary contributions (Samuelson, 1954). In light of this prediction, governments have historically followed the advice of economists like

Experiments Investigating Fundraising and Charitable Contributors
Research in Experimental Economics, Volume 11, 121–142
Copyright © 2006 by Elsevier Ltd.
All rights of reproduction in any form reserved
ISSN: 0193-2306/doi:10.1016/S0193-2306(06)11005-4

Adam Smith (1776) and used taxation to support public good provision. More recently, however, government cost-cutting and a general distaste for tax increases have contributed to the search for alternative provision mechanisms. Lotteries are one method of fund raising available both to governments unwilling to increase taxes (Mixon, Caudill, Ford, & Peng, 1997) and to smaller organizations without the powers of taxation.[1] Morgan (2000) shows that a fixed-prize lottery will increase public good provision beyond the level supported through voluntary contributions.[2] Lotteries – state-run, state-approved, or otherwise – are now used to fund a range of projects from government's general revenues to rather narrowly focused charitable activities. However, while lotteries support a wide variety of public projects, they certainly do not support all of them. Further, there is no reason to assume that those lotteries serve more-valued public activities. The effect of lotteries on social welfare in contexts with multiple public goods is an important open question. This paper initiates the behavioral investigation of this question by reporting the results of an experiment examining a lottery in an environment with two public goods.

Both the tendencies for participants to free ride and the use of lotteries as a fund-raising tool have been the focus of considerable attention among experimental economists. A broad experimental literature suggests that as a behavioral matter, free riding is generally less than complete. Subjects tend to persistently exceed theoretical predictions with their contributions to the public good (e.g., Chan, Mestelman, Moir, & Muller, 1996; Davis & Holt, 1993; Ledyard, 1995; Zelmer, 2003). Nevertheless, contributions fall short of the amount necessary for social efficiency. Recent experimental evidence supports the claim that lotteries are useful fund-raising devices. Morgan and Sefton (2000) show that self-funding lotteries increase public good provision beyond the level provided through voluntary contributions. The increase in revenues, however, is modest after accounting for the prize and the voluntary contributions crowded out by lottery contributions. Davis, Razzolini, Reilly, and Wilson (2005) compare lotteries to English auctions in an environment where participants have heterogeneous preferences for the prize. Their results are similar to Morgan and Sefton and further suggest that lotteries generally outperform auctions in terms of revenue generation for the public good. Dale (2004) provides experimental data suggesting that fixed-prize lotteries result in higher levels of public good provision than revenue-dependent lotteries (e.g., 50–50 draws). Dale also finds that with experience, net funding for the fixed-prize lottery differs only slightly from contribution levels elicited through voluntary contributions.[3]

To date, no experimental research has considered the effects of lotteries in an environment with multiple public goods. In this paper, I focus on perhaps the most interesting case where a lottery is used to fund a less-valued public good. This case is of considerable interest because lottery contributions to a less-valued public good may crowd out the well-documented behavioral tendency for participants to voluntarily contribute to more-valued public goods. Indeed, the results of this experiment suggest that this is exactly the case.

I organize the paper as follows. Section 2 analyzes the effects of lotteries in a two-public good environment. In this section I show that, as a theoretical matter, a lottery for either public good is self-funding and increases overall welfare when that good is socially desirable. This prediction requires that individuals contribute nothing to the public good, absent a lottery – a condition that runs counter to pertinent experimental literature. Section 3 outlines an experiment designed to test the consequences of a lottery supporting a less socially desirable public good on contributions and overall efficiency. Section 4 presents the experimental results and Section 5 concludes.

2. LOTTERY FUNDING WITH TWO PUBLIC GOODS

Here I extend the linear model, presented in both Morgan (2000) and Morgan and Sefton (2000), to include a second public good and explore the efficiency consequences of adding a single lottery to support each of the public goods in turn. Suppose N identical individuals have linear preferences over one private and two public goods expressed by

$$\pi_i = x_i + mG + kH \tag{1}$$

where x_i is i's private good consumption (normalized to have a return of 1), G and H represent aggregate contributions, and m and k are the marginal per capita returns (MPCR defined by Isaac & Walker, 1988) from public good G or H, respectively. Each agent maximizes Eq. (1) subject to the budget constraint,

$$w = x_i + g_i + h_i \tag{2}$$

by choosing g_i and h_i reflecting i's personal contribution to G and H, respectively. Combining Eqs. (1) and (2), agents have a single objective function

$$\pi_i = (w - g_i - h_i) + mG + kH \tag{3}$$

Assume standard public good conditions for both G and H (i.e., $0 < m < 1$, $Nm > 1$, $0 < k < 1$, and $Nk > 1$). Thus, while no individual finds it profitable to invest in either public good individually, society as a whole gains when either or both are provided. Further restrict $k < m$ so that good G is more socially desirable than good H (i.e., $Nm > Nk > 1$).

Maximizing Eq. (3) leads to the dominant solution Nash equilibrium with complete free riding in which agents consume only the private good (i.e., $g_i^N = h_i^N = 0$). At the Nash equilibrium, each person receives $\pi_i^N = w$ and the aggregate payoff is $\Pi^N = Nw$. At the social optimum, each agent contributes his entire endowment to the more socially desirable public good (i.e., $g_i = w$) resulting in an individual payoff of $\pi_i^S = Nmw$ and an aggregate payoff, $\Pi^S = N(Nmw) > \Pi^N$. Introducing a second public good into the linear environment in no way alters the static Nash prediction of zero voluntary contributions; free riding extends to multiple public goods.

Now add a self-funding lottery to support public good G. Tickets cost \$1 each and the probability of winning an exogenously determined prize (P) depends on the fraction of tickets purchased by consumer i (i.e., g_i/G). The payoff function in Eq. (3) is augmented to form an expected payoff

$$E(\pi_i) = (w - g_i - h_i) + (g_i/G)P + m(G - P) + kH \qquad (4)$$

The second term on the right-hand side in Eq. (4) is the expected value of the lottery, while the third term represents net funding for the provision of public good G.[4]

Assuming risk-neutral agents, maximization of Eq. (4) results in the first-order condition

$$\partial E(\pi_i)/\partial g_i = m + (G_{-i}/G^2)P - 1 = 0 \qquad (5)$$

where $G_{-i} = G - g_i$ represents total tickets purchased by others. Complete free riding is predicted toward H as $k - 1 < 0$ (i.e., $h_i^N = H^N = 0$). For $P > 0$, and with homogeneous agents, the Nash equilibrium ticket purchase for agent i is

$$g_i^N = [(N - 1)P]/[N^2(1 - m)] \qquad (6)$$

and

$$G^N = [(N - 1)P]/[N(1 - m)] \qquad (7)$$

in aggregate. Net provision of G follows directly

$$G^N - P = [(Nm - 1)P]/[N(1 - m)] \qquad (8)$$

which ensures that in equilibrium the funds raised through the lottery will exceed the prize if and only if the public good is socially desirable (i.e., $Nm > 1$).[5]

Equilibrium expected per capita payoff is

$$E(\pi_i) = w + [(Nm - 1)^2 P]/[N^2(1 - m)] \tag{9}$$

which exceeds the Nash equilibrium payoff, absent a lottery. The negative externality associated with the lottery (an individual purchasing an extra ticket decreases the expected payoff to others) offsets the positive externality associated with the public good, thereby offsetting agents' tendencies to free ride.[6] Using Eq. (9), the equilibrium aggregate payoff is

$$\Pi^{NLG} = Nw + P - G^N + Nm(G^N - P) = \Pi^N + (Nm - 1)(G^N - P) \tag{10}$$

If a single lottery is used to fund public good H, then all the previous results hold now for good H instead of good G. The equilibrium is described by $g_i^N = G^N = 0$ and,

$$h_i^N = [(N - 1)P]/[N^2(1 - k)] \tag{11}$$

The self-funding condition again requires that public good H is socially desirable (i.e., $Nk > 1$). Aggregate payoff at the Nash equilibrium is

$$\Pi^{NLH} = \Pi^N + (Nk - 1)(H^N - P) \tag{12}$$

For $0 < k < m < 1$, $Nm > Nk > 1$, and a constant prize (P) supporting one or the other public good, the equilibrium aggregate payoffs are ranked $\Pi^N < \Pi^{NLH} < \Pi^{NLG}$.[7]

To summarize, in a simple linear environment adding a second public good does not alter the standard Nash outcome of complete free riding toward both public goods. While a lottery supporting either public good increases aggregate payoff, the largest increase occurs when the lottery is applied to the most socially desirable public good.

3. EXPERIMENT DESIGN, CONJECTURES, AND PROCEDURES

Lotteries need not be applied to the most socially desired public good. Aside from the difficulty of ranking the social desirability of different public goods, some narrowly focused not-for-profit organizations that use lotteries for support may appeal to only a small fraction of the general population. This section develops an experimental design that allows some insight into the possible adverse consequences of lotteries on public good provision. Consider an environment with $N = 3$, participants each of who may invest privately or contribute to either or both of two public goods, G and H, with respective MPCRs of $m = 0.75$ and $k = 0.50$. Suppose further that a single lottery is implemented to raise funds for the less socially desirable good H. The expected payoff function is

$$E(\pi_i) = x_i + (h_i/H)P + 0.75(G) + 0.50(H - P) \qquad (13)$$

Each period subjects are given 20 tokens and must select g_i and h_i subject to the constraints $x_i + g_i + h_i = 20$, $x_i \geq 0$, $g_i \geq 0$, and $h_i \geq 0$. Given $N = 3$, $g_i^N = 0$, and from Eq. (11) $h_i^N = (4/9)P$.

Despite the equilibrium prediction of positive revenues net of the prize, net revenue may be negative as a behavioral matter if ticket purchases are less than the prize. When $(H - P) < 0$, all ticket purchases are refunded. Table 1 summarizes the experimental treatments and key theoretical predictions. In the baseline treatment ($P = 0$), the dominant solution is to free ride on others' contributions to either public good. Agents keep their endowment for private consumption ($g_i^N = h_i^N = 0$) and aggregate payoff is $\Pi^* = 60$, where Π^* is the aggregate payoff at the relevant Nash equilibrium. A social planner would have all agents contribute their entire endowment to public good G – the more socially desirable public good – resulting in an aggregate payoff of $\Pi^s = 135$. At the Nash equilibrium in the absence of a lottery, the predicted efficiency is $\xi^* = 100(\Pi^*/\Pi^S) = 44.4\%$. In the lottery treatment, $P = 22.5$, $g_i^N = 0$, $h_i^N = 10$, $H - P = 7.5$, and $\Pi^* = 63.75$, so at the equilibrium the efficiency is 47.2%.[8]

In a dynamic strategic environment, the appropriate unit of analysis is at the aggregate level (Selten, Abbink, Buchta, Sadrieh, 2003).[9] I offer these conjectures regarding aggregate contributions as points of reference. While they follow directly from the development in Section 2, as discussed below, intuition and previous experimental research suggests that none of them may be observed.

Table 1. Experimental Treatments and Theory Predictions.

	Baseline	Lottery
Groups (individuals)	5 (15)	5 (15)
P_H	0	22.5
g_i^N	0	0
h_i^N	0	10
$H^N - P_H$	0	$30 - 22.5 = 7.5$
Π^*	60	63.75
g_i^S	20	20
h_i^S	0	0
Π^S	135	135
$\xi^* = 100(\Pi^*/\Pi^S)$	44.4%	47.2%

In the baseline treatment, I conjecture that subjects completely free ride with respect to both public goods.

Conjecture 1. Absent a lottery, subjects completely free ride, so $G = H = 0$.

Conjecture 1 is a strict interpretation of the Nash equilibrium prediction. As past experiments have shown, subjects tend to persistently make contributions in excess of the equilibrium prediction. Isaac and Walker (1988) show that higher MPCR values are associated with larger contributions. While no experiments with two public goods have been conducted, it is reasonable to hypothesize that the public good with the higher MPCR might receive higher contributions.

The introduction of a lottery is predicted to increase ticket purchases and consequently net funding for good H as compared to voluntary contributions to good H in the baseline.

Conjecture 2. The introduction of a lottery supporting the less-valued good H increases both gross ticket sales and net provision of H. Specifically, when $P > 0$, $H^L > H^B$ and net $H^L >$ net H^B (where superscripts L and B refer to lottery and baseline, respectively).

Theory predicts complete free riding toward all public goods in the baseline and an increase in efficiency with the introduction of a lottery. Denoting efficiency as ξ ($\xi = \Pi^j/\Pi^S$, where $j =$ Baseline or Lottery), Conjecture 3 follows directly.

Conjecture 3. The introduction of a lottery increases efficiency. When $P > 0$, $>^L >>^B$.

Even if net provision of H increases, it is not clear that efficiency will increase for two reasons. First, suppose that in the baseline treatment subjects keep half of their endowment for private consumption (x_i) and split the remaining half between public goods G and H. If the introduction of the lottery causes people to substitute from x_i to h_i, efficiency increases. If the lottery causes people to substitute from g_i to h_i, efficiency falls. Second, in this experiment lottery cancellations can reduce total public good provision.

To evaluate these conjectures, an experiment consisting of 10 three-person groups was conducted in two 15-subject sessions in Trento, Italy, at the Computable and Experimental Economics Laboratory (CEEL). Subjects were recruited through poster advertisements. Each session was identical with the exception of the lottery prize for good H in the lottery treatment.

Subjects were individually seated at shielded computer terminals running *PGLottery* software with all screens and instructions in Italian.[10] A laboratory assistant read the instructions aloud, while subjects read an electronic version (that remained accessible to subjects for their review throughout the session). The instructions explained to participants that they were anonymously grouped with two other people in the room and that this grouping would remain constant throughout the 15-period session. The instructions also indicated that all subjects in each group faced identical payoff parameters. Because of the complexity of this environment, a Payoff Wizard was available, permitting subjects to calculate payoffs under a variety of 'what-if' scenarios based on hypothetical contribution decisions both for themselves and for others.[11] At the end of each period, a subject knew his own actions, the aggregate actions of others in his group, and his period and cumulative payoffs. In the lottery treatment, subjects were also told whether or not the lottery was cancelled. If the lottery proceeded, subjects were informed whether they won or lost. This information was summarized on each subjects' Decision History page available on their computer screens. Sessions lasted approximately 1.5 h. Average subject earnings in the baseline treatment were approximately €18 ($22.00 US at the time of the experiment), while in the lottery treatment average earnings were approximately €13 ($16.00 US at the time of the experiment).

4. RESULTS

In this section, I first provide an overview of the results using Figs. 1–3 and then turn to a more formal statistical evaluation of the conjectures using Tables 2–4. Each of the three figures presents a time series of aggregate results by treatment -- *Baseline* in the left panel and *Lottery* on the right. Data points are indicated by group number to visually capture group-specific effects. A median spline is plotted to indicate trend, while horizontal lines reflect key theoretical reference values. A treatment effect is immediately apparent in each of the three figures.

In Fig. 1, there are significant voluntary contributions to the more socially desirable good (*G*) in the baseline treatment (left panel). Ignoring endgame effects, voluntary contributions to *G* are relatively high and stable, but fall drastically with the introduction of a lottery supporting *H* (right panel), suggesting that crowding out is an issue.[12] Moreover, in the lottery treatment voluntary contributions to *G* start lower and contribution decline is much more monotonic through time.

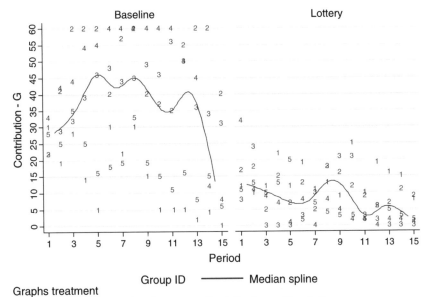

Fig. 1. Aggregate Contribution – Good *G*.

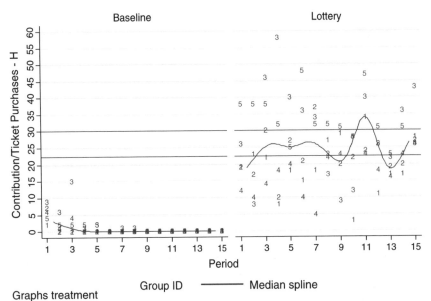

Fig. 2. Aggregate Contribution/Ticket Purchases – Good *H*.

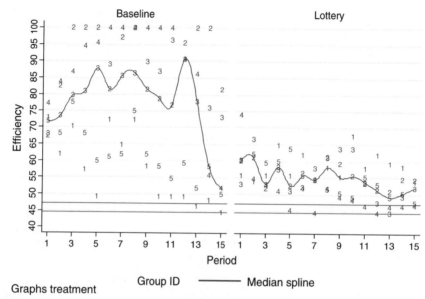

Fig. 3. Observed Efficiency.

Table 2. Averages by Treatment.

Period Range		G	H^{a}	net H^{b}	Efficiency
All	Baseline	33.87	0.89	0.89	76.13
	Lottery	9.13	24.69	5.31	54.87
3 through 13	Baseline	37.07	0.55	0.55	78.97
	Lottery	8.69	24.82	5.51	54.53

[a]In the baseline treatment, H is the aggregate voluntary contribution to H, while in the lottery treatment H is the aggregate ticket purchases in the lottery (i.e., gross rather than net ticket revenues).
[b]In the baseline treatment, net H is the aggregate voluntary contribution to H, while in the lottery treatment net H is the aggregate net funding for H (i.e., $H-P \geq 0$).

Fig. 2 describes contributions to (lottery ticket purchases for) good H. The top horizontal line reflects the Nash equilibrium prediction of lottery ticket purchases when $P = 22.5$, while the bottom line represents the lottery prize. In stark contrast to Fig. 1, there is virtually complete free riding toward H in the baseline treatment and a substantial increase in ticket purchases under the lottery treatment. In the right panel of Fig. 2, a large number of observations fall below the lower horizontal line indicating lottery cancellations.

Fig. 3 presents efficiency results. The top horizontal line represents the predicted efficiency at the Nash equilibrium in the lottery treatment, while the lower line is the predicted efficiency at the dominant strategy Nash equilibrium in the baseline treatment. Save for the final few periods, it is clear there are sizeable adverse efficiency consequences to the introduction of a lottery supporting the less-valued public good.

I now turn to a more formal statistical analysis of the conjectures. Table 2 presents pertinent summary data, while Tables 3 and 4 present statistical results corresponding to Conjectures 2 and 3. Tabular data and results are presented for all 15 periods and for periods 3–13 (to mitigate learning and endgame effects). Statistical analysis uses aggregate data averaged by group over the appropriate range of periods. Any statistical test involves five observations from each of the two treatments. With such a limited amount of data, it is important to use a range of statistical tests. Accordingly, Tables 3 and 4 report p-values (based upon two-sided hypothesis tests with a null hypothesis of no-treatment effect) from the parametric t-test for difference in means, the non-parametric Mann–Whitney test for difference in distributions, and the distribution-free Fisher exact-randomization test for difference in means (Moir, 1998).[13]

Result 1. In a baseline environment with two public goods, G and H, where G is more socially desirable than H, subjects contribute primarily to G. Contributions to the less-valued good, H, tend to zero and may be characterized as complete free riding.

Table 3. Statistical Test P-values for Treatment Effects: Funding for Good H.

	Contributions vs. Ticket Sales			Contributions vs. Net Provision		
Period range	E–R	t-test	$M-W$	E–R	t-test	$M-W$
All	0.0079	0.0001	0.009	0.0714	0.088	0.0758
3 through 13	0.0079	0.0001	0.0088	0.0159	0.0627	0.016

Table 4. Statistical Test P-values for Treatment Effects: Efficiency.

	$>^B$ vs. $>^L$		
Period range	E–R	t-test	$M-W$
All	0.0159	0.014	0.0163
3 through 13	0.0159	0.0154	0.0163

Average aggregate voluntary contribution to G across all periods is 33.87 tokens, approximately 56.5% of available endowments (Table 2). In the *final* period, not shown in Table 2, the average aggregate voluntary contribution to G is 17 tokens or 28.3% of available endowments. In contrast, the average aggregate voluntary contribution to H is only 5.6 tokens (9.3% of available endowments) in the *first* period (not shown), and averages only 0.89 (1.5% of available endowments) over all periods. Complete free riding is rarely, if ever, observed in linear public good experiments, especially at the aggregate level. The introduction of a second public good with a lower MPCR induces complete free riding behavior toward that good, at least here. From the ninth period onward, aggregate contributions to H are zero. The extreme free riding result toward good H in the baseline treatment suggests that it is neither lack of understanding nor error that causes people to stray from a dominant solution equilibrium in a linear public good experiment. Subjects know how to free ride, but they strategically choose not to.

Result 2. The introduction of a lottery supporting the less socially desirable public good H, increases contribution to that good. Relative to the baseline, both gross ticket purchases and net provision of H increase.

Table 3 presents test results supporting this claim. The null hypothesis of no-treatment effect is clearly rejected when comparing aggregate voluntary contributions to H in the baseline treatment to ticket purchases in the lottery treatment (left columns). The p-value is less than 1% for all three statistical tests. Adding a lottery causes people to purchase tickets in support of good H. Likewise, the null hypothesis of no-treatment effect is rejected when comparing aggregate voluntary contributions to H in the baseline treatment to net provision of H (i.e., $H-P$) in the lottery treatment (right columns). The p-values here are generally larger than in the comparison of contributions to ticket sales. This is a result of lottery ticket purchases less than the Nash equilibrium prediction of 30 in aggregate (53 out of 75 periods of observation have ticket sales less than 30) and a significant number of lottery cancellations.[14]

The relatively large number of instances where the lottery failed to generate revenues sufficient to cover provision of public good H represents one interesting aspect of these experimental results. The points below the lower horizontal line in the right panel of Fig. 2 document the instances where ticket purchases failed to cover the provision point minimum necessary to proceed with the lottery. This occurred in 33 out of 75 observations. This finding differs dramatically from Dale (2004), where the lottery was cancelled only twice in 135 periods, and in Morgan and Sefton (2000), where no lottery (with MPCR > 0) was ever cancelled.[15] On average, slightly more than two lotteries are cancelled each period. More disturbing, a regression of the number of lottery cancellations upon period indicates no significant time effect on lottery cancellations.[16]

Subjects in the lottery treatment seem to hone in on minimum provision point ticket purchases. It is evident in the right panel of Fig. 2 that both the median of, and variability in, aggregate ticket purchases decline over time. Subjects attempt to coordinate on a solution in which they jointly wager the minimum amount necessary to cover the prize. If this is the case, then selection of an optimal prize rule (i.e., prize = f(ticket sales)) is extremely important.

Result 3. The introduction of a lottery on a less socially desirable public good decreases efficiency.

Table 4 indicates that a null hypothesis of no-treatment effect is rejected (at a 2% level of significance) in all period subgroups. The reason efficiency declines with the lottery is twofold. First, as mentioned in Result 2, a significant number of lotteries are cancelled owing to insufficient funding, resulting in no net funding for H. Second, as is clearly evident in Fig. 1, the introduction of a lottery severely crowds out voluntary contributions to public good G. Across all periods, average aggregate contributions to G are 33.87 in the baseline and 9.13 in the lottery (see Table 2). In the baseline treatment, the individual Nash equilibrium prediction of complete free riding toward G (i.e., $g_i = 0$) occurs only 31 times in 225 observations, and $g_i \leq 5$ only 30% of the time. In the lottery treatment, complete free riding toward G occurs in 96 out of 225 observations and $g_i \leq 5$, 82% of the time. Crowding out, while noticeably present in the lottery treatment, is incomplete, leading to average efficiency in the lottery treatment of 54.5%, which is higher than the Nash equilibrium prediction of 47.2%.

5. CONCLUSIONS

Introducing multiple public goods in an environment comparable to the single public good environment studied by Morgan (2000) complicates the clean theoretical prediction of lotteries as welfare-improving fund-raising tools for a public good. While a lottery supporting a less socially desirable public good (the 'wrong' public good) is still welfare improving, it is not as welfare improving as instituting a lottery with the same prize in support of a more socially desirable public good (the 'right' public good). Morgan and

Sefton (2000) provide experimental results indicating that a lottery improves efficiency in a single public good environment and lend support to Morgan's theory. Dale (2004) and Davis et al. (2005) add further support in a single public good environment.

The results of the experiment reported here demonstrate that a lottery supporting the 'wrong' public good actually decreases overall efficiency. There are two reasons for this efficiency reduction. First, in the absence of a lottery, the 'right' public good receives significant voluntary contributions, while the 'wrong' public good receives virtually no voluntary funding. While further testing is necessary, the degree of voluntary contribution in these two public good environments seems to exceed contributions in single public good environments with comparable marginal per capita returns. Introducing a lottery supporting the 'wrong' public good crowds out these voluntary contributions to the 'right' public good and dramatically reduces efficiency. Crowding out is incomplete that keeps efficiency in the lottery treatment higher than otherwise. Second, unlike Morgan and Sefton, and later Dale, a significant number of lottery cancellations reduce the provision of public good H to zero and reduce efficiency.

The data from the current experiment suggest that in addition to any normative argument against lotteries, legitimate positive arguments questioning the unregulated proliferation of state and charitable lotteries also exist. Although my results cannot be taken as definitive, these experiments suggest that governments should consider carefully their policies toward lotteries and lottery regulation. At a minimum further-related research, both experimental and theoretical, is warranted.

NOTES

1. Funding public good provision through lotteries is not new. In 1569, the English government instituted a state lottery to raise funds for the "reparations of the havens and the strength of the realme and towards such other public good works" (Seville, 1999, p. 20).

2. Morgan's theoretical work has spawned efficiency-improving extensions. Amegashie and Myers (2000) show that a pre-lottery selecting a subset of people to enter a second and final lottery increases public good funding. Similarly if tickets entered into the lottery are an increasing function of the amount an agent spends on lottery tickets, public good funding increases. Apinunmahakul and Barham (2003) use a two-part tariff model to show a similar result.

3. Both the fixed-prize lottery and voluntary contribution mechanism generate greater levels of net public good funding in comparison to the revenue-dependent lottery.

4. These equilibrium results are not affected if one allows for negative levels of public good G (i.e., $G - P < 0$) as in Morgan or if under-funded lotteries have tickets refunded. Refunding tickets introduces an additional equilibrium in which each agent buys no tickets as each expects the lottery to be cancelled. In the experiment design reported later, a lottery produces positive net provision of a public good in equilibrium. Nonetheless, the design incorporates a refund if net provision is negative.

5. This lottery merely redistributes wealth among individuals. Morgan and Sefton (2000) argue that a series of smaller prizes could be used to mitigate concerns about the post-lottery income distribution. In practice, however, participants are attracted to large jackpots and charitable organizations appear far more interested in their receipts than in subsequent income distribution. For example, the Atlantic Lottery Corporation – a private company providing a substantial fraction of its profits to governments and charities in the Atlantic Canadian provinces – observes "Player reaction to large jackpots indicates they prefer to try for big jackpots. ... We tried a special draw of 10 prizes of $1 million each. Players did not respond with the enthusiasm they show when a jackpot grows." (http://www.alc.ca/English/FAQs/Games/#6, accessed 13 September 2005). Moreover, $\partial(G^N - P)/\partial P > 0$ so a fund manager, interested in maximizing funds for his charity, will want to offer larger prizes.

6. For a broader theoretical discussion on how lotteries and other mechanisms create a negative externality to partially offset the positive externality associated with a public good, see Amegashie (2004).

7. A lottery with prize P increases net funding by a larger amount, which is in turn valued more highly by society when the lottery is applied to the more socially desirable public good.

8. As a reference, had the same lottery prize of 22.5 been applied to public good G, then equilibrium efficiency would have been 79.2%.

9. Individual decisions in this experiment cannot be considered independent because subjects are partnered for the duration of the session. However, aggregate data are independent across groups as there is no strategic interaction across groups.

10. English instructions are included as an appendix.

11. Subjects scrolled through hypothetical contributions for x_i, g_i, and h_i and for X_{-i}, G_{-i}, and H_{-i}. In the absence of a lottery (i.e., $P = 0$), the Payoff Wizard calculated the resulting payoff. In the case of a lottery (i.e., $P > 0$), the Payoff Wizard alerted them as to whether the lottery would run (i.e., if $H > P$) and calculated the appropriate payoff. If the lottery would proceed, the Payoff Wizard displayed the expected payoff (based on the probability h_i/H), the payoff if they won, and the payoff if they lost.

12. Obviously there are group-specific dynamics. In the baseline treatment, groups 1 and 5 follow a trend much more commonly observed in public good experiments. Still, both of these groups voluntarily contribute more to G in the baseline treatment than most groups do under the lottery treatment.

13. The exact randomization difference of means test (E−R) calculates overall means by treatment, and uses the difference in these two means as the test statistic. The test is based upon a null hypothesis that assignment to treatment does not matter. If true, then the observed difference in means will not be large relative to all possible permutations of the data and resulting difference in means statistics. Two treatments, each with five observations, lead to 252 possible combinations of the data and 252 differences of means statistics. By ranking the observed difference in means

against all possible differences in means, an exact p-value based solely upon the observed data is calculated. Given the units of observation and a two-sided hypothesis test, the lowest possible p-value is 0.0079, indicative of the most extreme test statistic. The E–R test is advantageous as it rests on no distributional assumptions.

14. The comparable 'success' of this lottery in producing results significantly different from the baseline comes from strong free riding toward good H in the baseline treatment. Both Morgan and Sefton, and later Dale, realize only small gains over voluntary contributions in a single public good environment.

15. For the majority of treatments reported in both Morgan and Sefton, and in Dale, MPCR $= 0.75$. In the current paper, the lottery supports a good with MPCR $= 0.5$. The predicted efficiency properties with a high MPCR means that over-wagering in both the Morgan and Sefton and in the Dale environments is less costly than in the present case.

16. A simple linear regression reveals $cancellations = 2.97 - 0.096\ period$. A null hypothesis of mean cancellations equals zero is rejected ($p\text{-value} = 0.000$), but a null hypothesis of no time effect is not ($p\text{-value} = 0.141$). Low–adjusted R^2 values (0.0940) support this claim, but limited observations (15) mean more data are necessary to validate such a claim.

ACKNOWLEDGMENTS

This research was funded by UNBSJ University Research Fund 37-18. I thank Stuart Mestelman and R. Andrew Muller for permitting me to work at McEEL and Luigi Mittone for permitting me to research and conduct experiments at CEEL. I also thank Neil Buckley and Marco Tecilla for programming assistance. Finally, I thank without implicating Bram Cadsby, Peter Ibbott, Jason Childs, and Doug Davis for their comments on an earlier version of this paper. Please contact the author for a copy of the open source *PGLottery* software used in this experiment.

REFERENCES

Amegashie, J. (2004). *Negative externalities and the private provision of public goods: A survey.* Unpublished Working Paper. Department of Economics, Guelph University, Guelph.

Amegashie, J., & Myers, G. (2000). *Intense lottos and raffles.* Unpublished Working Paper 00-23. Department of Economics, Simon Fraser University, Burnaby.

Apinunmahakul, A., & Barham, V. (2003). *Financing public goods by means of lotteries: A comment.* Unpublished Working Paper. Department of Economics, University of Ottawa, Ottawa.

Chan, K., Mestelman, S., Moir, R., & Muller, R. A. (1996). The voluntary provision of public goods under varying income distributions. *Canadian Journal of Economics, 29*(1), 54–69.

Dale, D. J. (2004). Charitable lottery structure and fund raising: Theory and evidence. *Experimental Economics, 7*(3), 217–234.

Davis, D., & Holt, C. (1993). *Experimental economics*. Princeton: Princeton University Press.

Davis, D., Razzolini, L., Reilly, R., & Wilson, B. (2005). *Raising revenues for charities: Auctions versus lotteries*. Unpublished Working Paper. Virginia Commonwealth University, Richmond.

Isaac, R. M., & Walker, J. M. (1988). Group size effects in public goods provision: The voluntary contributions mechanism. *Quarterly Journal of Economics, 103*(1), 179–199.

Ledyard, J. (1995). Public goods experiments. In: J. Kagel & A. Roth (Eds), *Handbook of experimental economics* (pp. 111–194). Princeton: Princeton University Press.

Mixon, F. G., Jr., Caudill, S. B., Ford, J. M., & Peng, T. C. (1997). The rise (or fall) of lottery adoption within the logic of collective action: Some empirical evidence. *Journal of Economics and Finance, 21*(1), 43–49.

Moir, R. (1998). A Monte-Carlo analysis of the Fisher randomization technique: Reviving randomization for experimental economists. *Experimental Economics, 1*(1), 87–100.

Morgan, J. (2000). Financing public goods by means of lotteries. *Review of Economic Studies, 67*(234), 761–784.

Morgan, J., & Sefton, M. (2000). Funding public goods with lotteries: Experimental evidence. *Review of Economic Studies, 67*(234), 785–810.

Samuelson, P. A. (1954). The pure theory of public expenditure. *The Review of Economics and Statistics, 36*(4), 387–389.

Selten, R., Abbink, K., Buchta, J., & Sadrieh, A. (2003). How to play (3 × 3)-games. A strategy method experiment. *Games and Economic Behavior, 45*(1), 19–37.

Seville, A. (1999). The Italian roots of the lottery. *History Today, 49*(3), 17–20.

Smith, A. (1776). An inquiry into the nature and causes of the wealth of nations. In: E. Cannan (Ed.), *Library of Economics and Liberty* (5th ed., pp. 1904). London: Methuen and Co. Ltd. 20 July 2005. <http://www.econlib.org/library/Smith/smWN20.html>

Zelmer, J. (2003). Linear public goods experiments: A meta-analysis. *Experimental Economics, 6*(3), 299–310.

APPENDIX. NO LOTTERY – EXPERIMENT INSTRUCTIONS

This page is a link from the Decision page. It will open as a new window. You can return to it whenever you are at the Decision page.

Overview

Thank you for agreeing to be part of this experiment. Today you will be asked to make a number of choices. All of your choices are to be private. The choices you and others make will lead to payoffs expressed in lab dollars. Over the course of this session, your payoffs will be cumulated and used to determine the amount of money you will be paid at the end of the session. You will be paid in private, at the rate of 1 lab dollar equals 3.5 euro cents at the end of today's session. Throughout this session, you will be linked, via

computer to two other individuals. While the three of you will remain connected for the entire session, you will not know the identity of the other
individuals. The session will be divided into a total of 15 periods. At the
beginning of each period, you will be given 20 tokens. You must choose how
to allocate your tokens between three different options. Allocations may be
any non-negative integer (e.g., 0, 1, 2, ..., 20. A valid allocation decision will use
All of your available tokens. However, you are free to contribute any non-
negative amount (including zero) to each of the three options. Below we describe how payoffs are determined from allocation decisions for each option.

Good X

Your payoff from good X is determined solely by your own allocation
decision. For each token you allocate to X, you earn 1 lab dollar. Mathematically, if you allocate x tokens to good X, you earn 1^*x.

Good G

Your payoff from good G is determined by what you and the other two
individuals allocate to good G. For each token you allocate to good G, you
earn 0.75 lab dollars, *as do the other two individuals*. Mathematically, if we
let G represent the total allocation to good G by the three of you, you earn
0.75^*G as do the other two individuals.

Good H

Your payoff from good H is determined by what you and the other two
individuals allocate to good H. For each token you allocate to good H, you
earn 0.50 lab dollars, *as do the other two individuals*. Mathematically, if we
let H represent the total allocation to good H by the three of you, you earn
0.50^*H as do the other two individuals.

Total Payoff

In total, you earn $1^*x + 0.75^*G + 0.50^*H$ in lab dollars for a particular
allocation decision.

The Computer Interface

In each period, you will be informed of your identification number, the
current period, and the number of tokens you have available. You will be

provided with three boxes to enter your allocation to good X, good G, and good H. You increase your allocation to a good by clicking on the + button for that good. As you increase your allocation to a good, you will notice that your Tokens Available fall. Similarly, to decrease your allocation to a good, you click on the – button for that good. As you decrease your allocation to a good, you will notice that your Tokens Available rise. A valid decision will leave 0 Tokens Available. To change your decision once your Tokens Available is 0, you must first decrease you allocation to one good and then increase it for another. When you click on SUBMIT, the computer will check that Tokens Available is 0 and will ask you to make sure of your allocation decision. The computer will sum group allocations and report both your payoffs in the current period and your cumulative payoff. You can access a History page at either the Decision page or the Results page. The History page will open in a new window and describes the decisions made by you and others in each period up to the current period. It also lists your payoff in each period.

The Payoff Wizard

The environment in which you are being asked to operate is quite complex. In order to assist you, a Payoff Wizard is available at the bottom of the Decision page. In order to use the Payoff Wizard, you must enter valid allocation decisions for both G and H (X is determined automatically) for both yourself and the combined decisions of the two others. The Payoff Wizard reports your payoff based upon the allocation decisions you entered. It is important that you realize that these values are not your decisions, nor are they the decisions that others will make. They represent a *possible* set of decisions.

Questions

If you have any questions, now or at any time, please raise your hand and the experiment monitor will answer them.

LOTTERY – EXPERIMENT INSTRUCTIONS

This page is a link from the Decision page. It will open as a new window. You can return to it whenever you are at the Decision page.

Overview

Thank you for agreeing to be part of this experiment. Today you will be asked to make a number of choices. All of your choices are to be private. The choices you and others make will lead to payoffs expressed in lab dollars. Over the course of this session, your payoffs will be cumulated and used to determine the amount of money you will be paid at the end of the session. You will be paid in private, at the rate of 1 lab dollar equals 3.5 euro cents at the end of today's session. Throughout this session, you will be linked, via computer to two other individuals. While the three of you will remain connected for the entire session, you will not know the identity of the other individuals. The session will be divided into a total of 15 periods. At the beginning of each period, you will be given 20 tokens. You must choose how to allocate your tokens between three different options. Allocations may be any non-negative integer (e.g., 0, 1, 2, ..., 20). A valid allocation decision will use *All* of your available tokens. However, you are free to contribute any non-negative amount (including zero) to each of the three options. Below we describe how payoffs are determined from allocation decisions for each option.

Good X

Your payoff from good X is determined solely by your own allocation decision. For each token you allocate to X, you earn 1 lab dollar. Mathematically, if you allocate x tokens to good X, you earn 1^*x.

Good G

Your payoff from good G is determined by what you and the other two individuals allocate to good G. For each token you allocate to good G, you earn 0.75 lab dollars, *as do the other two individuals*. Mathematically, if we let G represent the total allocation to good G by the three of you, you earn 0.75^*G as do the other two individuals.

H-Raffle

Each token you allocate to *H*-Raffle purchases you one ticket in a raffle. If you win the raffle, then you get a fixed prize (the amount is displayed on your screen) expressed in lab dollars. The chance you have of winning the raffle depends upon the number of tickets you purchase as compared to the total number of tickets purchased by all three of you (i.e., h/H where h is your ticket purchase and H the total ticket purchase by all three of you). A raffle proceeds *only if* the total ticket purchase meets or exceeds the prize. In the event that a raffle is cancelled, your purchase of tickets in the H-raffle will be returned to you and converted to an allocation to good X. Mathematically, if the lottery is on, then you earn $(0.50^*(H - \text{prize}) + \text{prize})$ lab dollars if you win and $(0.50^*(H-\text{prize}))$ lab dollars if you lose. The other two individuals in your group earn a similar payoff depending on if they win or lose. There is only *one* winner per group.

Consider the following two examples in which prize equals 8 lab dollars. The numbers used are for demonstration purposes only.

(1) Suppose you use 4 tokens to purchase 4 tickets in the H-Raffle and the other two individuals use 5 and 3 tokens, respectively (i.e., $h = 4$ and $H = 4 + (5 + 3) = 12$). The raffle will go ahead as planned as $H > \text{prize}$ (i.e., $12 > 8$). You have a 4/12 chance of winning 8 lab dollars. If you win, your payoff will increase by $(0.50^*(12 - 8) + 8) = ((0.50^*4) + 8)$ lab dollars and if you lose, your payoff will increase by $(0.50^*(12 - 8)) = (0.50^*4)$ lab dollars.

(2) Suppose you use 2 tokens to purchase 2 tickets in the H-Raffle and the other two individuals use 1 and 4 tokens, respectively (i.e., $h = 2$ and $H = 2 + (1 + 4) = 7$). The raffle will be cancelled as $H < \text{prize}$ (i.e., $7 < 8$). In this instance, each of you will have your good X allocation increased by the number of tickets you had purchased.

Total Payoff

In total, you earn $1^*x + 0.75^*G + 0.50^*(H-\text{prize}) + \text{prize}$ in lab dollars for a particular allocation decision, but only if you win the raffle. If you lose the raffle, you earn $1^*x + 0.75^*G + 0.50^*(H-\text{prize})$ lab dollars. If $H < \text{prize}$, then the raffle is cancelled and you earn $1^*(x+h) + 0.75^*G$ lab dollars, where h is the number of raffle tickets you originally purchased but have now been returned.

The Computer Interface

In each period, you will be informed of your identification number, the current period, the raffle prize, and the number of tokens you have available. You will be provided with three boxes to enter your allocation to good X, good G, and the H-Raffle. You increase your allocation to a good by clicking on the + button for that good. As you increase your allocation to a good, you will notice that your Tokens Available fall. Similarly, to decrease your allocation to a good, you click on the − button for that good. As you decrease your allocation to a good, you will notice that your Tokens Available rise. A valid decision will leave 0 Tokens Available. To change your decision once your Tokens Available is 0, you must first decrease your allocation to one good and then increase it for another. When you click on SUBMIT, the computer will check that Tokens Available is 0 and will ask you to make sure of your allocation decision. The computer will sum group allocations, check to see if the raffle will proceed (returning tokens if necessary), determine the lottery winner, and report both your payoff in the current period and your cumulative payoff. You can access a History page at either the Decision page or the Results page. The History page will open in a new window and describes the decisions made by you and others in each period up to the current period. It also lists your payoff in each period.

The Payoff Wizard

The environment in which you are being asked to operate is quite complex. In order to assist you, a Payoff Wizard is available at the bottom of the Decision page. In order to use the Payoff Wizard, you must enter valid allocation decisions for both G and H (X is determined automatically) for both yourself and the combined decisions of the two others. The Payoff Wizard checks to see if total ticket purchases are sufficient to cover the prize. If $H <$ prize, then the Raffle Cancelled column is highlighted and your payoff is calculated as if all H allocations were returned. (*If you change either your H or others' H but total H < prize, you will see no change in the Payoff box in the Payoff Wizard under the Raffle Cancelled column. This is because all H allocations will be returned and allocated to good X*). If H is at least as large as prize, then the Raffle On column is highlighted and you see your expected (based upon the probability of winning) payoff, your payoff if you win, and your payoff if you lose. It is important that you realize that these values are not your decisions, nor are they the decisions that others will make. They represent a *possible* set of decisions.

Questions

If you have any questions, now or at any time, please raise your hand and the experiment monitor will answer them.

THE IMPACT OF SOCIAL COMPARISONS ON NONPROFIT FUND RAISING

Jen Shang and Rachel Croson

ABSTRACT

This paper examines the impact of social comparisons on fundraising and charitable contributions. We present results from a field experiment involving contributions to a public radio station. Some callers are told of the contribution decisions of others, and other callers are given no such information. We find that providing ambitions (high) social comparison information can significantly increase contributions.

Why individuals make charitable contributions and voluntarily provide public goods is an important question in modern society. Extensive research on voluntary contributions has been conducted by economists (Davis & Holt, 1993; Ledyard, 1995) and psychologists (Dawes, 1980).

Many theories have been proposed to explain why individuals give (or cooperate) when it is in their own (financial) interest to free or cheap ride. Explanations include altruism (e.g. Becker, 1974; Andreoni, 1988), warm glow, and warm-glow altruism (e.g. Andreoni, 1989, 1990), conditional co-operation (e.g. Fischbacher, Gachter, & Fehr, 2001), and reciprocity (e.g.

Experiments Investigating Fundraising and Charitable Contributors
Research in Experimental Economics, Volume 11, 143–156
Copyright © 2006 by Elsevier Ltd.
All rights of reproduction in any form reserved
ISSN: 0193-2306/doi:10.1016/S0193-2306(06)11006-6

Sugden, 1984). These motivations have been studied using experimental data from the lab and naturally occurring data.

Only very recently, field experiments have been introduced as a research tool in studying public goods provision and charitable contributions in economics (e.g. List & Lucking-Reiley, 2002; Eckel & Grossman, 2005, and other articles in this volume).[1] List and Lucking-Reiley study the effect of seed money and refunds in a university fund-raising campaign. They find that increasing the proportion of seed money increases both participation rates and the average amount of contribution, while instituting a refund only increases the average amount of contribution but not the participation rate. Eckel and Grossman study the effect of rebates as compared with matching in a public radio fund-raising campaign via mail. They find that matching and rebates solicit about the same number of contributions, but that matching generates higher average amounts contributed. Note that both of these two experiments manipulate the payoff structure faced by individual donors.

Instead of manipulating the payoff structure, our research introduces a new factor that influences contribution behavior: *social comparisons*. While previous research has suggested that social comparisons can have negative consequences for efficiency and social welfare, for example, by leading individuals to overconsume (e.g. Frank, 1999, 1985), this project identifies a positive impact of social comparisons; it can be used to enhance contributions to public goods.

In this article, we summarize our findings from three working papers, and report the results of a new field experiment in which social comparisons are manipulated and shown to increase average individual contribution in the field. Our setting is a fund-raising campaign for a public radio station.

We begin by introducing the concept of social comparisons and discussing how they might influence charitable giving. In the second section, we describe our previous research and its results. Section 3 descries the new field experiment and its results. We conclude with a brief summary describing our results, their implications for understanding charitable contributions, and their applications for nonprofit organizations more broadly.

SOCIAL COMPARISONS

Social comparisons were first studied by Festinger (1954). His original proposal was that people use three distinct processes to form an accurate view of themselves.[2] The first process involves using objective standards to evaluate their actions. For example, when I need to decide how much I should contribute to a local, public radio station, I can listen to the on-air fund-raising campaigns, and might donate the station-recommended amount. Second, people compare themselves to similar others, especially when an objective standard is not available or is not perceived as relevant. For example, I might believe that the station-recommend amounts are not objective (since they come from an interested party), so instead I might ask my friends how much they contributed and use that information to evaluate my own potential contribution levels. Third, people compare themselves not with similar others (others in their own position), but with individuals who have similar attributes. For example, if none of my friends contribute to the same station as I do, I might compare my contribution with other donors' contributions to judge the appropriateness of my actions.

The social comparisons studied in our research refer primarily to the third, more socially oriented comparison processes in Festinger's initial proposal. That is, we will use social comparisons to refer to the process, whereby people compare themselves to others who share attributes with themselves. In a nonprofit fund-raising context, this means that individuals compare their behavior with other donor's contributions to the same nonprofit.

Festinger's initial proposal later developed into a large stream of research on what kinds of social comparisons people seek in order to feel good about themselves (to achieve high self-evaluation or to accomplish self-enhancement, e.g. Taylor & Lobel, 1989). In contrast, our research does not examine the cause of social comparisons, nor are we interested in how people evaluate themselves. Rather, we are interested in how social comparisons influence contribution behavior. Our participants do not choose with whom they wish to compare themselves; they only decide what to do in response to social comparison information that we provide. We manipulate this information, and examine the consequences of this manipulation on individuals' behavior.

In this study, we communicate to contributors how much a previous donor had contributed in the social comparison conditions, while they get no such information in the control condition. We then look at the impact of this social comparison information on contribution behavior.

Social Comparisons in Nonprofit Fund Raising

In this research, we wanted to demonstrate the impact of social comparisons in public goods settings in a field setting. A related question has been studied in the lab using a dictator game (Cason & Mui, 1998). Subjects made two $40-dictator game decisions, one before and one after they learned the decision of another subject (or, in the control condition, another subject's birthday). Overall, participants become more self-regarding in the second decision, although this effect is significant in the control condition and insignificant in the experimental condition. Thus, the authors conclude that social comparison information can increase contributions, or at least retard the natural decrease of contributions. In our field study, we provide information on another (generous) donor and examine the impact of that information on the target donor's decision.

Only one very recent study has examined social comparisons in the field. Frey and Meier (2004) use a mail fund-raising campaign run by the university. Some students receive a letter telling them that 64% of other students had previously contributed (this represents the number who actually contributed in the last year). Other students receive a letter telling them that 46% of other students had previously contributed (this represents the number who actually contributed over the last 10 years). Seventy-seven percent of students in the 64% streatment (high social comparison) contribute to the fund, while 74.7% of students in the 46% treatment (low social comparison) contribute. After controlling for differences in previous contributions, this difference is statistically significant. While this paper examines the impact of social comparisons on *participation rate*, we will study the impact of social comparisons on *contribution amount*.

We sought a naturally occurring institution that captured the public good structure, where each individual has an incentive to free ride, but where the group as a whole is better off when everyone contributes. We identified public radio as one such setting. Each individual has an incentive to free ride, listen to the station, and not contribute to its continued functioning. However, the community as a whole is better off when the community is funded. This field setting offers us the potential to offer social comparison information to contributors in a natural way.

We collaborated with a public radio station to implement this experiment. This station has three on-air fund-drives per year. During the drive, listeners call into the station to make contributions. There are many recommended contribution levels being discussed on the air, $50 is required to become a basic member, listeners who give $60 and $75 receive additional gifts. Other gift levels kick in at $120, $180, $240, $360, $600, $840, $1000, and $2500. Because there are so many levels, Festinger's first category of objective comparison information is not salient in this situation.

Second, the listeners are geographically and socially distant. Thus, we hypothesize that the second social comparison process is similarly weak. We focus on the third, providing information about another donor's contribution.

OUR PREVIOUS WORK

Three previous papers of ours examine the impact of social comparisons in the field. This section reviews this research, beginning by introducing the experimental design that we use again in collecting the new data provided in this paper.

This research has been conducted in collaboration with a number of public radio stations during their annual on-air fund-drives. During the on-air drive, the station disc jockey intersperse music with appeals for donations. Listeners respond to the on-air appeals and call the station to make a pledge. Research assistants (RAs) answer the phone as volunteers for the station, ask the routine questions for the station and implemented the social comparison manipulation in the appropriate place in the conversation.

In particular, after answering the phone with the station's identifier: "Hello, STATION_NAME member line," RAs asked: "Are you a new member or a renewing member of STATION-NAME?" After the caller answered, RAs read (or did not read in the control condition) the social comparison manipulation: "We had another member, they contributed $x." We manipulated both the existence of this manipulation and the amount named. The question asked right after the manipulation was: "How much would you like to pledge today?" The dependent measure, the pledge amount, was then collected. We also ensured that another member had indeed contributed the amount we suggested earlier in the fund drive, so that our statements would not constitute deception.

We took a number of precautions to ensure random assignment and unbiased data collections. First, the RAs answering the phones were not the authors and were blind to the purposes of the experiment. They were also blind to the condition until the necessary point in the procedure. When each call arrived, the RAs chose the top "donor form" from a face-down pile. The donor form is based on the one usually used by the radio station, and includes places for the donor's name and contact information, payment information, etc. Each form also contained a sticker on which was printed "SAY NOTHING" for the control conditions and "We had another member, they contributed $x" for the various treatment conditions. Each sticker was covered with a post-it note. Thus, the RA could not tell which treatment the donor was in until they had reached the appropriate place in the script, removed the post-it note and then read the manipulation (or not, as the case may be). The forms were randomly shuffled within each RA, and repeating our analyses controlling for the particular RA who answered the phone does not change the results.

Our first paper (Shang & Croson, 2004a) reports the results of the first fund drive where we compare the control treatment (no social comparison) to our initial level of social comparison ($300). This paper focuses on the response of new donors to the social comparison manipulation. We chose $300 as an appropriate amount in consultation with the station, and from reading the literature on goal setting, which suggests that goals representing the 90–95 percentile of responses are most motivating (e.g. Locke & Latham, 1990). For this particular station, $300 represents the 94th percentile of contributions by new members. Two hundred and forty-eight new donors were in this experiment.

Our results were encouraging. This high social comparison significantly increased contributions by new members over the control condition. The average contribution was $119.70 in the $300 social information condition and $106.72 in the control condition. This is a $13 difference, and would translate into a 12% increase in revenue for the station had all callers been offered the social information. We thus demonstrated the impact of social comparisons on public goods provision in the field setting. This paper goes on to further develop the argument that the process underlying the increased contribution is indeed social comparisons and not some other process. A second experiment in this paper shows that when the donor and the social comparison target are of the same gender (more similar) the effect is larger than when they are of different genders (less similar) ($N = 79$, matched gender average contribution: $142, mismatched gender average contribution: $106). This first paper goes on to present lab studies and identify mediators of the social comparison effect.

Our second paper (Shang & Croson, 2004b) extends our findings from the first by looking at new and renewing members' contributions. We explore social comparison levels of $75 and $180 (50th percentile and 80th percentile, respectively), in addition to the previously effective $300. We show that while social comparisons directly affect new members' contributions (as shown in Shang & Croson, 2004a), with the 95th percentile being the most effective, they do not affect renewing members' contributions to the same degree (331 participating new members, 221 participating renewing members). This second paper also collects and analyzes "follow up" data; that is, the contributions of the new members in our experiment one year later. One might imagine a series of competing ex-ante hypotheses about the long-term effects of a social comparison manipulation like this. One possibility, based on cognitive dissonance, is that once an individual gives more because of this manipulation they will continue to give more. A second possibility, based on crowding out, is that after giving more this year they will be less likely to contribute in a subsequent year, or will contribute less. Finally, one might imagine that one year later, donors simply revert to the behavior that they would have exhibited without the manipulation. In fact, we find that new donors who had been assigned to the social comparison treatments give the same amount as those who had been assigned to the control treatment. However, they are twice as likely to make such a donation.

Our third paper (Shang & Croson, 2004c) focuses on renewing members and attempts to explain their lack of responsiveness found in the previous paper. In addition to the phone data from above, we also collect data from the renewal mail campaign used by the stations. Here, we manipulate a sentence on the response sheet where donors record their contributions. This sentence says "STATION_NAME received a contribution [of $x] from a member like you, and we invite you to join this member in renewing your membership today!" where the text in the brackets is included in the experimental conditions but not in the control conditions. Then the pledge amounts were collected with this sentence right below the manipulation: "Yes! Here is my contribution of _____." One hundred and twelve renewing members responded to the mailing (3056 mailers were sent out), and 91 received the phone manipulation, making 203 subjects altogether.

For renewing members, we compare not their absolute contribution, but the change in their contribution between this drive and the previous drive as a function of the social comparison condition. In particular, we record for each individual whether they received a social comparison that was higher or lower than what they had contributed the previous year. We find that those who receive an upward social comparison increase their contribution by $12.08 on average, and those who receive a downward social comparison decrease their contribution by $24.05 on average. Statistical tests confirm that these treatments are significantly different from each other.

In contrast to our previous work, this article presents the results of a new experiment designed to test the limits of social comparisons. Here we examine the effect of extreme social comparisons, choosing levels that are high relative to the typical contribution and to those examined in our previous work.

A NEW FIELD EXPERIMENT

This field experiment was conducted with an anonymous public radio station during their February on-air fund drive in 2004. We wanted to test the limits of our findings in Shang and Croson (2004a) by examining the impact of very high social comparison levels. In particular, we compare the control condition from the previous paper with a social comparison condition using $600 (the 97th percentile of contributions). The station was concerned about this high number "scaring off" new contributors, thus we offered it only to renewing members.

Method

Design. As in our previous studies, potential donors call to make contributions to the station during the on-air campaign. We provide renewing members with high social comparisons, and examine the impact on their pledges.

Results

Because our previous manipulations had been successful for increasing revenues for the station, they asked that we oversample the experimental condition. We thus used a ratio of 3:1 in preparing our experimental materials. For every one caller who randomly received the control condition, three callers would randomly receive the experimental condition. After preparing the response forms in the appropriate ratio, the forms were shuffled together to randomize. When the phone rang and the caller answered that they were the renewing member, the RA chose the top form from the (face down) pile and read the appropriate sentence. After this randomization, we had 56 callers in our control condition and 140 callers in our experimental condition during this drive. We first compare the amounts contributed directly in Fig. 1.

As can be seen in the figure, the average contribution in the control condition was $121, while the average contribution in the treatment condition was $172. This represents an increase of $52 per caller, about 43% by using a high social comparison number. A t-test finds this difference statistically significant ($t = 2.036$, $p = 0.022$).

For additional control, we also ran an OLS regression on the amounts contributed, including controls for the gender of the caller (previously observed to have some impact) and the day and hour that the call arrived. This particular station has extremely varied programming, and we wanted to control for the fact that callers who typically listen to music in the morning might be systematically different than callers who typically listen to news at night. Table 1 presents the result of the OLS regression with these additional controls. Our initial result remains statistically significant in the regression format.[3]

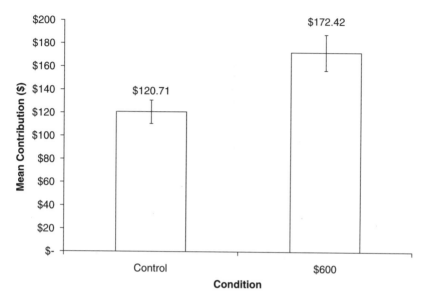

Fig. 1. Mean Contribution in Control and $600 Social Comparison Conditions.

Table 1. OLS Regression of Contribution on Treatment and Controls.

	Estimate	SE	*p*
$600 Treat	54.960	27.338	0.046
Male	14.023	24.731	0.571
Day		Yes	
Hour		Yes	
N	193		
R^2	0.074		

One final statistic of interest is the distribution of contributions in the two treatments. These distributions are shown in their entirety in Fig. 2, below and summarized in Fig. 3.

As expected, this distribution has spikes, including a large spike at $120, which represents $10 per month, includes a number of extra gifts and is a large attractor for renewing donors. There are smaller spikes at other gift levels including $75 and $240.

Differences between the two treatments are easier to see in Fig. 3. The first difference is the existence of contributions at or above $600 in the social

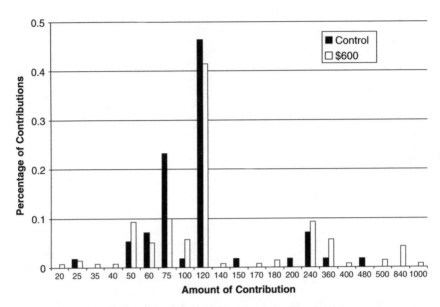

Fig. 2. Histogram of Contributions Received.

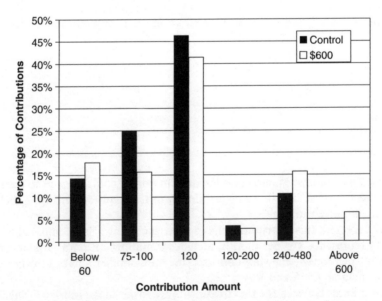

Fig. 3. Percentage of Contributions in Two Treatments, Collapsed.

comparison treatment that are not present in the control treatment. These contributions suggest that some callers are trying to match (or beat) the contributions made by the social comparison target. Note that all these high contributions are in the social comparison condition; one concern may be that our result occurred by accident, that we used the social comparison condition during times when high-value callers were likely to call, or that donors signaled their interest and were then placed in the social comparison condition. However, as explained above, our procedures precluded these explanations. Conditions were randomized within RA and within day/hour combinations. Furthermore, the RA did not know the condition of the caller until the post-it note was removed and read. Finally, the regression results show a significant difference in contribution amount, controlling for the day/hour of the call.

Of particular interest to us is the increase in the percentage of contributions that are $240 and above. These seem to be callers (albeit a fairly small number) who would otherwise have given lower amounts (e.g. between $75 and $120), and instead are influenced to increase their contribution by the existence of the social comparison target. We believe that this *shading* is the main source of the social comparison and provides evidence that social comparisons can impact decisions even though not all donors attempt to match or beat or beat the social comparison level. The existence of an ambitious social comparison can make some lower-level donors more generous.

Conclusions

Results from this study reinforce those in our previous research; social comparisons impact contributions. In this study, presenting target donors with information about a high social comparison significantly increases their own decision. This effect represents a potential increase in revenue of the nonprofit of 43%.

DISCUSSION AND FUTURE RESEARCH

Field experiments offer a unique opportunity to study the influence of social-psychological processes on public goods provision. In our study, we were able to remove the upper bound on giving typically imposed by dictator games experimenters in the laboratory and could observe donor behavior in a more natural and realistic setting.

However, field experiments have limitations as well. While one can demonstrate that an effect exists, it is much harder to conclude why the effect exists. We intend to further examine this question in the lab. For example, we would like to compare social comparison information like this with station-recommended contribution levels (which existed but were not manipulated in our study).

A second limitation of field experiments involves the generalizability of the results. It is possible that we observed our results due to the choice of this particular nonprofit radio station and this particular experimental implementation, and that they might not be observed elsewhere. For example, this experiment involved existing contributors to the station; would the results generalize to new members? Similarly, this manipulation was done via the phone; would the results generalize to mail or web contributions?

Our related research, however, suggests that the social comparison effect is indeed general. Shang and Croson (2004a) show the influence of social comparisons on new donors. Shang and Croson (2004b) demonstrate the robustness of this result using different social comparison levels and finding no long-term reduction in contributions one year later. Shang and Croson (2004c) find that renewing donors adjust their previous contribution in the direction of the social comparison target.

In summary, this research demonstrates the impact of social comparisons on charitable giving in a field study using a public radio station. Contemporary and future research explores the same effect in different domains, using different members and different social comparison levels. This stream of research more generally provides for a deeper understanding of what motivates individuals to contribute toward the funding of public goods and other charitable organizations.

NOTES

1. Research in psychology and marketing has used field experiments in studying charitable giving (for a review, see Weyant, 1996). Influence techniques studied include foot-in-the-door, door-in-the-face, low-ball, and legitimization-of-small-donation. The results, however, are mixed; some research shows positive effects (e.g. Brockner, Guzzi, Kane, Levin, & Shaplen, 1984), while others show no effects (e.g. Fraser, Hite, & Sauer, 1988).

2. Later this theory was extended into using social information to form an accurate view of the world outside of oneself (Suls, 2000).

3. We had over 80 dummy variables representing each hour of each day that we collected data. While some of these variables are themselves significant (e.g. people

give more during peak calling/commuting hours (from 8 am to 10 am and from 4 pm to 6 pm), there was no significant interaction between the treatment effect and these dummy variables. Furthermore, if we run the regression without these controls, the statistically significant effect remains. Results from the full regression are available for the interested reader upon request.

REFERENCES

Andreoni, J. (1988). Privately provided public goods in a large economy: The limits of Altruism. *Journal of Public Economics, 35*, 57–73.

Andreoni, J. (1989). Giving with impure altruism: Applications to charity and Ricardian equivalence. *Journal of Political Economy, 97*, 1447–1458.

Andreoni, J. (1990). Impure altruism and donations to public goods: A theory of warm-glow giving. *Economic Journal, 100*, 464–477.

Becker, G. (1974). A theory of social interactions. *Journal of Political Economy, 82*, 1063–1093.

Brockner, J., Guzzi, B., Kane, J., Levine, E., & Shaplen, K. (1984). Organizational fundraising: Further evidence on the effect of legitimizing small donations. *Journal of Consumer Research, 11*, 611–614.

Cason, T., & Mui, V.-L. (1998). Social influence in the sequential dictator game. *Journal of Mathematical Psychology, 42*, 248–265.

Davis, D., & Holt, C. (1993). *Experimental economics.* Princeton, NJ: Princeton University Press.

Dawes, R. (1980). Social dilemmas. *Annual Review of Psychology, 31*, 169–193.

Eckel, C. C., & Grossman, P. J. (2005). *Subsidizing charitable contributions: A field test comparing matching and rebate subsidies.* Working Paper, Virginia Polytechnic University.

Festinger, L. (1954). A theory of social comparison processes. *Human Relations, 7*, 117–140.

Fischbacher, U., Gachter, S., & Fehr, E. (2001). Are people conditionally cooperative? Evidence from a public goods experiment. *Economics Letters, 71*, 397–404.

Frank, R. (1985). *Choosing the right pond: Human behavior and the quest for status.* New York: Oxford University Press.

Frank, R. (1999). *Luxury fever: Money and happiness in an era of excess.* New York: The Free Press.

Fraser, C., Hite, R. E., & Sauer, P. L. (1988). Increasing contributions in solicitation campaigns: The use of large and small anchorpoints. *Journal of Consumer Research, 15*, 284–287.

Frey, B., & Meier, B. (2004). Social comparisons and pro-social behavior: Testing "conditional cooperation" in a field experiment. *American Economic Review, 94*, 1717–1722.

Ledyard, J. (1995). Public goods: A survey of experimental research. In: J. Kagel & A. E. Roth (Eds), *Handbook of experimental economics* (pp. 111–194). Princeton, NJ: Princeton University Press.

List, J., & Lucking-Reiley, D. (2002). The effects of seed money and refunds on charitable giving: Experimental evidence from a university capital campaign. *Journal of Political Economy, 110*, 215–233.

Locke, E., & Latham, G. (1990). *A theory of goal setting & task performance.* Englewood Cliffs, NJ: Prentice-Hall.

Shang, J., & Croson, R. (2004a). *Field experiments in nonprofit marketing: The impact of social information.* Working Paper, University of Pennsylvania.

Shang, J., & Croson, R. (2004b). *Social comparisons and the voluntary provision of public goods: Field experiments.* Working Paper, University of Pennsylvania.

Shang, J., & Croson, R. (2004c). *Social comparisons and social dilemmas: Evidence from the field.* Working Paper, University of Pennsylvania.

Sugden, R. (1984). Reciprocity: The supply of public goods through voluntary contributions. *Economic Journal, 94,* 772–787.

Suls, J. (2000). Opinion comparison: The role of the corroborator, expert, and proxy in social influence. In: J. Suls & L. Wheeler (Eds), *Handbook of social comparison: Theory and research.* New York: Kluwer.

Taylor, S., & Lobel, M. (1989). Social comparison activity under threat: Downward evaluation and upward contacts. *Psychological Review, 96,* 569–575.

Weyant, J. M. (1996). Application of compliance techniques to direct-mail request for charitable donation. *Psychology and Marketing, 13*(2), 157–170.

DO DONORS CARE ABOUT SUBSIDY TYPE? AN EXPERIMENTAL STUDY

Catherine C. Eckel and Philip J. Grossman

ABSTRACT

An individual should be indifferent between a rebate subsidy of rate s_r and a matching subsidy of rate $s_m = s_r/(1 - s_r)$, and the total amount received by the charity should be the same regardless of subsidy type. Recent laboratory and field experiments contradict these straightforward predictions of standard economic theory: subjects consistently make decisions that result in larger amounts going to the charity under a matching subsidy than under an equivalent rebate subsidy. This paper tests whether this result is due to rebate-aversion – a preference by donors for a match over a rebate subsidy. Consistent with theory, we find no significant preference for one or the other subsidy scheme. However, we do find that, as in previous studies, participants selecting the matching subsidy made decisions that resulted in approximately twice the donations of participants selecting the rebate subsidy donated.

1. INTRODUCTION

Experimental and field studies of charitable giving conducted over the past several years consistently show that a rebate subsidy leads to lower levels of

Experiments Investigating Fundraising and Charitable Contributors
Research in Experimental Economics, Volume 11, 157–175
Copyright © 2006 by Elsevier Ltd.
ISSN: 0193-2306/doi:10.1016/S0193-2306(06)11007-8

overall donations (the amount received by the charity) than an equivalent matching subsidy, despite the fact that both embody the same incentive structure for donating. A rebate subsidy refunds a portion of the contribution to the giver, thereby lowering the effective price of giving. The tax deductibility of charitable contributions under the U.S. Federal income tax system is an example. Matching subsidies are frequently offered by private employers who agree to send a matching amount for every dollar contributed to a charitable organization by an employee. It is straightforward to construct equivalent subsidies – a rebate subsidy of rate s_r and a matching subsidy of rate $s_m = s_r/(1-s_r)$ – that result in the same incentive structure for potential contributor. Nevertheless, the response of givers appears to vary with the form of the subsidy. This paper is one in a series that explores this somewhat puzzling result.

In the initial laboratory study (Eckel & Grossman, 2003), we reported results from experiments that directly compared several different subsidy levels. Our data indicated that contributions were significantly higher with matching subsidies than with equivalent rebate subsidies. Participants in that study otherwise responded to the subsidies as expected, giving more to charity when the price of giving was lower and when their endowment in the experiment was larger. Indeed, estimated income and price elasticities for the experimental data are similar to those found in studies using field data. However, the total contributions received by the charity were 23–86% larger under the matching subsidy than under the rebate, and this difference increased with the rate of subsidy.

To examine the external validity of our results, we implemented a field experiment in conjunction with Minnesota Public Radio's annual campaign. In that study, we also observed a similar differential response to rebate and matching subsidies (Eckel & Grossman, 2005a). Contributions to MPR were 10–29% higher under the match than the rebate. As in our earlier studies, the disparity was larger the higher the subsidy rate. While these differences are smaller than in the lab studies, they are substantial, and statistically significant. In the field, the contributions carried larger dollar values than in the lab and used the donor's own money rather than endowments from the experimenter. However, the pattern of results remains, suggesting that they cannot be attributed to the limiting aspects of a lab setting.[1]

Several additional studies have returned to the lab to further explore the result. Davis, Millner, and Reilly (2005) replicate Eckel and Grossman (2003) and examine participants' "pass ratio" (the ratio of the dollar amount passed to the charity under the matching condition, exclusive of subsidy, to the dollar amount passed under a comparable rebate condition). They infer that participants use a "constant percentage" pass rule. They argue that some confused, or inattentive, participants see the different decisions as identical thus giving the same response (in percentage terms). Other confused participants, while not understanding the differences, reason that they are different and require different answers. They give randomly different responses but, on average, pass the same constant percentage.

Attempting to eliminate confusion, Davis et al. (2005) present for each allocation decision a table, which shows participants how much they would earn and how much the charity would receive. The extra information increased the number of optimizing decisions, moving the results closer to that predicted by theory (i.e., the pass rates for the rebate conditions increased and the pass rates for the match conditions decreased). They conclude that participants, in large part, ignored, did not care about, or did not understand the implications for the charities of their decisions under the two subsidy types.

The laboratory studies above present participants with a menu of both rebate and matching subsidy choices, of which one is chosen for payment. This approach introduces the possibility that participants are confused and fail to distinguish sufficiently between the two types of subsidies, biasing the results. For example, a subject might read the following statements as equivalent, and try to be consistent by making the same choice under each condition, when in fact the first implies a "price" of giving of 0.75 per dollar of donations received by the charity and the second a price of 0.80.

> For every token you pass to the other player, the experimenter will refund to you one-quarter token.

> For every token you pass to the other player, the experimenter will match it with one-quarter additional token.

(A price of 0.75 would entail a 1/3 token subsidy per token passed.) This false equivalence could lead subjects to underestimate the price of giving under the match subsidy and contribute to the pattern of results that we observe. In Eckel and Grossman (2006), we simplify the design to eliminate this potential source of confusion. Each participant still makes multiple decisions that vary in price and endowment, but not subsidy type. A given subject faces decisions that are either all rebate choices or all matching choices. Rather than diminishing the difference in response, this approach enhances the differences in response, ranging from 7% to 140% larger contributions for matching than rebate subsidies. This suggests that while confusion about the difference between subsidy types may have contributed to the previous results, it is not the sole source of the difference we observe.

Davis and Millner (2005) tested rebate and matching subsidies for a private good: chocolate bars. Participants made purchase decisions given (a) rebates from listed price, (b) matching quantity offers, and (c) simple price reductions. As in the previous studies, the rebates were "instant" – subjects did not have to wait for the rebate. Consistent with previous results they find that participants purchased significantly more chocolate bars under the matching sales format. This result implies that the phenomenon is not due to some inherent aspect involved in giving to charity, as we had speculated in our 2003 paper, but is more widespread. Interestingly, Davis and Millner (2005) report more bars purchased under a straight price reduction than under the comparable rebate subsidy. Their findings suggest that people simply may not like rebates – that they are rebate-averse.[2] They suggest such a preference may have arisen because of past negative experiences with rebates; rebates are less certain, have higher transactions costs, and, for mail-in rebates, represent future rather than immediate payment. (Note that it was clear to participants that all matches and rebates occurred within the time frame of the experiment, so these issues should not have been relevant in the lab.)

In these previous studies, the donor had no choice about which type of subsidy he received. This paper directly tests whether donors are rebate-averse or indifferent between a rebate subsidy and the functionally equivalent matching subsidy. We present this choice in a very simple framework: subjects choose between regimes involving either a 50 percent rebate or a 1 for 1 match. We also test whether the level of giving differs for the two subsidies. To foreshadow our results, we find no significant difference in the choice of subsidy, but, consistent with our earlier work, still find giving to be significantly greater under the matching subsidy than the rebate subsidy.

The next section describes the experiment, Section 3 presents the results, and Section 4 concludes.

2. EXPERIMENTAL DESIGN AND PROCEDURES

All sessions of the experiment were conducted at Saint Cloud State University. Participants were recruited by e-mail. Announcements about the opportunity to participate in forthcoming experiments were made in a variety of undergraduate and graduate classes. Interested parties were instructed to respond by e-mail. Date, time, and place information was e-mailed to all respondents and participants were selected for participation on a first-come, first-served basis.

Both sessions of the experiment followed a standard procedure. Participants were seated one to a table in a large room. Consent forms were distributed, signed by the participants, and collected. A group monitor was chosen at random to observe and assist in conducting the experiment; the monitor received a flat fee of $20. The experimenter distributed a packet containing written instructions, a slip of paper printed with a random five-digit code number, and an allocation problem decision sheet (APDS) (samples are included in the appendix). Participants were told to retain the paper with the code number. The APDS included, on one side, a list of 10 charities with a description of the services provided by the charities. Participants recorded their decisions on the opposite side. The design balanced the choices by appearance: for half of the decision forms the matching subsidy choice was on the left; for the other half of the decision forms the rebate subsidy choice was on the left.

Participants were told to read the instructions and raise their hands if they had any questions. The experimenter answered any questions in private. After completing the instructions, a participant first selected a charity from the list to receive any contributions he wished to make. The participant then selected whether he wished to play the "match game" or the "rebate game." At that point, the participant then determined how he wished to allocate his $20 endowment between himself and his charity of choice. After completing these decisions, the participant deposited his allocation decision sheet in a box in the center of the room (the box was no closer than 10 ft to the nearest participant).

After all decisions were made, participants' earnings and contributions to the charities were calculated. Earnings were sealed in envelopes marked with the participants' specific code numbers and placed on a table to be picked up.

While the experimenters calculated participants' earnings and contributions to the charities, a survey of socioeconomic characteristics was distributed. Students were told that the information collected from the surveys was for research purposes only. After entering their code numbers and completing the survey, the participants placed the forms in the box in the center of the room.

After the contributions to each charity were totaled, the experimenter wrote checks to the charities and sealed them in envelopes. The monitor signed a statement verifying the payments made and the procedures. Both monitor and experimenter walked to a mailbox and deposited the envelopes.

The APDS presented the participant first with the choice of 10 charities. As in our previous papers, the charities were selected to reflect as broad a range of services and client groups as possible. The new sample of charities included international, national, and local organizations; health, environmental; and social service charities. A brief description of each charity was given to the participants. After selecting a charity, the participants then selected whether they wanted to play the "match game" or the "rebate game." The match game matched one for one, any donation made by the participants. The rebate game rebated to the donor $0.50 for every $1.00 donation. Finally the participants indicated how they wished to allocate their $20 endowments.

3. RESULTS

A total of 124 participants participated in four sessions; 120 made decisions, 4 served as monitors. Table 1 provides a summary of the socioeconomic characteristics for the participant pool. The average age of participants was 20. Men comprised 63 percent of the sample. Approximately one-third was majoring in economics or business, and approximately three-quarters had at most only one economics course.

3.1. Does the Subsidy Choice Influence the Amount of Giving?

We first test whether participants selecting the matching subsidy donate more than participants selecting the rebate subsidy. An issue raised by Davis et al. (2005) is "when considering the donation what exactly should be the focus of any analysis?" Davis et al. (2005) focused on the amount passed by the donor; Eckel and Grossman (2003, 2005a, b) focused on the amount received by the charities (including any matching contribution). For completeness, we report (for all participants and for donors only) summary statistics for both the amount passed as well as the total amount received by the charities.

Consistent with the Davis et al. (2005) notion of a "constant percentage" pass rule, the mean pass amounts do not differ significantly between those participants choosing the rebate subsidy and those participants choosing the matching subsidy ($5.44 vs. $5.26, see Table 2). Perhaps a better test of the constant percentage pass test is the amount passed considering only subjects who donated positive amounts. By his act of donating, a donor indicates that his selected charity is consistent with his altruistic tendencies. A non-donor may have failed to donate, not because he has no altruistic tendencies, but rather because the sample of charities did not include a charity

Table 1. Summary Statistics ($N = 120$).

Mean Age	20.3
(Std. Dev.)	(2.3)
Male	63.3%
Religion Services	
○ Never attend	36.7%
○ Less than once a month	30.8%
○ At least once a month	18.3%
○ Once a week	8.3%
○ More than once a week	5.8
Non-Caucasian	15.8%
Class	
○ Freshman	41.7%
○ Sophomore	25.8%
○ Junior	18.3%
○ Senior	12.5%
○ Graduate Student	1.7%
Employed	
○ No	35.6%
○ Part-time	55.6%
○ Full-time	8.9%
Economics/Business	32.5%
# Econ Classes	
○ 0−1	75.0%
○ 2−4	20.8%
○ >4	4.2%
Charity	
○ American Cancer Society	26.7%
○ American Red Cross	15.0%
○ Big Brothers Big Sisters	10.8%
○ Big River Sierra Club	5.8%
○ Central Minnesota Task Force on Battered	6.7%
Women	8.3%
○ Doctors Without Borders	18.3%
○ Feed The Children	2.5%
○ Minnesota AIDs Project	0.8%
○ Oxfam America	5.0%
○ YMCA	
Mean Response (Std. Dev.)	
○ Procedures preserved anonymity?	4.50
	(0.79)
○ Your donation went to your charity?	4.45
	(0.78)
○ Instructions were clear?	4.42
	(0.90)
○ Recipients of donation are deserving?	4.74
	(0.67)

Table 2. Amount Passed and Amount Received for All Participants and for Donors Only.

Sample	Amount Passed		Means Test t-statistic (p-value $<$)	Amount Received		Means Test t-statistic (p-value $<$)
	Rebate	Match		Rebate	Match	
	$5.44	$5.26	0.19	$5.44	$10.53	3.31
	(4.72)	(5.19)	(0.85)	(4.72)	(10.37)	(0.002)
Donors Only	$6.28	$7.97	1.79	6.28	15.94	6.09
	(4.51)	(4.35)	(0.08)	(4.51)	(8.70)	(0.001)

consistent with his concerns. Data from the post-experiment manipulation check provides support for this notion. Responses to specific statements were elicited using a Likert scale ranging from 1 (strongly disagree) to 5 (strongly agree). To the statement "The recipients of donation to your designated charity are deserving of support," the mean response of donors is 4.84; the mean response of non-donors is 4.38. The difference is significant (*t-statistic* = 2.35, p-value < 0.03).

More importantly, while members of both groups clearly considered their designated charities to be deserving of support, the assessment need not translate into actual giving. A common response by donors to the post-experiment, open-ended request that subjects explain their decision process was that they gave because of some personal experience with the charity (i.e., a donor might select the American Cancer Society because a family member had, or has, cancer). A non-donor might acknowledge that a charity is worthy of support but still prefer to direct their support to another charity (i.e., one non-donor selected the American Red Cross, strongly agreed that the charity was deserving but gave nothing saying he preferred to give his money to Mothers Against Drunk Driving).

Considering only subjects who donated positive amounts, the difference in the amount passed increases. Those donors selecting the rebate subsidy passed $6.28 on average; those donors selecting the matching subsidy passed $7.97. A means test rejects the null hypothesis of no difference at the 8 percent level (*t-statistic* = 1.79). While this result is statistically weak, it is worth noting that this result is opposite to our expectations. Standard theory would predict that the amount passed under a rebate subsidy should be greater than the amount passed under the strategically equivalent matching subsidy; the more appropriate one-tailed test rejects this alternative hypothesis at the 4 percent level. This conclusion assumes, of course, that participants understood the instructions. Results of a post-experiment manipulation check discussed below support this assumption.

The mean total amounts received by the charities differ significantly both for all participants ($5.44 under the rebate vs. $10.53 under the match), as well as for positive donors only ($6.28 rebate vs. $15.94 match). One possible explanation for the larger amount received under the match scheme than the rebate scheme is that the maximum possible amount received differs (i.e., $40 under the matching scheme vs. $20 under the rebate scheme).[3] However, a closer examination of the data reveals that for only three participants was the amount received by the charity in excess of $20.[4] Constraining these three to a maximum amount received of $20 does little to qualify our conclusions. Mean amounts received from all participants still differ significantly ($5.44 under the rebate vs. $9.58 under the match).

We next test whether the difference in amounts received by the charities holds up when we control for other possible determinants of giving by estimating the two-limit, censored Tobit regression:

$$\text{DONATION}_i = a_0 + a_1 \text{MATCH}_i + a_2 X_i + \varepsilon_i$$

where $i = 1, \ldots, 120$ (index of participants), and variables are defined as follows:

DONATION	=	total amount received by the selected charity;
MATCH	=	matching subsidy selected $= 1$, 0 otherwise;
X	=	matrix of control variables including:
AGE	=	participant's age;
SEX	=	male $= 1$, 0 otherwise;
RELIGION	=	attend religious services at least once a month $= 1$, 0 otherwise;
ECON	=	number of economics classes taken;
ACS	=	donation to the American Cancer Society $= 1$, 0 otherwise;
ARC	=	donation to the American Red Cross $= 1$, 0 otherwise;
BIGBRO	=	donation to Big Brothers Big Sisters $= 1$, 0 otherwise;
BIGRIV	=	donation to the Big River Sierra Club $= 1$, 0 otherwise;
TASKFORCE	=	donation to the Central Minnesota Task Force on Battered Women $= 1$, 0 otherwise;
DOCTORS	=	donation to Doctors without Borders $= 1$, 0 otherwise;
CHILDREN	=	donation to Feed the Children $= 1$, 0 otherwise;
MNAIDS	=	donation to the Minnesota AIDs Project $= 1$, 0 otherwise; and
OXFAM	=	donation to the Oxfam America $= 1$, 0 otherwise.

The YMCA served as the control charity. The censored upper limit is $20 for participants selecting the rebate and $40 for participants selecting the match.

Table 3 reports the results for several variations of the basic model. Column 1 excludes all of the control variables; column 2 includes the socioeconomic variables; and column 3 includes the socioeconomic variables and the charity identifiers. In all three regressions, the MATCH variable has a positive and significant coefficient supporting the conclusion that participants give significantly more under a matching subsidy scheme than under a strategically equivalent rebate subsidy scheme.

3.2. Is a Participant's Donation a Function of Understanding?

Since participants who better understand how the subsidy schemes work may choose and give differently than those who do not understand how the schemes work, we consider whether self-reported understanding of the subsidy schemes influences giving. In a post-experiment survey, we asked participants for their responses to four manipulation check statements including the statement: "The instructions for the experiment were clear and easy to follow." Responses were on a five-point Likert scale ranging from 1 (strongly disagree) to 5 (strongly agree). Of the 119 participants responding, 87 percent responded to this statement either agree (4) or strongly agree (5). Only five participants responded disagree (2) or strongly disagree (1). The mean response was 4.42. We find no significant correlation between a participant's response and either the amount passed or the amount received by the charities (the respective correlation coefficients are −0.00747 and −0.00711). Furthermore, a χ^2 contingency table test finds no significant relationship between a participant's selected subsidy and her response to the statement ($\chi^2(4) = 1.54$, p-value < 0.82).

3.3. Does the Subsidy Choice Influence whether a Participant Donates?

It is possible that the decision whether to contribute is influenced by the subsidy scheme selected. The calculation of own earnings is marginally easier for the matching subsidy ($20 − donation) than for the rebate subsidy ($20 − 0.5 ∗ donation). Additional calculation costs may lead to a decision not to contribute.

To test the null hypothesis that the choice of subsidy scheme is independent of the decision to donate we conducted two tests. First we conducted a Fisher's exact probability test for the equality of distributions.[5] The test statistic $T_3 = 4.91$, p-value < 0.001, supports rejection of the null hypothesis of independence. This indicates that people choosing the rebate subsidy were more likely to make a positive contribution. Next we estimated

Table 3. Two-limit, Censored Tobit Results.

Variable	Coefficient (marginal effect) (*t*-statistic)		
	Model 1	Model 2[a]	Model 3[a]
MATCH	4.084*	3.436*	4.956*
	(2.995)	(2.563)	(3.844)
	(2.18)	(1.81)	(2.80)
AGE		−0.418	−0.294
		(−0.312)	(−0.228)
		(1.03)	(−0.74)
MALE		−5.073*	−3.088*
		(−3.784)	(−2.395)
		(2.60)	(1.68)
RELIGION		−0.804	−0.423
		(−0.600)	(−0.328)
		(0.42)	(0.24)
ECON		0.639	0.904
		(0.477)	(0.701)
		(0.99)	(1.47)
ACS			6.856*
			(1.78)
ARC			9.706*
			(2.40)
BIGBRO			6.587
			(1.56)
BIGRIV			1.242
			(0.24)
TASKFORCE			17.157*
			(3.63)
DOCTORS			13.174*
			(2.92)
CHILDREN			11.001*
			(2.76)
MNAIDS			−2.181
			(0.30)
OXFAM			4.665
			(0.49)
CONSTANT	4.709	16.334	3.214
	(3.82)	(1.96)	(0.38)
LLF	−362.71	−357.25	−344.98
N	120	119	119

*Significant at the 95 percent level, one-tailed test.
[a]One participant did not give age.

the Logit regression:

$$\text{DONY (donation made} = 1)$$
$$= \beta_0 + \beta_1 * \text{MATCH (matching subsidy selected} = 1)$$

The complete regression results (t-statistics in parentheses) are

$$\text{DONY} = \underset{(5.20)}{1.863} - \underset{(2.60)}{1.198} * \text{MATCH}$$

The estimated coefficient for β_1 is significantly different from zero suggesting that those participants who selected the matching subsidy are significantly less likely to donate to their selected charity. (Note we cannot rule out that those intending to contribute zero have a preference for the matching subsidy that is not related to payoffs.)

3.4. Are Participants Rebate-Averse?

As the subsidies are designed, the cost of giving $1 to a charity is $0.50 in both treatments. Since the incentive structure is the same, participants should be indifferent to the two subsidy schemes. However, participants are likely to have had more real world experiences, and potentially negative experiences with rebate subsidies (i.e., mail-in rebate offers on many common electronic products and other common household goods). Recipients of rebate subsidies typically incur costs not incurred by recipients of matching subsidies, such as the cost of filling in and mailing forms, delays in payment, and uncertainty that the rebate will actually be received (i.e., the individual may never complete and mail the necessary forms, forms or rebate payment can be lost in the mail, and errors may occur in processing). Real world matching subsidies are typically immediate (i.e., buy one get one free offers) incurring no extra costs or uncertainty. While these factors are not relevant in the experiment setting, past experiences may color a participant's choice.

This sort of real world experiences does not seem to have influenced the choices of the participants. Of the 120 participants, 53 selected the matching subsidy and 67 selected the rebate subsidy. We test the null hypothesis that participants are indifferent between the two subsidy schemes and are unable to reject it at the 95 percent confidence level ($t = 1.28$, p-value $= 0.11$). We also repeat this test, excluding subjects who give zero. Among participants who gave positive amounts, 35 chose the matching subsidy and 58 chose the rebate subsidy. This difference indicates a statistically significant preference in favor of the rebate subsidy ($t = 2.27$, p-value $= 0.004$). We find no indication that participants are averse to the rebate subsidy.

3.5. Does the Order of Choices Significantly Influence the Participants' Subsidy Choice?

Recall that for half of the participants the rebate choice was listed on the left of the decision sheet, and for the other half the match choice was listed on the left. To test for an order effect, we estimated the Logit regression:

$$\text{MATCH (matching subsidy selected} = 1)$$

$$= \alpha_0 + \alpha_1 * \text{RFIRST (rebate subsidy on left} = 1)$$

The Complete regression results (*t*-statistics in parentheses) are

$$\text{MATCH} = \underset{(1.29)}{-0.336} - \underset{(0.55)}{0.203} * \text{RFIRST}$$

The estimated coefficient for α_1 is insignificantly different from zero suggesting no order effects.

4. CONCLUSION

Standard economic theory suggests that (1) an individual should be indifferent between a rebate subsidy of rate s_r and a matching subsidy of rate $s_m = s_r/(1-s_r)$, and (2) the total amount received by the charity should be the same regardless of subsidy type. Recent laboratory and field experiments contradict the second prediction.

In the laboratory studies cited, participants were presented with a series of choices involving either a match or a rebate subsidy; they were unable to choose the subsidy scheme they preferred. The studies thus did not test the first prediction of theory, that participants would be indifferent between the two subsidy schemes. In the experiment reported in this paper, participants were permitted to select between a 50 percent rebate subsidy and an equivalent 100 percent matching subsidy. Consistent with theory, we find no significant preference for one or the other subsidy scheme. Participants were slightly more likely to choose the 50 percent rebate subsidy than the 100 percent matching subsidy, but the difference was not statistically significant. Theory also predicts that the total contributions to a charity should not differ between equivalent subsidy schemes. Consistent with previous studies, we find that the decisions of participants selecting the matching subsidy resulted in total donations that were on average approximately twice the donations under the rebate subsidy ($10.53 vs. $5.44, respectively), a significant difference.

As noted above, Davis et al. (2005) raise the question whether analysis should focus on the amount passed by the donor, or the amount received by the charities. We find their result quite provocative, and it has shaped our subsequent investigations. For the most part, we continue to focus on the outcome rather than the pass rate for three reasons. First, from the charities' perspective, the amount received is what is important. Charities are unlikely to want to correct "confusion" that results in donations that are larger than they might otherwise be. So even if the result were due to confusion, it is a happy confusion from the point of view of a charity, and one that could be exploited. Second, the lab results are replicated in field experiments where donors have a stronger incentive to understand the implications of their actions since they are "playing" with their own money and for higher stakes. Third, to take the chocolate bar analogy, what seems important is the amount of chocolate (or charitable activity) that leaves the store with the purchaser along with the amount of money left in his pocket. These are real differences in outcomes. Our data, and that of Davis and his coauthors, suggest that there is a real difference in the way people respond to a subsidy framed as a rebate and one framed as a match. While confusion (or inattention) played a role as a partial explanation for our initial reported findings, the evidence does not support an ultimate conclusion that it is the only or even the dominant explanation. Across all of the experiments, in the lab and in the field, for public goods and private goods, the designs are unable to remove or fully explain the difference in outcomes between the rebate and match mechanisms.

The findings reported in this paper, as well as those in the Eckel and Grossman (2003, 2005a, b), Davis et al. (2005), and Davis and Millner (2005) papers, have implications for the government, non-profit, and for profit sectors of the economy. For government and the non-profit sectors, the results suggest that replacing the current system of tax rebates with an equivalently matching subsidy system would increase contributions to charitable organizations. For the for-profit sector, the results suggest that matching offers may be a more effective sales generating mechanism than refund coupons and mail-in rebate offers.

NOTES

1. Preliminary results from a second field experiment are consistent with the MPR findings (results available upon request of the authors).
2. Davis and Millner (2005) found no evidence of rebate-aversion with respect to charitable contributions when they reexamined the data from Davis et al. (2005).

3. If a donor contributes the full $20 endowment, the charity receives $40 (the $20 contribution plus the $20 match) under the matching scheme but only $20 (the $20 contribution) under the rebate scheme.

4. One $30 and two $40.

5. The large sample approximation, which has the standard normal distribution, was used (see Conover, 1999).

ACKNOWLEDGMENTS

This research was supported by grants from the John D. and Catherine T. MacArthur Foundation, Network on Preferences and Norms, and the National Science Foundation (SBR-0136684). We would like to thank Doug Davis, Mark Isaac, Gwendolyn Morrison, and an anonymous referee for their helpful comments.

REFERENCES

Conover, W. J. (1999). *Practical nonparametric statistics* (3rd ed.). New York: Wiley.

Davis, D. D., & Millner, E. L. (2005). Rebates and matches and consumer behavior. *Southern Economic Journal, 72*(2), 410–422.

Davis, D. D., Millner, E. L., & Reilly, R. J. (2005). Subsidy schemes and charitable contributions: A closer look. *Experimental Economics, 8*, 85–106.

Eckel, C. C., & Grossman, P. J. (2003). Rebates and matching: Does how we subsidize charitable contributions matter? *Journal of Public Economics, 87*, 681–701.

Eckel, C. C., & Grossman, P. J. (2005a). *Subsidizing charitable contributions: A field test comparing matching and rebate subsidies.* SCSU Working Paper.

Eckel, C. C., & Grossman, P. J. (2005b). Subsidizing charitable giving with rebates or matching: Further laboratory evidence. *Southern Economic Journal, 72*(4) (April), (Forthcoming).

APPENDIX. SAMPLE INSTRUCTIONS AND FORMS

Code Number_____

Instructions

You are asked to participate in a study of decision-making. The study will last about 30 min. You will receive compensation for your participation, which will be paid to you in cash at the end of the study. How you will be compensated is explained below.

One of the persons in the room will be chosen at random to be the monitor for today's study. The monitor will be paid $20. The monitor will verify that the instructions, as they appear here, have been followed.

To insure the anonymity of all participants' decisions, each participant has been assigned randomly a five-digit code number. This number can be found at the top of this sheet "Instructions." The code number is also written on the attached claim check. *Please keep this claim check and remember this number.* You will collect your compensation for participating by this code number.

Each participant has been given an "Allocation Problem Decision Sheet." The allocation problem decision sheet includes a list of 10 charities with a brief description of the services each provides. You will select *one, and only one*, of these 10 charities be paired with.

Each participant begins with an endowment of $20. After you have selected the charity you wish to be paired with, you will select which of the two games you wish to play.

Choice A is the match game. In this game, for any contribution you decide to make from your $20 endowment it will be matched by the experimenter one for one.

Choice B is the rebate game. In this game, for any contribution you decide to make from your $20 endowment the experimenter will rebate to you 50 percent of your contribution.

Examples of Allocation Problems

Match Game Example: You have selected to play the match game and have contributed $8 of your endowment to your selected charity. Your earnings will be $12 (= $20−$8); the charity will receive a total of $16 (= your $8 contribution plus the additional $8 matching contribution from the experimenter).

Rebate Game Example: You have selected to play the rebate game and have contributed $8 of your endowment to your selected charity. Your earnings will total $16; the $12 (= $20−$8) you kept for yourself plus the $4 rebate from the experimenter (= 0.5*$8). The charity will receive your $8 contribution.

Important Note: In all cases you can choose any amount to keep and any amount to pass, but the amount you keep plus the amount you pass *must* equal your endowment.

After you have selected the charity you wish to be paired with, which game you wish to play, and how much of your endowment to keep for yourself and how much you wish to pass to your charity of choice, please place the Allocation Problem Decision Sheet in the box in the center of the room. Please return to your seat.

After you have completed these tasks, the experimenters will hand out a questionnaire. Please note that the questionnaire will be used for research purposes only. Please enter your code number in the space provided. After completing the questionnaire, please place the questionnaire in the box in the middle of the room.

While you are completing the questionnaire, the monitor and experimenter will determine your compensation and donation to the charity. Your compensation will be sealed in an envelope with your code number on its face. You may pick up your envelope at the end of the study by presenting your claim check to the persons assisting with the experiment.

The monitor and experimenters will also calculate the total donation to each of the charities. The experimenters will make out checks for these amounts, and place them in addressed and stamped envelopes. The monitor and an experimenter will go to the nearest mailbox and drop the envelope in the mailbox.

After signing the form that verifies that the study was conducted according to instructions, the monitor is free to leave.

If you have any questions about the procedures, please ask now.

Before beginning, please answer the following four questions. *You will be paid $0.50 for each correct answer.*

1. Assume you have elected to play the REBATE GAME and you have allocated your $20 as follows: Keep $12 for yourself and pass $8 to your chosen charity.

How much, in total, will the charity   _____
receive?

How much, in total, will you receive?   _____

2. Assume you have elected to play the **MATCH GAME** and you have allocated your $20 as follows: Keep $12 for yourself and pass $8 to your chosen charity.

How much, in total, will the charity   _____
receive?

How much, in total, will you receive?   _____

Code Number_____

Allocation Problem Decision Sheet

For this study, each of you will be paired with a charity of your choice. Following is a list of 10 possible charities. Please select the charity you wish to be paired with by placing an X in the box next to your choice.

American Cancer Society
Provides many services to cancer patients and their families such as information, medical equipment, transportation to treatment locations, and a support system

American Red Cross
Offers blood donation information and services, disaster relief, many helpful educational classes, as well as HIV/AIDS support groups

Big Brothers Big Sisters
Provides one-to-one mentoring for youth and children residing in a one parent family for the purpose of creating caring, confident, and competent young adults

Big River Sierra Club
Protects and preserves environmentally sensitive areas

Central Minnesota Task Force on Battered Women
Offers safe shelter to battered women and their children, as well as food and clothing, assistance with legal, medical, and financial problems, and information/support groups

Doctors Without Borders
Doctors and nurses volunteer to provide urgent medical care in some 70
countries to civilian victims of war and disaster regardless of race, religion,
or politics

Feed The Children
One of Americas most effective charities providing food, clothing, medical
care, education, and emergency relief to children in the United States and
overseas since 1979

Minnesota Aids Project
Provides referrals to HIV sensitive physicians, help obtain/maintain medical
coverage, support groups, legal services, life enhancement programs, toll
free information and referral line, and transportation services

Oxfam America
Invests privately raised funds and technical expertise in local organizations
around the world that hold promise in their efforts to help poor move out of
poverty; committed to long-term relationships in search of lasting solutions
to hunger, poverty, and social inequities

YMCA
Provides parent visitation monitoring services and physical fitness services

I wish to play the (circle one):   Match Game   Rebate Game

Of your **$20.00** endowment, how much do you wish to keep for yourself,
and how much do you wish to pass to your charity of choice?

Keep for Self:	$
Pass to Charity:	$
Total:	$ 20.00

IDENTIFYING ALTRUISM IN THE LABORATORY [☆]

Glenn W. Harrison and Laurie T. Johnson

ABSTRACT

Recent attempts to measure altruism toward other players or charities suffer from a potential confound: the act of giving is typically correlated with the size of the pie left on the experimenter's table. Altruistic acts could thus be more generous if subjects prefer that monies go toward other players, or charities, than be left on the table. On the other hand, revealed altruism could be lower if subjects are more altruistic toward the residual claimant than they are toward the agent to whom they are being asked to give. We demonstrate this point with simple laboratory experiments that derive from popular recent designs. We find a significant effect from the hypothesized confound, with revealed altruism dependent upon who is specified as the residual claimant.

Recent attempts to measure altruism toward other players or charities suffer from a potential confound: the act of giving is typically correlated

[☆] Supporting data and instructions are stored at the ExLab Experimental Social Sciences Digital Library at http://exlab.bus.ucf.edu.

Experiments Investigating Fundraising and Charitable Contributors
Research in Experimental Economics, Volume 11, 177–223
ISSN: 0193-2306/doi:10.1016/S0193-2306(06)11008-X

with the size of the pie left on the experimenter's table. Altruistic acts could thus be more generous if subjects prefer that monies go toward other players, or charities, than be left on the table. On the other hand, revealed altruism could be lower if subjects are more altruistic toward the residual claimant than they are toward the agent to whom they are being asked to give. In either case, what is not spent out of the experimenter's budget constraint implies that there is money going "somewhere else," other than to the subjects. Hence the choice of a particular "somewhere else" can matter for elicited preferences. Subjects' concerns about the disposition of the residual claim of the experimenter are related to their concerns about the total surplus that they get to divide, but are distinct.[1]

We illustrate this point with some simple laboratory experiments that derive from popular designs. We find that there is a significant effect from this confound, and that the results are surprising (to us, at least). The extent of revealed altruism depends upon who is specified as the residual claimant.

If this were "just another context effect" then it would be useful to know about for those claiming some universal or generic tendency to altruism, but not fundamental. We believe that this is a potential confound of greater relevance. In a wide range of experiments there is no doubt that subjects depart dramatically from what are taken to be the game-theoretic predictions by engaging in what is variously labeled "cooperation," "altruism," "reciprocity" or "confusion." *In virtually all cases the data show that subjects make more money than the predictions would suggest.* This fact, itself, should give us some pause to reflect on whether we have actually modeled the right objective function in the experiment.[2]

In Section 1 we define the basic experimental games used previously to measure altruism, and then discuss the problem of interpreting behavior from them. In Section 2 we discuss the broader methodological relevance of our hypothesized confound. In Section 3 we design an experiment that allow us to assess the existence of the potential confound, and in Sections 4 and 5 report the results of a laboratory experiment using that design. We find that the confound does dramatically change the measured extent of revealed altruism, in some cases increasing it and in other cases decreasing it. We conclude that altruism exists,[3] but that it is clearly contextual and varies from individual to individual. More important, we identify some general confounds that should be addressed in all experiments that measure altruism, as well as in other experiments.

1. GIFT-GIVING GAMES AND THEIR INTERPRETATION

1.1. The Dictator Game

Most of the gift-giving games used in experiments take the form of modifications of the Dictator game, introduced as such by Forsythe, Horowitz, Savin, and Sefton (1994). In that game, which we refer to as simply "Dictator," two players are paired at random. Each receives some initial endowment, and one player can pass any fraction of his endowment to the other player. The player receiving the gift has no response to make in a game-theoretic sense, so there is no element of strategy in the behavior of the first player. Extensions of Dictator that allow for responses of the second player include the Ultimatum game (where the second player can reject the proposal, in which case neither player receives anything) and the Trust game (where the second player decides how much of the gift, after it has been scaled up by some fixed ratio, to send back to the first player).

The results from Dictator are that players often send a positive fraction of their initial endowment to the other player, which is inconsistent with the first player having preferences defined solely over his own payoffs. Thus, passing behavior under Dictator is viewed as evidence that some subjects may have some "altruistic preferences" in the context of the traditional laboratory experiment.[4]

The importance of context has been examined in several experiments, and not surprisingly the evidence suggests that framing does matter. For example, Hoffman, McCabe, Shachat, and Smith (1994) demonstrate that the seemingly innocuous use of the word "divide" in bargaining game instructions, and the use of random initial endowments, could lead to deviations from theoretical predictions. Similarly, the experiments of Cherry, Frykblom, and Shogren (2002) included a treatment in which subjects earned their initial bargaining stake as the result of a non-trivial quiz. Those subjects that did better in the quiz earned $40, and the others earned $10. In the control experiment subjects were simply endowed with these different amounts. The responses were striking: offers to the other player were much less generous when subjects had earned the initial stake, whether or not the responses were "double-blind." There are other examples of the effects of framing and context in related settings, such as Andreoni (1995b), Sonnemans, Schram, and Offerman (1998) and Small and Loewenstein (2003), but the implication is that one has to take it into account in experiments. We therefore echo the conclusion of Eckel and Grossman (1996b, 188ff.) in a similar context:

> It is received wisdom in experimental economics that abstraction is important. Experimental procedures should be as context-free as possible, and the interaction among subjects should be carefully limited by the rules of the experiment to ensure that they are playing the game we intend them to play. For tests of economic theory, these procedural restrictions are critical. As experimenters, we aspire to instructions that most closely mimic the environments implicit in the theory, which is inevitably a mathematic abstraction of an economic situation. We are careful not to contaminate our tests by unnecessary context. But it is also possible to use experimental methodology to explore the importance and consequence of context. Economists are becoming increasingly aware that social and psychological factors can only be introduced by abandoning, at least to some extent, abstraction. This may be particularly true for the investigation of other-regarding behavior in the economic arena.

1.2. Aversion to Inefficiency

We focus on one generic aspect of the context or frame of the standard gift-giving task, which we call "inefficiency aversion." In most of the gift-giving experiments, any monies passed by the first player to the second are scaled up by the experimenter. Thus $1 sent from the first player to the second player (or charity) might become $3 in the hands of the second player (or charity). We examine specific instances of these games below.

This design feature became explicit with Eckel and Grossman (1996a, 1996b). They correctly observed that there is at least one important confound making comparisons of Ultimatum bargaining outcomes and Dictator outcomes problematic: the relative price of fairness. Specifically, in the Ultimatum game ("Ultimatum") the foregone expected earnings of holding on to money is higher than in Dictator, since the more the subject holds on to the more likely it is that the other player will reject the proposal.[5] Since this confound depends on the subjective expectations of the players and risk attitudes, it is not well controlled for, even if we do know that it can only be higher in Ultimatum than in Dictator.[6] Hence they proposed explicitly controlling for the relative price of giving with the gift-giving designs now popular.

Consider a game in which there are two players, rather than one player and a charity. If the subject being asked to make the allocation places no value on the monies retained by the experimenter at the end of the game, but does place a positive value on the monies being allocated to himself or the other player, then such players would like to see those monies allocated away from the experimenter. More generally, if the subject just places a higher value (in terms of his own subjective evaluations) on monies being in the hands of either subject rather than the experimenter, then there is a motive to pass money to the other player. The possibility of this type of weighted utility function means that one does not have to assume irrationality: subjects might realize that monies *not* spent on them will still exist, but nonetheless experience a subjective loss in utility if the money ends up with the experimenter instead of the other player. To take an extreme example, what if the experimenter announces that he brought $3,000 to the session beyond the fixed show-up fees, since there were 10 pairs and he might have to pay out up to $3,000, but that he planned on donating the money he retained at the end to the *National Rifle Association* or the *American Civil Liberties Union*.[7] Subjects have a wide range of attitudes toward these organizations, running the gamut from love to hate. Quite apart from other-regarding preferences toward the other player, and any other confounds,[8] this planned disposition of any funds not retained by the subjects would be expected to influence behavior within the game, with at least some subjects wanting to minimize (or maximize) the residual donations by the experimenter.[9] The way to do that, in fact the only way given the structure of this game, is to pass (keep) money to (from) the other player and behave "as if" altruistic (selfish).[10]

Subjects may or may not be averse to inefficiency as we have defined it. Just as the general term "risk aversion" allows for risk loving behavior as well as risk neutrality, we view the notion of inefficiency aversion as including subjective preferences in which some subjects prefer to see monies left in the hands of the experimenters or are indifferent. We presume that subjects may want to maximize earnings on behalf of subjects as a whole, but stress that this is just a presumption that has to be evaluated in the context of each experiment.

Although it might be tempting to call this "just another framing effect," we believe it is also more fundamental from a traditional perspective. The budget constraint binding the experimenter implies a task representation to subjects, if we rule out deception, and that task representation might influence behavior. Consider the context of an experimenter in a poor country that is visiting from a rich country. Whittington (2002, 356ff.) discusses the difficulties faced when deciding how much one should pay a survey enumerator in a poor, less-developed country, suggesting as a rule of thumb that they be paid no more than 5–10 times the local wage. His experiences could almost count as a field experiment itself:

> But these general guidelines are no substitute for a high level of political sensitivity in settling on and/or negotiating monetary compensation for enumerators. Particularly in situations where applicants for positions as enumerators have no experience working with foreign donors or international agencies, their expectations about wages can be very high. Potential enumerators may, for example, expect to be paid international wage rates.

> I have had [...] experiences in which I got off on the wrong foot because of initial negotiations over wages. Both were in rural situations in which local wage rates for unskilled labor were exceedingly low (less than US$1 per day). Once in Haiti I literally had a group of potential enumerators react violently to a proposal I made for wage rates that I considered very generous. I managed to leave, but not before a crowd of potential enumerators attacked my car.

Think of his initial proposal as a "generous offer" in a field Ultimatum bargaining game as he represented the pie, and these attacks as rejections from subjects that the pie was fairly divided. This is just a difference in expectations, which are known from controlled laboratory experiments[11] to have a dramatic and predictable effect in Ultimatum, but it derived from the task representation. At the very least, control over task representation might be lost in contexts that provoke subjects to think about the residual surplus (money not spent from the experimenter's budget).

The possibility that the disbursement of the residual claim in an experiment might affect responses is clearly identified by Levine (1998). Assuming no role for the beliefs of player i about the altruism of the other player in a two-person game,[12] he follows Ledyard (1995) and proposes a utility function for player i as

$$v_i = u_i + a_i + u_j$$

where u_i is the direct utility of player i from his own monetary payoff, and $a_i \in (-1, 1)$ is a coefficient of altruism. If a_i is positive the player is said to be altruistic, if it is zero he is selfish, and if it is negative he is said to be spiteful. With this background, Levine (1998, p. 598) then has an unusually careful discussion of how one interprets experimental payoffs in terms of utility, a critical issue for any attempt to identify altruism:

> In studying experiments, we will identify the participants' utility with their monetary income from the experiment. [...] It is important to note, however, that the money that is not received by the participants reverts to the experimenter, and there is no reason for the subjects to feel differently about the experimenter than the other subjects. However, it does not seem sensible to identify the utility of the experimenter with the amount of money that reverts to him. Instead, we will assume that the marginal utility of the experimenter for money that is not disbursed to the subjects is zero, so that in effect, from the subject's point of view, the money is thrown away, and the altruism coefficient a_i does not matter. Notice that it is possible to design experiments to control more carefully for the effect of money that is not received by the subjects. Rather than having the money revert to the experimenter, one subject can be chosen to be the residual claimant, with all money not disbursed to the subjects being given to the residual claimant, who does not otherwise participate in the experiment. In this case, the utility of

money not going to the participants other than the residual claimant can also be identified with money income, and the residual claimant should be viewed by the other subjects as having the population mean value of a_i. According to the theory, this should have an effect on the outcome of the experiment.

Our experiments can be seen as tests of this hypothesis.[13]

1.3. Giving to Others

Building on Eckel and Grossman (1996a, 1996b, 1998), Andreoni and Miller (2002) implement a simple experiment to elicit altruistic preferences. Our design is based on their experiment. The instructions for the main task in our version are brief:

> In this experiment you are asked to make a series of choices about how to divide points between yourself and one other subject in the room. You and the other subject will be paired randomly and you will not be told each other's identity.

> As you divide the points, you and the other subject will each earn money. Every point that you earn will be worth 10, 20, 30 or 40 cents, depending on the choice. For example, if you earn 58 points you will make $5.80 in the experiment if your points are worth 10 cents for that choice. Similarly for the earnings of the other player.

> Each choice you make is similar to the following:

> **Divide 50 points:** *Hold* _____ @ **$0.10 each, and** *Pass* _____ @ **$0.20 each.**

> In this choice you must divide 50 points. You can keep all of the points, keep some and pass some, or pass all of the points. In this example, you will receive 10 cents for every point you hold, and the other player will receive 20 cents for every point you pass. For example, if you hold 50 and pass 0 points, you will receive 50 × $0.10 = $5.00, and the other player will receive no points and $0. If you hold 0 and pass 50 points, you will receive no points and $0, and the other player will receive 50 × $0.20 = $10.00. However, you could choose any number between 0 and 50 to hold. For instance, you could choose to hold 29 tokens and pass 21. In this case you would earn 29 points, or 29 × $0.10 = $2.90, and the other subject would receive 21 × $0.20 = $4.20.

> Here is another example.

> **Divide 50 points:** *Hold* _____ @ **$0.30 each, and** *Pass* _____ @ **$0.10 each.**

> In this example every point you hold earns you 30 cents, and every point you pass earns the other subject 10 cents.

> Important note: In all cases you can choose any number to hold and any number to pass, but the number of points you hold plus the number of points you pass must equal the total number of points to divide.

> Please do not talk. Are there any questions?

The actual tasks given to subjects by Andreoni and Miller (2002) were randomized across subjects in terms of order, but consisted of the following in most of their experiments:

1. Divide 75 points: *Hold* _____ @ $0.10 each, and *Pass* _____ @ $0.20 each.
2. Divide 40 points: *Hold* _____ @ $0.10 each, and *Pass* _____ @ $0.30 each.
3. Divide 75 points: *Hold* _____ @ $0.20 each, and *Pass* _____ @ $0.10 each.
4. Divide 60 points: *Hold* _____ @ $0.10 each, and *Pass* _____ @ $0.20 each.
5. Divide 40 points: *Hold* _____ @ $0.30 each, and *Pass* _____ @ $0.10 each.
6. Divide 60 points: *Hold* _____ @ $0.10 each, and *Pass* _____ @ $0.10 each.
7. Divide 100 points: *Hold* _____ @ $0.10 each, and *Pass* _____ @ $0.20 each
8. Divide 60 points: *Hold* _____ @ $0.20 each, and *Pass* _____ @ $0.10 each.
9. Divide 80 points: *Hold* _____ @ $0.10 each, and *Pass* _____ @ $0.20 each.
10. Divide 40 points: *Hold* _____ @ $0.40 each, and *Pass* _____ @ $0.10 each.
11. Divide 40 points: *Hold* _____ @ $0.10 each, and *Pass* _____ @ $0.40 each.

These questions serve to "capture" the indifference curve between own payoffs and payoffs to the other player, in the spirit of Revealed Preference theory. As the price of giving to the other player dropped, one would expect to see choices that imply that no less was allocated to the other player. Thus, answers to decision #10 and #11 would be expected to show that the pass rate in #11 is no less than the pass rate in #10. In the extreme, with sufficiently high substitutability in the preferences of the player between own payoff and payoff to the other player, one would see a 0% pass rate in #10 and a 100% pass rate in #11.

Each choice also implies different payoffs to the experimenter, depending on how the subjects view this task. The maximal payout by the experimenter was for decision #7, and would be $20 if the subject passed 100% of the 100 points to the other player. So if the subject only cared about extracting money from the experimenter for either player, the same responses would be observed as if the player had been altruistic (and had high enough elasticity of substitution between the payoffs of the two players). Thus one cannot say if the observed behavior in this example is due to altruism toward the other player or inefficiency aversion.

The smallest payout by the experimenter was for decision #6, and would be $6.00 irrespective of how the subject allocated the endowment of points. So in this instance any allocation to the other player is a sign of some altruism.

What does the data from the Andreoni and Miller (2002) experiments suggest? Figs. 1 and 2 display the pass rate, calculated as the percentage of the initial endowment of points that the subject passed to the other player.[14] As Fig. 1 illustrates, many subjects were stingy! Around 48% of responses involved passing nothing to the other player. By itself this is not a problem

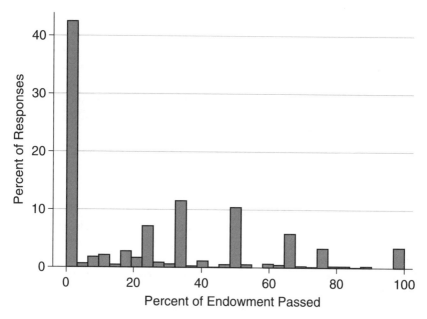

Fig. 1. Pass Rate in Andreoni and Miller Experiments.

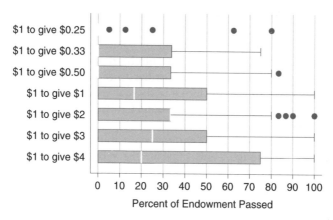

Fig. 2. Pass Rate As Price of Giving Varies.

for their design. If a given subject never gave to the other player, however, there is no interesting test of consistency with rationality in the sense defined by the axioms of Revealed Preference – nor is there a violation, of course, since this subject could just care less about the well-being of the other player.

It turns out that 23% of the responses were from subjects who gave nothing to the other player in *all* decisions. The responses of these players should not be discarded, but they should be identified since they are not particularly interesting for some purposes (e.g., the tests of rationality underlying consistency with the axioms of Revealed Preference).[15] We focus in our design on the range of prices that generate significant contributions, to better identify the extent of altruism.[16] From Fig. 2 we see that this interesting range is where the experimenter subsidizes the act of giving, which is also precisely where the confound of concern here is the most important.

1.4. Giving to Charities

Eckel and Grossman (2003) extended the Dictator game considered above, and in their earlier work on altruism toward other individuals, to consider charitable contributions to organizations. They allowed subjects to pick 1 of 10 designated charities that met tax eligibility standards for exemptions in Texas, where the experiments were conducted. Their design then matched the earlier Dictator games: subjects had differing endowments across decisions, and differing rates at which their contributions would end up in the pocket of their designated charity.

Eckel and Grossman (2003) were particularly interested in the effects of "rebates" or "matching subsidies" on charitable contributions – in theory, the two should have the same effect if chosen appropriately, as they were in their design. A matching subsidy works by some external body providing a match to the charitable contributions of the donor, so that every dollar contributed generates more than one dollar to the charity. A rebate works by the charity itself, or some external body such as the government through tax exemptions, effectively returning monies to the donor in some proportion to the amounts donated.[17]

Eckel and Grossman (2003) found that contribution rates, or *pass rates* as defined earlier, are roughly the same in the rebate or matching subsidy treatments. In both cases the pass rates are remarkably close to 50%. This implies a much higher *dollar contribution* under the matching subsidy treatment, simply from the arithmetic of the two subsidy rules and the control for identical initial endowments. They conclude that matching subsidies might be an attractive way to replace rebates based on tax exemptions, which is desirable as part of some broad-based reform of the tax system to encourage uniformity.

One possible explanation for this framing effect is that subjects might perceive the matching subsidy as entailing a contribution from somebody else who might otherwise not make a contribution, and fail to perceive the rebate subsidy in the same manner. If the subject valued the contribution to the charity more than the income level of that third party, the subsidy offers a way for the subject to increase their own utility at the expense of the third party. This would be an example of subjects applying a weighted utility function, discussed earlier.

Davis, Millner, and Reilly (2003, 2005) focus on the fact that the pass rates were remarkably similar under the two treatments, and hypothesize instead that this framing result might be due to a simple calculation error by the subjects. They modified the original design to make the effects of the two treatments blindingly transparent to subjects, and found that pass rates are indeed closer to predicted levels. Their results are consistent with some calculation error, but do not eliminate it.

One particularly striking methodological contribution of Davis, Millner, and Reilly (2003) is a recognition of the potential importance of sample composition effects *and* a general way of dealing with them. They find a statistically significant sex effect, such that women are more altruistic in each of their treatments.[18] However, since their three treatment samples contained 58%, 65% and 37% females, respectively, they would have observed a difference in average pass rates if they failed to condition on the sample composition differences. They did so, using a statistical model of predicted pass rates that includes controls for sex, and report the conditional pass rates assuming identical sample compositions in each treatment.[19] We generalize their approach.

2. HOW GENERAL IS THIS POTENTIAL PROBLEM?

Standard practice in experimental economics is to start with words that essentially state the following, taken from Plott (1982, p. 1524):

> This is an experiment in the economics of market decision-making. Various research foundations have provided funds for this research. The instructions are simple and if you follow them carefully and make good decisions you might earn a considerable amount of money which will be paid to you in cash.

How might the subject interpret these instructions? One plausible way is to view the experimental task *initially* as a game between the subjects as a whole ("Us") and the experimenter or research foundation ("Him"). The instructions do go on to describe the specific experimental task, which typically pits one subject against another subject to some extent. But this could reasonably be viewed by the subject as a two-stage game. The first stage is where the subjects as a group have to find strategies to extract money from the experimenter or research foundation, and the second stage is where the subjects individually try to maximize their own share of the extraction. The first stage suggests a cooperative solution, and the second stage typically suggests a non-cooperative solution.[20]

There are several striking examples in experimental economics of standard games that seem to "tempt" subjects to represent the task in this manner: the centipede game of McKelvey and Palfrey (1992), the trust or investment game of Berg, Dickhaut, and McCabe (1995), the public goods game of Andreoni (1995a, 1995b) and Fehr and Gächter (2000), the common pool resource extraction game of Ostrom, Walker, and Gardner (1992), the matching pennies game of Goeree and Holt (2001) and Goeree, Holt, and Palfrey (2003), the travelers' dilemma game of Capra, Goeree, Gomez, and Holt (1999) and Goeree and Holt (2001), and the principal-agent, gift-exchange games of Fehr, Kirchsteiger, and Riedl (1993), Fehr, Gächter, and Kirchsteiger (1997) and Fehr and Falk (1999). In all cases the deviations generally observed are correlated with the subjects as a whole extracting money from the experimenter, at least relative to the theoretical prediction used to identify "deviations."

The claim that a wide class of experimental games fail to control for a potential confound is not intended to offer a single, "magic bullet" explanation for all of the anomalies identified from those games. Some apparent anomalies can be accounted for, but others cannot. Moreover, the fact that they can be accounted for within standard theory does not mean that the alternative explanations are wrong. Finally, the explanation for anomalies from the perspective of traditional theory might entail interactions between several explanations, and could be contextual. These methodological points might seem obvious if it were not for the fact that the literature often stakes out "all or nothing, corner-solution" positions in which traditional theory is either completely false or completely true.[21] Let the data decide, when the experimental data are interpreted rigorously *and* one allows for heterogeneity in behavior (e.g., Fehr & Schmidt, 1999, p. 818; Bolton & Ockenfels, 2000, Assumption 4, p. 172; Charness & Rabin, 2002, p. 818).

3. EXPERIMENTAL DESIGN

In all treatments we had one subject that was the Dictator. In treatments O and O(C) we also had one subject that was a Peasant (recipient of the

Dictator's giving). Each had separate tasks, although we focus here on the Dictators. The Peasants were placed in a separate room from the Dictators.

The basic design we use builds on Andreoni and Miller (2002), as discussed and illustrated above. Each subject makes 10 decisions, each of which entails an allocation of points to himself and an allocation to pass. In treatment O the points passed are assigned to another player in the other room, following Andreoni and Miller (2002). In treatment C the points passed are assigned to a specific charity, in the spirit of Eckel and Grossman (2003). In each case we say "nothing" about what happens to the residual, although it is clear that the experimenter is effectively paying more to the subjects when a point is allocated to an account that has a larger multiplier.

In treatment O(C) we follow treatment O, but add some text to say that the experimenter has allocated up to a certain amount for each player pair, and that anything left over after the session will be sent to a specific but unnamed charity.[22] Similarly, in treatment C(O) we follow treatment C, but add some text to say that the experimenter has allocated up to a certain amount for each player pair, and that anything left over after the session will be assigned to another player selected at random. Thus one player in treatment C(O) would receive the complete residual from the entire session.

In *all* treatments the following text was used:

> We will select one of your decisions to actually implement at the end of the session. We have allowed for up to $32 to be paid out for the decision that is selected, multiplied by the number of pairs of subjects here today. This is the maximum amount that can be paid out, depending on your choices and the roll of the die selecting the decision to be implemented. Depending on your choices, and the decision picked to be implemented, we might not need to pay out as much as $32 per pair.

This text effectively informed the subject that we had the cash to make the payments necessary under the rules of the task. We decided to be explicit in this matter in our control treatments since we had to be explicit about it our research treatments, and we wanted the sole difference between the treatments to be the consequences of leaving money on the (experimenter's) table. If we had not been so explicit, there would have been two differences between our control and research treatments: the reminder that we planned conservatively in terms of the "cash box," and a statement about the disposition of residuals. The comparable text in treatment O(C) *included the above text* plus this extra explanation at the end of the paragraph.

> Any monies left will be paid to a public charity. The name and address of the charity is in a sealed envelope which we will open at the end of the session. We will write a check to the charity at the end of the session, seal it in an envelope, and you can come with us to the nearest public mailbox to see it mailed.

In treatment C(O) we added this extra text instead:

Any monies left will be paid to one other subject in the room, selected at random.

So the only difference between the experiments in this respect was the addition of the extra text for the O(C) and C(O) treatments.

We deliberately chose residual claimants for these tests that would be transparently understood, plausible in the context of our experiment, and generate differences in preferences across our sample. One could easily imagine variants that would not elicit large differences in preferences. In the O(C) treatment, for example, what if we confronted students in Colorado with residuals that would be contributed to the United Way of Florida in one situation and then to United Way of Georgia in another situation? There might still be a large difference between preferences for the residual in O as compared to these two together, but a priori one could expect that differences between the two United Way treatments would be minimal. Since our objective was simply to identify if the specification of the residual claimant could matter at all, these clear extremes were appropriate. They were also appropriate in the sense that such contrasts are likely to be present in the field, as noted earlier. Any field application would have to evaluate what alternatives were appropriate for that context. We also expect that the sensitivity of results will depend on the sample, and indeed stress below the need to condition inferences on comparable samples. In general, we expect these specification and sampling issues to become more important in field settings than in laboratory settings due to the greater heterogeneity of contexts and samples that one is likely to encounter in the field.

Each subject was asked to make choices patterned after Andreoni and Miller (2002), but only included returns to giving of 1 or more:

1. Divide 75 points: *Hold* _____ @ $0.20 each, and *Pass* _____ @ $0.40 each.
2. Divide 40 points: *Hold* _____ @ $0.20 each, and *Pass* _____ @ $0.60 each.
3. Divide 75 points: *Hold* _____ @ $0.20 each, and *Pass* _____ @ $0.20 each.
4. Divide 60 points: *Hold* _____ @ $0.20 each, and *Pass* _____ @ $0.40 each.
5. Divide 40 points: *Hold* _____ @ $0.50 each, and *Pass* _____ @ $0.50 each.
6. Divide 100 points: *Hold* _____ @ $0.10 each, and *Pass* _____ @ $0.20 each.
7. Divide 60 points: *Hold* _____ @ $0.20 each, and *Pass* _____ @ $0.30 each.
8. Divide 80 points: *Hold* _____ @ $0.20 each, and *Pass* _____ @ $0.40 each.
9. Divide 40 points: *Hold* _____ @ $0.20 each, and *Pass* _____ @ $0.50 each.
10. Divide 40 points: *Hold* _____ @ $0.20 each, and *Pass* _____ @ $0.80 each.

Three versions of these questions were employed in each session, varying the order of each question.

4. PROCEDURES

The experiments were conducted over two consecutive days in late January 2004 at the University of Denver. This is a small, private college, with an undergraduate enrollment of 4,500 in 2003. Residents of Colorado make up roughly 45% of each class, and undergraduate tuition costs around $25,000 per year. Subjects were recruited in classes with large sections, and all subjects were undergraduates.

We had 173 subjects across all treatments. In treatments C, O, C(O) and O(C) we had 28, 58, 31 and 56 subjects, respectively, so that we would have roughly 30 proposers in each treatment. Subjects were randomly assigned to a treatment, and did not know anything about the purpose of the experiment when recruited to specific sessions. Each of the C and C(O) sessions was conducted in one large classroom, and sessions O and O(C) in two large, adjacent classrooms. All subjects met in one classroom initially in sessions O and O(C), and were then taken to the other room if they randomly received an "odd numbered" subject ID number. These simple logistics served to make it clear to all subjects that there were "real people" in the other room, since this was referred to in the instructions. In fact, many of the subjects separated in this manner knew each other, adding to the credibility that there was another person in the other room.

The instructions were relatively brief, and we read them out aloud as the subjects had an opportunity to read along. This serves to slow down those subjects who want to just skip through the instructions and make their decisions, so that all subjects have an equal opportunity to "internalize" the instructions. One monitor was the experimenter for Dictators in all sessions, and another monitor was the experimenter for Peasants in the O and O(C) sessions.

Our sample demographics matched the general undergraduate mix at the University of Denver. Over 61% of the sample was female. Only 2.3% were black, and 8.1% were Hispanic. Freshmen and Sophomores made up 33% and 46% of the sample, respectively. Although age ranged from 18 to 24, 84% of the sample was aged 18, 19 or 20, so there is relatively little variation in this characteristic. The complete list of individual demographic questions is provided in Appendix A.

To avoid any confounds from specific knowledge, we did not identify the charity that we were using. We did provide an opportunity to all subjects to examine the check being written to the charity, and to come with us to mail it immediately after the session concluded. In fact, the charity was the *American Civil Liberties Union of South Carolina Foundation*, a 501(c)3 non-profit organization, and payments totaling $1,143 were made to them as the result of the experiment. The subjects did not know this until after all choices were made, and no subject expressed any concern with this charity.[23]

Each subject received $10 for showing up and participating in the experiment. This was slightly on the generous side compared to most laboratory experiments with a convenience sample of students, but we were unsure about the response of students at the University of Denver to standard recruitment procedures. Moreover, the base student population was relatively small, adding to our concern about enrollment. Finally, there had been no fresh snow on the local ski resorts for some weeks, heightening our concern that Mother Nature would increase the opportunity cost of attending the experiment at the last minute.[24]

Average payments, in addition to the show-up fee, were $20.67. However, this includes one "happy, happy" subject in the C(O) treatment that received a payout of $441 in addition to the show-up fee. Removing him, the average was $18.25. Individual payments ranged from a low of $0.20 to a high of $32, again in addition to the show-up fee.

5. RESULTS

We evaluate results in two stages. The first is to examine the raw results, which we refer to as "apparent altruism." We believe that these results are misleading, because of significant demographic effects and our sample sizes. Hence we consider the effects of our treatments after conditioning on observable demographics, and statistically "equalizing" the effect of those demographics across treatments. We refer to these results as "revealed altruism," to recognize explicitly that they are not apparent from the raw data. The statistical specification we use is a two-limit Tobit model, recognizing that pass rates can neither be below 0 nor above 100.

5.1. Apparent Altruism

Behavior is best examined in terms of pass rates, defined as the percent of the endowment which is passed, in order to normalize across the different endowments in each decision. In treatments C and C(O) the average pass rate was 48.9% and 47.6% respectively, with overall standard deviations of 28% in each case.[25] Of course, these large standard deviations reflect expected variations with treatments, such as the price of giving, which we control for below. In treatments O and O(C) the average pass rate was only 33.2% and 29.3% respectively, with overall standard deviations of 27% and 25%.

Fig. 3 displays the *unconditional* pass rates observed in our experiments, based on a tabulation of the raw data.[26] The pass rate is shown on the vertical axis. The horizontal axis shows the price of giving, which is just the ratio of the money received by the other party to the money sent. Thus if $1 was passed and became $3 when received by the other party, the return to giving is 3. The top two lines, in gray, show the pass rates for treatments C and C(O); the bottom two lines, in black, show the pass rates for treatments O and O(C).

Fig. 3 displays unconditional behavior in the sense that we do not condition on the fact that our samples differed across the four sessions. For example, women made up 71% of the samples for the C and O(C) treatments, but only 55% of the sample for the O treatment and 51% of the sample for the C(O) treatment. If altruistic preferences differ for men and women, as one would expect from the previous literature, then this difference in sample composition could easily distort inferences from raw data such as in Fig. 3. With sufficient sample sizes and random assignment to treatment, this would not be an issue. But when there are many possible characteristics that can affect responses, other than sex, the sample sizes needed for randomization to be effective are enormous.[27]

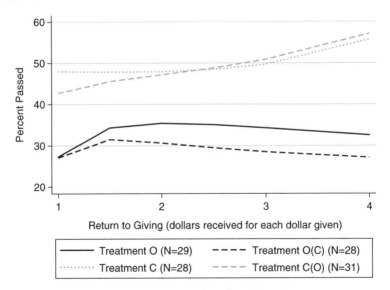

Fig. 3. Apparent Altruism from Raw Data.

5.2. Revealed Altruism

Fig. 4 reports conditional behavior assuming that responses can be characterized by a statistical model of behavior that controls for differences in individual sample characteristics. Table 1 reports the statistical specification underlying these displays, so that one can test for significance of effects. We focus on a standard array of "objective" observable characteristics, as well as a random effects specification to control for any unobserved individual heterogeneity beyond those characteristics.[28] Specifically, we include sex, age, race,[29] personal and household income[30] and a measure of multiple-person households.[31] We also include controls for the return to giving,[32] the initial endowment of points and interactions between the return to giving and sex.[33] As noted above, the estimation procedure is a two-limit Tobit model, recognizing that pass rates cannot be below 0 or above 100. To generate Fig. 4, each model is *estimated* on the sample in just one treatment, and then *predicted* pass rates[34] are calculated using those estimated coefficients and the common sample characteristics across all four treatments. Thus, we ensure that the sample composition is controlled for when generating predicted pass rates.

Five features of Fig. 4 are important. First, the use of common, synthetic samples generates differences in the responses when one compares the same treatment in Figs. 3 and 4. For example, pass rates for treatment C are much

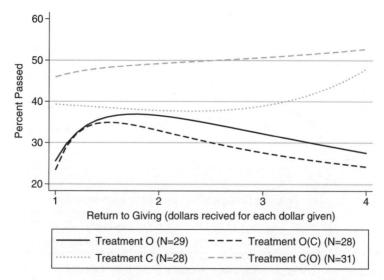

Fig. 4.   Revealed Altruism.

Table 1. Estimation Results from Panel Tobit Model of the Pass Rate.

Variable	Coefficient	SE	z	$P > |z|$	95% Confidence Interval	
Primary treatments						
Efficiency	−28.91	3.56	−8.12	0.000	−35.89	−21.92
Charity	26.40	3.28	8.05	0.000	19.97	32.83
Charity × efficiency	17.36	3.69	4.7	0.000	10.12	24.60
Design controls						
Return	51.74	19.30	2.68	0.007	13.92	89.57
Return2	−20.30	8.76	−2.32	0.020	−37.47	−3.14
Return3	2.66	1.18	2.25	0.024	0.34	4.98
Endowment	0.07	0.06	1.12	0.262	−0.05	0.19
Individual subject controls for sex						
Endowment × female	−0.15	0.07	−2.2	0.028	−0.28	−0.02
Return × female	−4.08	1.59	−2.57	0.010	−7.20	−0.97
Efficiency × female	23.65	3.95	5.99	0.000	15.92	31.38
Charity × female	−17.99	3.39	−5.31	0.000	−24.63	−11.35
Female	13.71	6.89	1.99	0.046	0.21	27.21
Additional individual subject controls						
Non-White	−20.59	2.40	−8.57	0.000	−25.30	−15.88
Age	0.08	0.72	0.12	0.906	−1.32	1.49
Work	11.01	1.84	6	0.000	7.41	14.61
Income1	−20.57	2.41	−8.53	0.000	−25.29	−15.84
Income2	−6.77	2.00	−3.37	0.001	−10.69	−2.84
Hhd	5.02	2.35	2.14	0.032	0.42	9.62
Constant	−15.23	18.63	−0.82	0.414	−51.74	21.28
Estimates of error terms						
σ_u	26.80	0.91	29.43	0.000	25.01	28.58
σ_e	19.36	0.47	40.9	0.000	18.43	20.29
ρ	0.66	0.02			0.62	0.69

Note: Unless otherwise noted, all variables are binary dummy variables. Charity denotes the C or C(O) treatments; efficiency denotes the O(C) and C(O) treatments; return is the multiplier on contributions, or the monetary "return" to giving; endowment is the token endowment for a specific choice; female denotes females; non-White denotes self-reported ethnicity; age is measured in years; Income1 (Income2) denotes parent or own income in 2003 over $65,000 and less than $100,000 (over $100,000); Hhd indicates if the subject lives in a household with someone else; σ_u the error term for the unobserved individual effect; σ_e the general error term; and ρ the proportion of the total error term $\sigma_u + \sigma_e$ that is due to σ_u. *P*-values reported as 0.000 are actually values that are less than 0.0005.

lower when one accounts for the fact that it had a different sample than other treatments. Similarly, pass rates for treatments O and O(C) in Fig. 4 are generally lower than in their unconditional counterparts in Fig. 3. This finding is consistent with other experimental research, and highlights the general methodological point that one simply cannot detect such differences if questions about individual characteristics are not asked. Many experiments do not include a questionnaire on individual characteristics, or limit attention to just one or two characteristics. For some purposes, where there is little *a priori* belief that responses will vary with observable characteristics, this is a reasonable economy in terms of experimental procedure. On the other hand, questionnaires do not take a long time to complete, and often serve to allow subjects time to settle into the experiment before the main tasks begin.

Second, Fig. 4 also reveals that altruism toward an unspecified generic charity tends to be greater than altruism toward another subject, and this general preference holds at all levels of the return to giving when one controls for the efficiency confound. This result is consistent with evidence reviewed earlier, particularly Eckel and Grossman's (1996b), but is the first time that it has been demonstrated for subjects drawn from the same population at the same time, in essentially the same experimental task, and with the same level of knowledge about the specific recipient. Hence there are no other confounds that might affect this conclusion.[35] The implication is that there is no single "propensity to be altruistic," but that it depends on the context and on the type of recipient. This is not surprising, but worth documenting carefully so that claims of altruism in one setting are not automatically assumed to apply in different settings.

Our third result, related to our central thesis, is the general pattern of preferences reflected in the revealed altruism results being consistent with the existence of residual claimant effects. Comparing treatments C and O, when the residual claims are the same and rebound to the experimenter, we observe that subjects tend to prefer giving to a charity than to some other subject. This effect is particularly clear for higher returns to giving, although it also holds for the lowest return to giving. Hence when we substitute the charity for the experimenter in treatment O(C) we observe a *reduction* in contributions to the other subject by comparison to treatment O from the two bottom lines of Fig. 4. Conversely, when we substitute some other subject for the experimenter in treatment C(O), we observe an *increase* in contributions to the charity by comparison to treatment C from the two top lines of Fig. 4. The implication is that subjects, on average, rank contributions to a charity over contributions to the experimenter, and then rank contributions to the experimenter over contributions to another subject. Although this particular pattern is not required for our hypothesis about the residual claim to be valid, it happens to be qualitatively consistent internally as well as with related experimental data.

Fourth, we observe weak evidence in three cases for a "relative price" effect on giving, but strong evidence in one case. Treatments C, O and O(C) exhibit evidence for increased giving when the return is higher. But this evidence only appears for high levels of the return in the case of treatment C, and for low levels of the return in the case of treatments O and O(C). On the other hand, we observe a striking effect in treatment C(O), in which increases in the return to giving to a charity generate increases in amounts allocated.[36]

Finally, we obtain strikingly disparate predictions of the effect of the efficiency treatment depending on the context. In the case of altruism toward charity, revealed altruism is higher in the efficiency treatment than in the control treatment. In contrast, in the case of altruism toward another person, revealed altruism is lower in the efficiency treatment. Of course, these claims about increasing or decreasing the quantitative level of revealed altruism apply only to the comparisons employed here. Our general point is that the measured extent of altruism will likely be sensitive to the way in which the residual claimant is defined, and that this will likely interact with subject pool differences.

6. CONCLUSIONS

Behavior in most of the games studied by economists is complex. Ultimatum games offer a cocktail of potential confounds when analyzed rigorously, including risk attitudes, altruism, reciprocity norms, expectations, intentions and the ability to backward induct (see Harrison & McCabe, 1996). Public good contribution games and trust games offer a similar witches' brew, making it hard to convincingly identify what is driving behavior (see Palfrey & Prisbey, 1997; Cox, 2004). And yet these games, and the others identified in Section 2, are the staple of increasingly elaborate and tightly specified models measuring other-regarding preferences, which require striking leaps of faith in joint hypothesis tests.

We focus on one of the least confounded game forms, the Dictator game with varying multipliers, because it offers the humble prospect of allowing the experimenter to measure altruism in an individual. We encounter a generic methodological confound from the role that the "third man" plays in the experiment: the disposition of the residual claims provided by the experimenter matter. Subjects are playing a general equilibrium game, which we have been analyzing as a partial equilibrium game, and inferential loose ends are the result.

We conclude that altruism does indeed exist, but that it is contextual and varies considerably across a given subject pool and specification of residual claimant. Addressing the potential methodological confounds in previous work could affect inferences on the extent of altruism – in some cases it is smaller than prevailing procedures would suggest, but in some cases it is actually larger. This potential methodological confound applies to a wide range of experimental designs.

NOTES

1. Several studies correctly note that concerns about maximizing the total surplus might be a confound when drawing inferences about altruism, fairness or reciprocity. For example, see Frank (1998), Kritikos and Bolle (2001), Charness and Grosskopf (2001), Charness and Rabin (2002), Engelmann and Strobel (2004) and Morganstern (2004). In all cases they hold the disposition of the residual claim constant.

2. Crisp statements of this idea have appeared, most notably in Levine (1998, p. 598) and Camerer (2003, p. 220), but without much development. Although the connections are not immediately obvious, we believe that there have also been precursors in the experimental literatures on "noisy equilibria," "social preferences" and "tournaments."

3. Some commentators view the existence of altruistic preferences as "proving" that traditional economic theory is false in some fundamental way. What it shows is that certain specific assumptions, such as individual preferences being defined solely over own payoffs, are false in some settings and for some people. However popular and inappropriate those assumptions have been, they are not fundamental. Two examples of appropriate interpretations, at the undergraduate and graduate textbook level, may be useful to note. Jack Hirshleifer's (1976) *Price Theory and Applications* (72ff.) contained a simple exposition of altruistic preferences as early as 1976. And in 1978 Layard and Walter's (1978) *Microeconomic Theory* stated simply that "Clearly we are in no way assuming that people are materialistic or selfish. Someone else's welfare may be good for me, be it that of a famine victim in Africa or bureaucrats in Bengal" (p. 126).

4. Without too much exegesis, altruism can be thought of as a more general notion that subsumes other motives identified in the experimental literature, such as fairness or reciprocity. In fact, the word itself has an interesting and surprisingly recent history, first gaining use in English around 1853. The *Oxford English Dictionary* (Second Edition) defines it as "devotion to the welfare of others, regard for others, as a principle of action; opposed to egoism or selfishness." It comes directly from the French word *altruisme*, which in turn was formed by Auguste Comte (1798–1857), a French philosopher regarded as the founder of sociology. Comte was a strong opponent of the view that one could usefully distinguish economic and social aspects of life, and was critical of the writings of many economists for apparently doing so (see Scharff, 2002). Comte based the French word on the Italian *altrui*, which means "of or to others, what is another's." Thus the task of measuring

altruistic behavior is separate from the task of identifying possible motives for altruism, unless assumptions about the structure of those motives are used to help in the identification inference. We prefer a more agnostic approach, which implies that we have nothing to say about those motives. For this reason, and following Andreoni and Miller (2002), we do not attempt to differentiate "pure altruism" from "impure altruism" as these terms have been defined by Andreoni (1990).

5. It is *empirically* more likely: the subgame-perfect Nash Equilibrium predicts that it is equally unlikely.

6. The fact that it is higher could actually be an attraction to risk-lovers, of course.

7. The NRA nominally supports the Second Amendment of the United States Constitution, which provides that individuals have a right to bear arms; see http://www.nra.org/. The ACLU supports the Constitution more generally; see http://www.aclu.org/. Each has some vocal critics in the U.S. media, which presumably indicates that some fraction of the population is also critical of them.

8. In the context of Trust games, for example, there is also a potential confound from uncontrolled attitudes to risk.

9. Since these are public organizations to those the subjects could send their earnings, responses will be censored for those subjects that are planning to contribute to the organization after the experiment.

10. Engelmann and Strobel (2004) make the same point, and design experiments to identify the importance of the aversion to inefficiency relative to other motives. Unfortunately, virtually all of their treatments consider situations in which the decision-maker is indifferent between the choices of interest if motivated solely by own payoff. The exceptions are their treatments N_x, N_y and N_{yi}, and in treatment N_x the allocation that maximizes own payoff and group payoff are the same. In fact, only 55 of their 409 observations are inconsistent with subjects choosing an allocation that maximizes their own payoff, so any evidence for "altruism" in the remaining 354 observations was completely costless to the subject. In their treatment N_y (N_{yi}) subjects faced a multiplier of 4 (9), in the sense that every currency unit they gave up generated 4 (9) currency units for the other two players together. In these two treatments there was considerable evidence of (costly) altruism that cannot otherwise be explained by self-interest. Others that point explicitly to the potential role of inefficiency aversion include Frank (1998), Kritikos and Bolle (2001), Charness and Grosskopf (2001), Charness and Rabin (2002), Cox (2004) and Morganstern (2004).

11. Harrison and McCabe (1996).

12. Levine (1998) does in fact allow for more than two players as well as a role for the altruism for the other players in defining the utility of player i, arguing that this is needed to explain behavior in strategic games such as Ultimatum. In his notation, the case we consider is when $\lambda = 0$. It is noteworthy that although the altruism coefficient is subject-specific, this model assumes that the regard players have for the altruism of other players is the same for all players.

13. There have been some tests of the effect of alternative dispositions of excess contributions in public goods contribution games that set some threshold for production of the public good. For example, Smith (1980) considered alternative monetary rebate rules, and Marks and Croson (1998) consider alternatives ways of using the money in addition to a monetary rebate and "no rebate." The evidence suggests that these treatments generate differences in the level of contributions and their

variance. In the context of Ultimatum game experiments, Frank (1998) told subjects that he would burn any residual! In his experiments he used regular stamps as the experimental *numéraire*. It is arguable that the novelty of seeing cash or cash-like stamps actually put to fire might have been a confound that blunted any net effect. In some nations it is illegal to deliberately destroy legal tender.

14. Their experiment used an endowment of tokens, which were converted to points at the exchange rates shown in the instructions, and then these points were converted to currency at a fixed rate of 10 cents per point. We simplify things by instructing the subjects directly in points.

15. It would be appropriate to re-run the tests undertaken by Andreoni and Miller (2002) with these subjects removed. However, since they find so few violations of rationality with them included, there is not likely to be much change if one does.

16. Multipliers that effectively tax transfers intended to redistribute might engender relatively little altruism, but they are of considerable practical relevance. In public finance, a multiplier less than one corresponds to there being a marginal efficiency cost of redistribution due to the use of a distortionary taxation and/or subsidy scheme for implementing the transfers. Ballard (1988) employs a computable general equilibrium model of the United States to calculate that every dollar transferred from the richest income groups to the poorest groups costs the former between $1.50 and $2.30, so that the marginal efficiency cost of the $1 transferred is between $0.50 and $1.30. Of course, these specific numbers are sensitive to the distortions assumed and used in the transfer policy, but the marginal efficiency cost is generally positive for all relevant policies considered by Ballard (1988). Thus, further study of that domain is worthy, even if it is unlikely to generate considerable levels of altruism in the stark, abstract setting of the laboratory.

17. Although tax exemptions are the important real-world metaphor for the rebate subsidy, and are sizeable, they amount to a *virtual* rebate in the sense that they are rarely actually rebated. An actual rebate would occur if someone made a sizeable donation to a tax-exempt organization but did not allow for that in their regular tax payments to the government, resulting in a physical rebate check being sent back to the taxpayer as a tax refund. Most taxpayers presumably allow for the effects of large donations by taking appropriate deductions throughout the year. This field counterpart of the experimental treatment may be of some importance when subjects are deciding how to respond to rebates in the laboratory.

18. This *a priori* likelihood was well known, given the earlier work of Brown-Kruse and Hummels (1993), Bolton and Katok (1995), Eckel and Grossman (1998) and Andreoni and Vesterlund (2001) with closely related games. Ortmann and Tichy (1999, p. 328) went further and recognized the need for experimenters to "... take gender effects into account when they choose their subjects and/or control for these effects when they evaluate their results."

19. The complete statistical analysis is presented in the longer, working paper version in Davis, Millner, and Reilly (2003). Following the procedures of Harrison and Lesley (1996), one could also use the same methods to predict population responses by substituting population averages for observable characteristics. This requires the maintained assumption that the marginal effect of the observed characteristic is reliably estimated from the lab, sample responses. This may be a strong and untenable assumption, given the self-selection and narrow range of

characteristics inherent in the population that is sampled in the customary laboratory experiment.

20. There have been some experiments in which the trade-off between conflict and cooperation has been directly studied. Durham, Hirshleifer, and Smith (1998) tested the theoretical framework of Hirshleifer (1989, 1991), allowing subjects to choose to allocate experimental tokens into two accounts. One account would expand the group pie, and the other account would increase that individual's share of the pie.

21. Camerer (2004, p. 159) poses the methodological issue as follows, in the context of a discussion about risk attitudes as a potential confound: "... I have chosen examples in which there are several studies or one conclusive one, showing regularities in field data that cannot be easily reconciled with expected utility theory. However, these regularities can be explained by adding extra assumptions. The problem is that these extras are truly ad hoc because each regularity requires a special assumption. Worse, an extra assumption that helps explain one regularity may contradict another. For example, assuming people are risk-preferring (or have convex utility for money) can explain the popularity of long shot horses and lotto, but that assumption predicts stocks should return less than bonds, which is wildly false." There are several problems with this position. First, risk preferences are not a "special assumption" being added in an ad hoc manner; implicitly, Camerer (2004) has assumed risk neutrality when alleging an anomaly in these instances, and *that* is certainly a special assumption. Second, the people that typically engage in one economic activity could be different from the people that engage in the other activity, and simply have different risk preferences. Third, is the outcome domain the same for the first set of gambles and the second set? If not, then there is no problem from a traditional perspective allowing differences in risk attitudes for the same decision-maker in different domains.

22. Eckel and Grossman (1996b, fn. 9, 185) note that one adds a confound by comparing altruism toward an *unknown* individual with altruism toward a *known* charity. They conjecture that their results, showing greater contributions to the charity than the individual, are not due to this confound. Our results confirm their conjecture. Small and Loewenstein (2003) examine this issue by carefully designing an experiment in which the recipient can be identified as a specific individual or family, but no information about the recipient was provided. They find an effect on apparent altruism. More generally, Frohlich, Oppenheimer, and Moore (2001) question the control afforded by anonymous designs, arguing that "double blind" procedures may lead the subjects to view the experiment itself as a game and doubt the existence of the recipient. In such a case the apparent self-interest may just be confounded by the (mistaken) belief that there is "nobody out there" to receive any contribution.

23. The choice of this charity was motivated, in part, by its use in another series of experiments conducted in South Carolina.

24. Fortunately for us, there was no snow until the day after the experiment.

25. The data consist of a panel, so we report overall standard deviations. The formal statistical analysis corrects for correlated observations from the same subject.

26. Detailed results for pass rates and earnings are displayed in Appendix B. The lines in Fig. 3 are based on fractional polynomial fits of the observed choices, but essentially reflect the unconditional averages at each price.

27. For example, Davis, Millner, and Reilly (2003) collected information on the sex, age, race, marital status, family structure, education level, and major of their subjects, but only corrected for sample composition effects of sex. A panel Tobit model replicating their results (their Table 7) is easily extended to show significant effects on pass rates of age, race, education level and major. Whether or not there are large sample composition effects in terms of these variables, the logic of their correction for sample composition effects extends obviously.

28. Our data constitutes a panel, with 10 observations for each individual.

29. Classified as "white" and "non-white" only, given the paucity of breakdowns in the latter group.

30. One dummy variable picks out if the own income or parental income is greater than $65,000 but less than $100,000, and another dummy variable picks out if either is greater than $100,000.

31. A dummy variable picking out if the subject lives with one or more people in the same household.

32. Taking on values 1, $1\frac{1}{2}$, 2, $2\frac{1}{2}$, 3, $3\frac{1}{2}$ and 4. This variable is also controlled for in quadratic and cubic forms.

33. The last interaction is implied by the findings of Eckel and Grossman (1996a) and Andreoni and Vesterlund (2001).

34. There are several ways in which one can generate predicted values using the Tobit model, depending on how one recognizes the effects of censoring at the limits. We assume that the predicted value takes on the limit value if it would otherwise be below or above. Thus we implicitly use the estimated model to construct the linear prediction and then truncate at the limit points if appropriate, where the linear prediction assumes that the random effect for each individual is zero. This procedure is consistent with the latent process that is assumed to be generating the data employed in the Tobit model. An alternative procedure is to predict the expected value conditional on the pass rate being censored. Finally, one can predict the pass rate and ignore the effects of the limit points. These alternatives lead to more or less dampened effects than our preferred prediction procedure, as one might expect *a priori*. There are also other statistical ways to control for sample effects across treatments, such as fixed-effects estimation on each treatment.

35. One possible confound, controlled for by Eckel and Grossman (1996b) following Hoffman, McCabe, Shachat, and Smith (1994), is the *experimenter's* knowledge of specific contributions by each subject. They implemented a double-blind procedure, which ensures that this will not be possible, and which should have been understood as such by the subjects. We are interested in developing experimental procedures for detecting altruism that can be used as components of larger, field experiments trying to identify "trust," and it is desirable that one not add the extra layer of complexity needed for a double-blind design. Moreover, we needed to collect information on the individual characteristics of subjects, and we do not know of an attractive double-blind design that allows one to do that and claim that one cannot use the characteristics to identify (perhaps probabilistically) an individual subject. The only procedures that would permit such an investigation would require "randomized responses" to the questions identifying characteristics, or "randomized questions" with the same response domain, and that would dramatically expand the sample size needed (e.g., Goodstadt & Gruson, 1975). Of course, one is able to collect

information on individual characteristics in extreme cases in which *all* individuals have one or other characteristic, as in the same-sex double-blind experiments of Eckel and Grossman (1996b). They recognize (fn. 9) that one cannot generally identify individual characteristics and associate them with specific individual responses in double-blind experiments.

36. The apparent decline in pass rates for higher returns to giving in C(O) is not statistically significant.

37. A box plot shows the median line, then the interquartile range (the 25th and 75th percentiles) as a box, then the adjacent values as "whiskers" and then outlying observations as dots. See Chambers, Cleveland, Kleiner, and Tukey (1983) for explanations of the box plot.

ACKNOWLEDGMENTS

We are grateful to James Andreoni, Philip Grossman, Andreas Ortmann, Elisabet Rutström, Dale Stahl, a referee and the editor for helpful comments.

REFERENCES

Andreoni, J. (1990). Impure altruism and donations to public goods: A theory of warm-glow giving. *Economic Journal, 100*(June), 464–477.

Andreoni, J. (1995a). Cooperation in public-goods experiments: Kindness or confusion? *American Economic Review, 85*(4), 891–904.

Andreoni, J. (1995b). Warm-glow versus cold-prickle: The effects of positive and negative framing on cooperation in experiments. *Quarterly Journal of Economics, 110*(1), 1–21.

Andreoni, J., & Miller, J. (2002). Giving according to GARP: An experimental test of the consistency of preferences for altruism. *Econometrica, 70*(2), 737–753.

Andreoni, J., & Vesterlund, L. (2001). Which is the fair sex? Gender differences in altruism. *Quarterly Journal of Economics, 116*(1), 293–312.

Ballard, C. L. (1988). The marginal efficiency cost of redistribution. *American Economic Review, 78*(5), 1019–1033.

Berg, J. E., Dickhaut, J., & McCabe, K. (1995). Trust, reciprocity, and social history. *Games and Economic Behavior, 10*, 122–142.

Bolton, G. E., & Katok, E. (1995). An experimental test for gender differences in beneficent behavior. *Economics Letters, 48*, 287–292.

Bolton, G. E., & Ockenfels, A. (2000). ERC: A theory of equity, reciprocity, and competition. *American Economic Review, 90*(1), 166–193.

Brown-Kruse, J., & Hummels, D. (1993). Gender effects in laboratory public goods contribution: Do individuals put their money where their mouth is? *Journal of Economic Behavior and Organization, 22*, 255–267.

Camerer, C. F. (2003). *Behavioral game theory*. Princeton: Princeton University Press.

Camerer, C. F. (2004). Prospect theory in the wild: Evidence from the field. In: C. F. Camerer, G. Loewenstein & M. Rabin (Eds), *Advances in behavioral economics*. Princeton: Princeton University Press.

Capra, C. M., Goeree, J. K., Gomez, R., & Holt, C. A. (1999). Anomalous behavior in a traveler's dilemma. *American Economic Review, 89*(3), 678–690.

Chambers, J. M., Cleveland, W. S., Kleiner, B., & Tukey, P. A. (1983). *Graphical methods for data analysis.* Monterey, CA: Wadsworth.

Charness, G., & Grosskopf, B. (2001). Relative payoffs and happiness: An experimental study. *Journal of Economic Behavior and Organization, 45,* 301–328.

Charness, G., & Rabin, M. (2002). Understanding social preferences with simple tests. *Quarterly Journal of Economics, 117*(3), 817–869.

Cherry, T. L., Frykblom, P., & Shogren, J. F. (2002). Hardnose the Dictator. *American Economic Review, 92*(4), 1218–1221.

Cox, J. C. (2004). How to identify trust and reciprocity. *Games and Economic Behavior, 46*(2), 260–281.

Davis, D. D., Millner, E. L., & Reilly, R. J. (2003). *Subsidy schemes and charitable contributions: A closer look.* Working Paper, Department of Economics, Virginia Commonwealth University.

Davis, D. D., Millner, E. L., & Reilly, R. J. (2005). Subsidy schemes and charitable contributions: A closer look. *Experimental Economics, 8*(2), 85–106.

Durham, Y., Hirshleifer, J., & Smith, V. L. (1998). Do the rich get richer and the poor poorer? Experimental tests of a model of power. *American Economic Review, 88*(4), 970–983.

Eckel, C. C., & Grossman, P. J. (1996a). The relative price of fairness: Gender differences in a punishment game. *Journal of Economic Behavior and Organization, 30,* 143–158.

Eckel, C. C., & Grossman, P. J. (1996b). Altruism in anonymous Dictator games. *Games and Economic Behavior, 16,* 181–191.

Eckel, C. C., & Grossman, P. J. (1998). Are women less selfish than men? Evidence from Dictator experiments. *Economic Journal, 108,* 726–735.

Eckel, C. C., & Grossman, P. J. (2003). Rebate versus matching: Does how we subsidize charitable contributions matter. *Journal of Public Economics, 87,* 681–701.

Engelmann, D., & Strobel, M. (2004). Inequality aversion, efficiency, and maximin preferences in simple distribution experiments. *American Economic Review, 94*(4), 857–869.

Fehr, E., & Falk, A. (1999). Wage rigidity in a competitive incomplete contract market. *Journal of Political Economy, 107*(1), 106–134.

Fehr, E., & Gächter, S. (2000). Cooperation and punishment in public goods experiments. *American Economic Review, 90*(4), 980–994.

Fehr, E., Gächter, S., & Kirchsteiger, G. (1997). Reciprocity as a contract enforcement device: Experimental evidence. *Econometrica, 65,* 833–860.

Fehr, E., Kirchsteiger, G., & Riedl, A. (1993). Does fairness prevent market clearing? An experimental investigation. *Quarterly Journal of Economics, 108,* 437–459.

Fehr, E., & Schmidt, K. (1999). A theory of fairness, competition, and cooperation. *Quarterly Journal of Economics, 114,* 817–868.

Forsythe, R., Horowitz, J. L., Savin, N. E., & Sefton, M. (1994). Fairness in simple bargaining games. *Games and Economic Behavior, 6*(3), 347–369.

Frank, B. (1998). Good news for experimenters: Subjects do not care about your welfare. *Economic Letters, 61,* 171–174.

Frohlich, N., Oppenheimer, J., & Moore, J. B. (2001). Some doubts about measuring self-interest using Dictator experiments: The costs of anonymity. *Journal of Economic Behavior and Organization, 46,* 271–290.

Goeree, J. K., & Holt, C. A. (2001). Ten little treasures of game theory and ten intuitive contradictions. *American Economic Review, 91*(5), 1402–1422.

Goeree, J. K., Holt, C. A., & Palfrey, T. R. (2003). Risk averse behavior in generalized matching pennies games. *Games and Economic Behavior, 45*, 97–113.

Goodstadt, M. S., & Gruson, V. (1975). The randomized response technique: A test on drug use. *Journal of the American Statistical Association, 70*(352), 814–818.

Harrison, G. W., & Lesley, J. C. (1996). Must contingent valuation surveys cost so much? *Journal of Environmental Economics and Management, 31*, 79–95.

Harrison, G. W., & McCabe, K. A. (1996). Expectations and fairness in a simple bargaining experiment. *International Journal of Game Theory, 25*(3), 303–327.

Hirshleifer, J. (1976). *Price theory and applications* (1st ed.). Englewood Cliffs, NJ: Prentice-Hall.

Hirshleifer, J. (1989). Conflict and rent-seeking success functions: Ratio vs. difference models of relative success. *Public Choice, 63*, 101–112.

Hirshleifer, J. (1991). The paradox of power. *Economics and Politics, 3*, 177–200.

Hoffman, E., McCabe, K., Shachat, K., & Smith, V. L. (1994). Preferences, property rights, and anonymity in bargaining games. *Games and Economic Behavior, 7*(3), 346–380.

Kritikos, A., & Bolle, F. (2001). Distributional concerns: Equity- or efficiency-oriented. *Economics Letters, 73*(3), 333–338.

Layard, P. R. G., & Walters, A. A. (1978). *Microeconomic theory*. St. Louis: McGraw-Hill.

Ledyard, J. (1995). Public goods: A survey of experimental research. In: J. Kagel & A. E. Roth (Eds), *Handbook of experimental economics*. Princeton: Princeton University Press.

Levine, D. K. (1998). Modeling altruism and spitefulness in experiments. *Review of Economic Dynamics, 1*, 593–622.

Marks, M., & Croson, R. (1998). Alternative rebate rules in the provision of a threshold public good: An experimental investigation. *Journal of Public Economics, 67*, 195–220.

McKelvey, R. D., & Palfrey, T. R. (1992). An experimental study of the centipede game. *Econometrica, 60*, 803–836.

Morganstern, A. (2004). Efficiency concerns and incentive provision – an experimental study. *Economics Letters, 83*, 335–341.

Ortmann, A., & Tichy, L. K. (1999). Gender differences in the laboratory: Evidence from prisoner's dilemma games. *Journal of Economic Behavior and Organization, 39*, 327–339.

Ostrom, E., Walker, J., & Gardner, R. (1992). Covenants with and without a sword: Self-governance is possible. *American Journal of Political Science, 86*(2), 404–417.

Palfrey, T. R., & Prisbey, J. E. (1997). Anomalous behavior in public goods experiments: How much and why? *American Economic Review, 87*(5), 829–846.

Plott, C. R. (1982). Industrial organization theory and experimental economics. *Journal of Economic Literature, 20*, 1485–1527.

Scharff, R. C. (2002). *Compte after positivism*. New York: Cambridge University Press.

Small, D. A., & Loewenstein, G. A. (2003). Helping a victim or helping the victim: Altruism and identifiability. *Journal of Risk and Uncertainty, 26*(1), 5–16.

Smith, V. L. (1980). Experiments with a decentralized mechanism for public good decisions. *American Economic Review, 70*(4), 584–599.

Sonnemans, J., Schram, A., & Offerman, T. (1998). Public goods provision and public bad prevention: The effect of framing. *Journal of Economic Behavior and Organization, 34*, 143–161.

Whittington, D. (2002). Improving the performance of contingent valuation studies in developing countries. *Environmental and Resource Economics, 22*(1–2), 323–367.

APPENDIX A. EXPERIMENTAL INSTRUCTIONS

A.1. Welcome to the Experiment

This is an experiment in the economics of decision-making. Your participation in this experiment is voluntary. However, we think you will find the experiment interesting. You will be paid $10 at the end of the experiment for your participation, and you might also earn money throughout different parts of the experiment. Please be careful to respect the privacy of other participants during the experiment, and refrain from interacting with them.

Before proceeding with tasks for which you will be paid additional money, we first need to collect some basic information about you. Please take a few moments to fill out the form. Your answers to these questions will be kept confidential, and will be used for statistical purposes only. We will be using the attached identification number to keep track of who answered which questions, but we will not be identifying your responses with your SSN or your name.

You should raise your hand when you are finished with this form so that the assistants can collect it. Once all the forms have been collected, we will proceed with the rest of the experiment. We will wait for everyone to have time to finish each task, so there is no need to hurry.

ID _____

Some Questions About You

In this survey most of the questions asked are descriptive. We will not be grading your answers and your responses are completely confidential. Please think carefully about each question and give your best answers.

1. What is your AGE? _____ years

2. What is your sex? (Circle one number)
01 Male
02 Female

3. Which of the following categories best describes you? (Circle one number)
01 White   06 Hispanic
02 African-American   07 Hispanic

03	African	08	Mixed Race
04	Asian-American	09	Other
05	Asian		

4. What is your major? (Circle one number)
01 Accounting
02 Economics
03 Finance
04 Business Administration, other than Accounting, Economics, or Finance
05 Education
06 Engineering
07 Health Professions
08 Public Affairs or Social Services
09 Biological Sciences
10 Math, Computer Sciences, or Physical Sciences
11 Social Sciences or History
12 Humanities
13 Psychology
14 Other Fields

5. What is your class standing? (Circle one number)

01	Freshman	04	Senior
02	Sophomore	05	Masters
03	Junior	06	Doctoral

6. What is the *highest* level of education *you* expect to complete? (Circle one number)
01 Bachelor's degree
02 Master's degree
03 Doctoral degree
04 First professional degree

7. What was the *highest* level of education that your *father* (or male guardian) completed? (Circle one number)
01 Less than high school
02 GED or High School Equivalency
03 High school
04 Vocational or trade school
05 College or university
06 Post Graduate

8.   What was the *highest* level of education that your *mother* (or female guardian) completed? (Circle one number)
01   Less than high school
02   GED or High School Equivalency
03   High School
04   Vocational or trade school
05   College or university
06   Post Graduate

9.   What is your citizenship status in the United States? (Circle one number)
01   US Citizen
02   Resident Alien
03   Non-Resident Alien
04   Other Status

10.   Are you a foreign student on a Student Visa? (Circle one number)
01   Yes
02   No

11.   Are you currently... (Circle one number)
01   Single and never married?
02   Married?
03   Separated, divorced or widowed?

12.   On a 4-point scale, what is your current GPA if you are doing a Bachelor's degree, or what was it when you did a Bachelor's degree? This GPA should refer to all of your coursework, not just the current year. (Circle one number)
01   Between 3.75 and 4.0 GPA (mostly A's)
02   Between 3.25 and 3.74 GPA (about half A's and half B's)
03   Between 2.75 and 3.24 GPA (mostly B's)
04   Between 2.25 and 2.74 GPA (about half B's and half C's)
05   Between 1.75 and 2.24 GPA (mostly C's)
06   Between 1.25 and 1.74 GPA (about half C's and half D's)
07   Less than 1.25 (mostly D's or below)
08   Have not taken courses for which grades are given.

13.   How many people live in your household? Include yourself, your spouse and any dependents. Do not include your parents or roommates unless you claim them as dependents. _____

14. Please circle the category below that describes the total amount of INCOME earned in 2003 by the people in your household (as "household" is defined in question 13). (Consider all forms of income, including salaries, tips, interest and dividend payments, scholarship support, student loans, parental support, social security, alimony, child support and others.) (Circle one number)
01 $15,000 or under
02 $15,001–$25,000
03 $25,001–$35,000
04 $35,001–$50,000
05 $50,001–$65,000
06 $65,001–$80,000
07 $80,001–$100,000
08 Over $100,000

15. Please circle the category below that describes the total amount of INCOME earned in 2003 by your parents. (Consider all forms of income, including salaries, tips, interest and dividend payments, social security, alimony, child support, and others.) (Circle one number)
01 $15,000 or under
02 $15,001–$25,000
03 $25,001–$35,000
04 $35,001–$50,000
05 $50,001–$65,000
06 $65,001–$80,000
07 $80,001–$100,000
08 Over $100,000
09 Don't Know

16. Do you work part-time, full-time, or neither? (Circle one number)
01 Part-time
02 Full-time
03 Neither

17. Before taxes, what do you get paid? (fill in only one)
01 _____ per hour before taxes
02 _____ per week before taxes
03 _____ per month before taxes
04 _____ per year before taxes
05 _____ not applicable

18.   Do you currently smoke cigarettes? (Circle one number)
01   Yes
02   No
    If yes, approximately how much do you smoke in one day? _____ packs

18b. Who was the lecturer in the class that you were in when you signed up
for this experiment? (Circle one number)

01	Arthur Gilbert	07	Laurie Johnson
02	George Potts	08	Irvin Jones
03	Paul Colomy	09	Keith Miller
04	Terrency Toy	10	Tracy Ehlers
05	Sheldon York	11	None of the above, or cannot recall
06	Michael Monahan		

**For the remaining questions, please select the one response that best matches
your reaction to the statement.**

19. "I believe that fate will mostly control what happens to me in the years
ahead."

Strongly Disagree	Disagree	Slightly Disagree	Slightly Agree	Agree	Strongly Agree

20. "I am usually able to protect my personal interests."

Strongly Disagree	Disagree	Slightly Disagree	Slightly Agree	Agree	Strongly Agree

21. "When I get what I want, it's usually because I'm lucky."

Strongly Disagree	Disagree	Slightly Disagree	Slightly Agree	Agree	Strongly Agree

22. "In order to have my plans work, I make sure that they fit in with the
desires of people who have power over me."

Strongly Disagree	Disagree	Slightly Disagree	Slightly Agree	Agree	Strongly Agree

23. "I have mostly determined what has happened to me in my life so far."

Strongly Disagree	Disagree	Slightly Disagree	Slightly Agree	Agree	Strongly Agree

24. "Whether or not I get into a car accident depends mostly on the other
drivers."

Strongly Disagree	Disagree	Slightly Disagree	Slightly Agree	Agree	Strongly Agree

25."Chance occurrences determined most of the important events in my past."

| Strongly Disagree | Disagree | Slightly Disagree | Slightly Agree | Agree | Strongly Agree |

26."I feel like other people will mostly determine what happens to me in the future."

| Strongly Disagree | Disagree | Slightly Disagree | Slightly Agree | Agree | Strongly Agree |

27."When I make plans, I am almost certain to make them work."

| Strongly Disagree | Disagree | Slightly Disagree | Slightly Agree | Agree | Strongly Agree |

28."Getting what I want requires pleasing those people above me."

| Strongly Disagree | Disagree | Slightly Disagree | Slightly Agree | Agree | Strongly Agree |

29."Whether or not I get into a car accident depends mostly on how good a driver I am."

| Strongly Disagree | Disagree | Slightly Disagree | Slightly Agree | Agree | Strongly Agree |

30."Often there is no chance of protecting my personal interests from bad luck."

| Strongly Disagree | Disagree | Slightly Disagree | Slightly Agree | Agree | Strongly Agree |

31."When I get what I want, it's usually because I worked hard for it."

| Strongly Disagree | Disagree | Slightly Disagree | Slightly Agree | Agree | Strongly Agree |

32."Most of my personal history was controlled by other people who had power over me."

| Strongly Disagree | Disagree | Slightly Disagree | Slightly Agree | Agree | Strongly Agree |

33."Whether or not I get into a car accident is mostly a matter of luck."

| Strongly Disagree | Disagree | Slightly Disagree | Slightly Agree | Agree | Strongly Agree |

34."I think that I will mostly control what happens to me in future years."

| Strongly Disagree | Disagree | Slightly Disagree | Slightly Agree | Agree | Strongly Agree |

35. "People like myself have very little chance of protecting our personal interests when they conflict with those of strong pressure groups."

| Strongly Disagree | Disagree | Slightly Disagree | Slightly Agree | Agree | Strongly Agree |

36. "It's not always wise for me to plan too far ahead because many things turn out to be a matter of good or bad fortune."

| Strongly Disagree | Disagree | Slightly Disagree | Slightly Agree | Agree | Strongly Agree |

O, OC

At the beginning of the experiment you selected an ID number by picking an envelope from us. Would those of you that selected an *odd* ID number please proceed to a separate room? You will undertake the rest of the experiment there, with the experimenter that is going with you. Thank you! The rest of you should remain here.

O

In this experiment you are asked to make a series of choices about how to divide points between yourself and one other subject in the *other* room. You and the other subject will be paired randomly and you will not be told each other's identity.

As you divide the points, you and the other subject will each earn money. Every point that you earn will be worth 10, 20, 30 or 40 cents, depending on the choice. For example, if your points are worth 10 cents each and you earn 58 points you will make $5.80 for that choice. Similarly for the earnings of the other player.

Each choice you make is similar to the following:

Divide 50 points: *Hold* _____ @ $0.10 each, and *Pass* _____ @ $0.20 each.

In this choice you must divide 50 points. You can keep all of the points, keep some and pass some, or pass all of the points. In this example, you will receive 10 cents for every point you hold, and the other player will receive 20 cents for every point you pass. For example, if you hold 50 and pass 0 points, you will receive 50 × $0.10 = $5.00, and the other player will receive no points and $0. If you hold 0 and pass 50 points, you will receive no points and $0, and the other player will receive 50 × $0.20 = $10.00. However, you could choose any number between 0 and 50 to hold. For instance, you could choose to hold 29 tokens and pass 21. In this case you would earn 29 points, or 29 × $0.10 = $2.90, and the other subject would receive 21 × $0.20 = $4.20.

Here is another example:

Divide 50 points: *Hold* _____ @ **$0.30 each, and** *Pass* _____ @ **$0.30 each.**

In this example every point you hold earns you 30 cents, and every point you pass earns the other subject 30 cents.

Important note: In all cases you can choose any number to hold and any number to pass, but the number of points you hold plus the number of points you pass must equal the total number of points to divide.

We will select one of your decisions to actually implement at the end of the session. We have allowed for up to $32 to be paid out for the decision that is selected, multiplied by the number of pairs of subjects here today. This is the maximum amount that can be paid out, depending on your choices and the roll of the die selecting the decision to be implemented. Depending on your choices, and the decision picked to be implemented, we might not need to pay out as much as $32 per pair.

Please do not talk. Are there any questions?

_____

C

In this experiment you are asked to make a series of choices about how to divide points between yourself and a public charity. The name and address of the charity is in a sealed envelope, which we will open at the end of the session. We will write a check to the charity at the end of the session, seal it in an envelope, and you can come with us to the nearest public mailbox to see it mailed.

As you divide the points, you and the charity will each earn money. Every point that you earn will be worth 10, 20, 30 or 40 cents, depending on the choice. For example, if your points are worth 10 cents each and you earn 58 points you will make $5.80 for that choice. Similarly for the earnings of the charity.

Each choice you make is similar to the following:

Divide 50 points: *Hold* _____ @ **$0.10 each, and** *Pass* _____ @ **$0.20 each.**

In this choice you must divide 50 points. You can keep all of the points, keep some and pass some, or pass all of the points. In this example, you will receive 10 cents for every point you hold, and the charity will receive 20 cents for every point you pass. For example, if you hold 50 and pass 0 points, you will receive $50 \times \$0.10 = \$5.00$, and the charity will receive no points and $0. If you hold 0 and pass 50 points, you will receive no points and $0, and the charity will receive $50 \times \$0.20 = \$10.00$. However, you could choose any number between 0 and 50 to hold. For instance, you could choose to hold 29 tokens and pass 21. In this case you would earn 29 points, or $29 \times \$0.10 = \$2.90$, and the charity would receive $21 \times \$0.20 = \$4.20$.

Here is another example:

Divide 50 points: *Hold* _____ @ **$0.30 each, and** *Pass* _____ @ **$0.30 each.**

In this example every point you hold earns you 30 cents, and every point you pass earns the charity 30 cents.

Important note: In all cases you can choose any number to hold and any number to pass, but the number of points you hold plus the number of points you pass must equal the total number of points to divide.

We will select one of your decisions to actually implement at the end of the session. We have allowed for up to $32 to be paid out for the decision that is selected, multiplied by the number of subjects here today. This is the maximum amount that can be paid out, depending on your choices and the roll of the die selecting the decision to be implemented. Depending on your choices, and the decision picked to be implemented, we might not need to pay out as much as $32 per pair.

Please do not talk. Are there any questions?

OC

In this experiment you are asked to make a series of choices about how to divide points between yourself and one other subject in the *other* room. You and the other subject will be paired randomly and you will not be told each other's identity.

As you divide the points, you and the other subject will each earn money. Every point that you earn will be worth 10, 20, 30 or 40 cents, depending on the choice. For example, if your points are worth 10 cents each and you earn 58 points you will make $5.80 for that choice. Similarly for the earnings of the other player.

Each choice you make is similar to the following:

Divide 50 points: *Hold* _____ @ **$0.10 each, and** *Pass* _____ @ **$0.20 each.**

In this choice you must divide 50 points. You can keep all of the points, keep some and pass some, or pass all of the points. In this example, you will receive 10 cents for every point you hold, and the other player will receive 20 cents for every point you pass. For example, if you hold 50 and pass 0 points, you will receive $50 \times \$0.10 = \$5.00$, and the other player will receive no points and $0. If you hold 0 and pass 50 points, you will receive no points and $0, and the other player will receive $50 \times \$0.20 = \$10.00$. However, you could choose any number between 0 and 50 to hold. For instance, you could choose to hold 29 tokens and pass 21. In this case you would earn 29 points, or $29 \times \$0.10 = \$2.90$, and the other subject would receive $21 \times \$0.20 = \$4.20$.

Here is another example:

Divide 50 points: *Hold* _____ @ **$0.30 each, and** *Pass* _____ @ **$0.30 each.**

In this example every point you hold earns you 30 cents, and every point you pass earns the other subject 30 cents.

Important note: In all cases you can choose any number to hold and any number to pass, but the number of points you hold plus the number of points you pass must equal the total number of points to divide.

We will select one of your decisions to actually implement at the end of the session. We have allowed for up to $32 to be paid out for the decision that is selected, multiplied by the number of pairs of subjects here today. This is the maximum amount that can be paid out, depending on your choices and the roll of the die selecting the decision to be implemented. Depending on your choices, and the decision picked to be implemented, we might not need to pay out as much as $32 per pair. Any monies left will be paid to a public charity. The name and address of the charity is in a sealed envelope which we will open at the end of the session. We will write a check to the charity at the end of the session, seal it in an envelope, and you can come with us to the nearest public mailbox to see it mailed.

Please do not talk. Are there any questions?

CO

In this experiment you are asked to make a series of choices about how to divide points between yourself and a public charity. The name and address of the charity is in a sealed envelope which we will open at the end of the session. We will write a check to the charity at the end of the session, seal it in an envelope, and you can come with us to the nearest public mailbox to see it mailed.

As you divide the points, you and the charity will each earn money. Every point that you earn will be worth 10, 20, 30 or 40 cents, depending on the choice. For example, if your points are worth 10 cents each and you earn 58 points you will make $5.80 for that choice. Similarly for the earnings of the charity.

Each choice you make is similar to the following:

Divide 50 points: *Hold* _____ @ **$0.10 each, and** *Pass* _____ @ **$0.20 each.**

In this choice you must divide 50 points. You can keep all of the points, keep some and pass some, or pass all of the points. In this example, you will receive 10 cents for every point you hold, and the charity will receive 20 cents for every point you pass. For example, if you hold 50 and pass 0 points, you will receive $50 \times \$0.10 = \$5.00$, and the charity will receive no points and $0. If you hold 0 and pass 50 points, you will receive no points and $0, and the charity will receive $50 \times \$0.20 = \$10.00$. However, you could choose any number between 0 and 50 to hold. For instance, you could choose to hold 29 tokens and pass 21. In this case you would earn 29 points, or $29 \times \$0.10 = \$2.90$, and the charity would receive $21 \times \$0.20 = \$4.20$.

Here is another example:

Divide 50 points: *Hold* _____ @ **$0.30 each, and** *Pass* _____ @ **$0.30 each.**

In this example every point you hold earns you 30 cents, and every point you pass earns the charity 30 cents.

Important note: In all cases you can choose any number to hold and any number to pass, but the number of points you hold plus the number of points you pass must equal the total number of points to divide.

We will select one of your decisions to actually implement at the end of the session. We have allowed for up to $32 to be paid out for the decision that is selected, multiplied by the number of subjects here today. This is the maximum amount that can be paid out, depending on your choices and the roll of the die selecting the decision to be implemented. Depending on your choices, and the decision picked to be implemented, we might not need to pay out as much as $32 per pair. Any monies left will be paid to one other subject in the room, selected at random.

Please do not talk. Are there any questions?

P–O and OC

In this experiment we are going to ask you to predict the choices of the people in the other room. In a moment we will show you the instructions that they are being asked to follow. They will make 10 choices, as explained in the instructions we will give you. You should write down on the Decision Sheet your prediction of the *average* response to each choice from all of the people in the other room. In other words, for choice #1, write down what you predict the average response will be. Similarly for choices 2 through 10.

You will be rewarded based on your accuracy. As the instructions will explain, one of these 10 choices will be picked at random for implementation, and we will use that choice to decide who was the most accurate at predicting the choices made in the other room.

The person that predicts the average response most accurately will receive $20, and the three people that predict the average response best after that person will each receive $10. In the event of a tie, we will toss coins to see who gets the rewards. So the best four predictions will get a reward.

These rewards are in addition to any money you may receive from the decisions of the people in the other room.

The subjects in the other room do not know that you are being paid to predict their responses.

Please do not talk between yourselves. Here are the instructions given to the subjects in the other room. Please read them quietly, and write down your predictions. Do you have any questions?

ID: A_____

Decision Form

Directions: Please fill in the blanks below. Make sure that the amount of points listed under *Hold* plus the number listed under *Pass* equals the *total* number of points available. At the end of the experiment we will pick one of these decisions at random to actually implement.

1. Divide 75 points: *Hold* _____ @ $0.20 each, and *Pass* _____ @ $0.40 each.
2. Divide 40 points: *Hold* _____ @ $0.20 each, and *Pass* _____ @ $0.60 each.
3. Divide 75 points: *Hold* _____ @ $0.20 each, and *Pass* _____ @ $0.20 each.
4. Divide 60 points: *Hold* _____ @ $0.20 each, and *Pass* _____ @ $0.40 each.
5. Divide 40 points: *Hold* _____ @ $0.50 each, and *Pass* _____ @ $0.50 each.
6. Divide 100 points: *Hold* _____ @ $0.10 each, and *Pass* _____ @ $0.20 each.
7. Divide 60 points: *Hold* _____ @ $0.20 each, and *Pass* _____ @ $0.30 each.
8. Divide 80 points: *Hold* _____ @ $0.20 each, and *Pass* _____ @ $0.40 each.
9. Divide 40 points: *Hold* _____ @ $0.20 each, and *Pass* _____ @ $0.50 each.
10. Divide 40 points: *Hold* _____ @ $0.20 each, and *Pass* _____ @ $0.80 each.

ID: B_____

Decision Form

Directions: Please fill in the blanks below. Make sure that the amount of points listed under *Hold* plus the number listed under *Pass* equals the *total* number of points available. At the end of the experiment we will pick one of these decisions at random to actually implement.

1. Divide 40 points: *Hold* _____ @ $0.20 each, and *Pass* _____ @ $0.80 each.
2. Divide 40 points: *Hold* _____ @ $0.20 each, and *Pass* _____ @ $0.50 each.
3. Divide 80 points: *Hold* _____ @ $0.20 each, and *Pass* _____ @ $0.40 each.
4. Divide 40 points: *Hold* _____ @ $0.50 each, and *Pass* _____ @ $0.50 each.
5. Divide 60 points: *Hold* _____ @ $0.20 each, and *Pass* _____ @ $0.30 each.
6. Divide 100 points: *Hold* _____ @ $0.10 each, and *Pass* _____ @ $0.20 each.
7. Divide 60 points: *Hold* _____ @ $0.20 each, and *Pass* _____ @ $0.40 each.
8. Divide 75 points: *Hold* _____ @ $0.20 each, and *Pass* _____ @ $0.20 each.
9. Divide 40 points: *Hold* _____ @ $0.20 each, and *Pass* _____ @ $0.60 each.
10. Divide 75 points: *Hold* _____ @ $0.20 each, and *Pass* _____ @ $0.40 each.

ID: C_____

Decision Form

Directions: Please fill in the blanks below. Make sure that the amount of points listed under *Hold* plus the number listed under *Pass* equals the *total* number of points available. At the end of the experiment we will pick one of these decisions at random to actually implement.

1. Divide 100 points: *Hold* _____ @ $0.10 each, and *Pass* _____ @ $0.20 each.
2. Divide 40 points: *Hold* _____ @ $0.20 each, and *Pass* _____ @ $0.60 each.
3. Divide 60 points: *Hold* _____ @ $0.20 each, and *Pass* _____ @ $0.30 each.
4. Divide 60 points: *Hold* _____ @ $0.20 each, and *Pass* _____ @ $0.40 each.
5. Divide 40 points: *Hold* _____ @ $0.20 each, and *Pass* _____ @ $0.50 each.
6. Divide 75 points: *Hold* _____ @ $0.20 each, and *Pass* _____ @ $0.40 each.
7. Divide 75 points: *Hold* _____ @ $0.20 each, and *Pass* _____ @ $0.20 each.
8. Divide 40 points: *Hold* _____ @ $0.20 each, and *Pass* _____ @ $0.80 each.
9. Divide 40 points: *Hold* _____ @ $0.50 each, and *Pass* _____ @ $0.50 each.
10. Divide 80 points: *Hold* _____ @ $0.20 each, and *Pass* _____ @ $0.40 each.

ID: AP_____

Decision Form

Directions: Please fill in the blanks below. Make sure that the amount of points listed under *Hold* plus the number listed under *Pass* equals the *total* number of points available. You should write down what you think the *average* response in the other room will be to each decision.

1. Divide 75 points: *Hold* _____ @ $0.20 each, and *Pass* _____ @ $0.40 each.
2. Divide 40 points: *Hold* _____ @ $0.20 each, and *Pass* _____ @ $0.60 each.
3. Divide 75 points: *Hold* _____ @ $0.20 each, and *Pass* _____ @ $0.20 each.
4. Divide 60 points: *Hold* _____ @ $0.20 each, and *Pass* _____ @ $0.40 each.
5. Divide 40 points: *Hold* _____ @ $0.50 each, and *Pass* _____ @ $0.50 each.
6. Divide 100 points: *Hold* _____ @ $0.10 each, and *Pass* _____ @ $0.20 each.
7. Divide 60 points: *Hold* _____ @ $0.20 each, and *Pass* _____ @ $0.30 each.
8. Divide 80 points: *Hold* _____ @ $0.20 each, and *Pass* _____ @ $0.40 each.
9. Divide 40 points: *Hold* _____ @ $0.20 each, and *Pass* _____ @ $0.50 each.
10. Divide 40 points: *Hold* _____ @ $0.20 each, and *Pass* _____ @ $0.80 each.

ID: BP_____

Decision Form

Directions: Please fill in the blanks below. Make sure that the amount of points listed under *Hold* plus the number listed under *Pass* equals the *total* number of points available. You should write down what you think the *average* response in the other room will be to each decision.

1. Divide 40 points: *Hold* _____ @ $0.20 each, and *Pass* _____ @ $0.80 each.
2. Divide 40 points: *Hold* _____ @ $0.20 each, and *Pass* _____ @ $0.50 each.
3. Divide 80 points: *Hold* _____ @ $0.20 each, and *Pass* _____ @ $0.40 each.
4. Divide 40 points: *Hold* _____ @ $0.50 each, and *Pass* _____ @ $0.50 each.
5. Divide 60 points: *Hold* _____ @ $0.20 each, and *Pass* _____ @ $0.30 each.
6. Divide 100 points: *Hold* _____ @ $0.10 each, and *Pass* _____ @ $0.20 each.
7. Divide 60 points: *Hold* _____ @ $0.20 each, and *Pass* _____ @ $0.40 each.
8. Divide 75 points: *Hold* _____ @ $0.20 each, and *Pass* _____ @ $0.20 each.
9. Divide 40 points: *Hold* _____ @ $0.20 each, and *Pass* _____ @ $0.60 each.
10. Divide 75 points: *Hold* _____ @ $0.20 each, and *Pass* _____ @ $0.40 each.

ID: CP_____

Decision Form

Directions: Please fill in the blanks below. Make sure that the amount of points listed under *Hold* plus the number listed under *Pass* equals the *total* number of points available. You should write down what you think the *average* response in the other room will be to each decision.

1. Divide 100 points: *Hold* _____ @ $0.10 each, and *Pass* _____ @ $0.20 each.
2. Divide 40 points: *Hold* _____ @ $0.20 each, and *Pass* _____ @ $0.60 each.
3. Divide 60 points: *Hold* _____ @ $0.20 each, and *Pass* _____ @ $0.30 each.
4. Divide 60 points: *Hold* _____ @ $0.20 each, and *Pass* _____ @ $0.40 each.
5. Divide 40 points: *Hold* _____ @ $0.20 each, and *Pass* _____ @ $0.50 each.
6. Divide 75 points: *Hold* _____ @ $0.20 each, and *Pass* _____ @ $0.40 each.
7. Divide 75 points: *Hold* _____ @ $0.20 each, and *Pass* _____ @ $0.20 each.
8. Divide 40 points: *Hold* _____ @ $0.20 each, and *Pass* _____ @ $0.80 each.
9. Divide 40 points: *Hold* _____ @ $0.50 each, and *Pass* _____ @ $0.50 each.
10. Divide 80 points: *Hold* _____ @ $0.20 each, and *Pass* _____ @ $0.40 each

APPENDIX B. DETAILED STATISTICAL RESULTS

Figs. A1–A4 display box plots of the distribution of apparent pass rates for each treatment and return to giving.[37] These plots reveal that the variations in apparent pass rates displayed in the text are primarily due to variations in one tail or the other of the distribution, rather than shifts in the whole distribution. This points to the possibility that some characteristic of the individual helps explain changes in altruism as the return to giving or the treatment changes. This is borne out by the statistical analysis reported in the text, and the estimation results reported below for each treatment. These estimates underlie the predictions in Fig. 4.

Fig. A5 displays a scatterplot of earnings for each player in each treatment. These earnings are denominated in dollars and cents. In general they indicate that subjects did not, as a whole, seek to equalize earnings, since the tendency is for the Dictator to get more in relation to the Peasant. However, within each scatterplot it is easy to see that some subjects may have been equalizing earnings, even if it is not the dominant tendency.

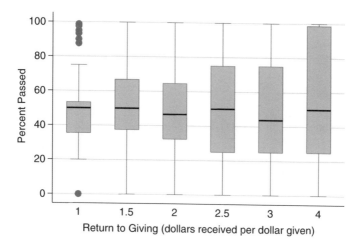

Fig. A1. Apparent Altruism in Treatment C.

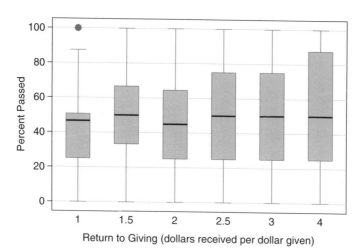

Fig. A2. Apparent Altruism in Treatment C(O).

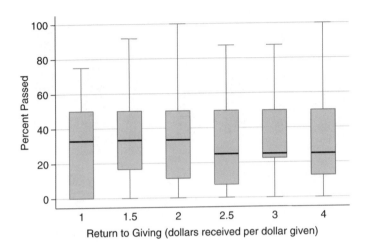

Fig. A3.   Apparent Altruism in Treatment O.

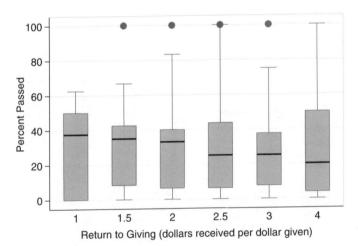

Fig. A4.   Apparent Altruism in Treatment O(C).

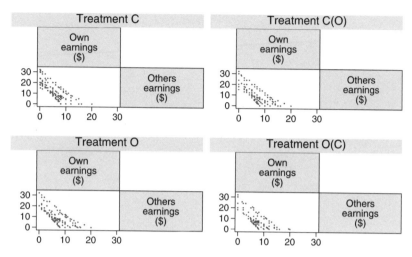

Fig. A5. Scatterplots of Earnings.

THE VOLUNTARY PROVISION OF A PUBLIC GOOD WITH BINDING MULTI-ROUND COMMITMENTS

Matthew A. Halloran, James M. Walker and Arlington W. Williams

ABSTRACT

This paper examines binding multi-round commitments (MRCs) to the group account in a repeated voluntary contributions mechanism (VCM) game. Before each five-round interval, subjects in a four-person group are given the option to commit a portion of their endowments to the group account for each of the next five rounds. Decision rounds proceed, with each subject's commitment acting as the binding minimum of his group-account allocation for each round. The opportunity to make MRCs does not increase mean allocations to the group account relative to a control treatment. However, commitments do have implications for reciprocal behavior within groups, leading to higher outcome variances across groups in the MRCs treatment.

Experiments Investigating Fundraising and Charitable Contributors
Research in Experimental Economics, Volume 11, 225–246
ISSN: 0193-2306/doi:10.1016/S0193-2306(06)11009-1

1. INTRODUCTION

The experimental environment known as the voluntary contributions mechanism (VCM) has been studied extensively in an attempt to understand factors affecting the severity of the free-rider problem in the voluntary provision of a public good. In the traditional VCM, subjects are assigned to a group, and each receives an identical endowment of tokens. Each subject then simultaneously chooses to allocate a portion of his endowment in the group account and the remainder in his private account. A token placed in the group account yields a positive return to each group member, regardless of their own allocation. A token placed in a subject's private account yields a positive return only to that subject. In the most commonly studied form of the VCM, the return from the group account and the return from the private account are symmetric across individuals, and are structured so that the group optimum is for all tokens to be allocated to the group account. At the same time, if all subjects' preferences are based solely on monetary returns, and this is common information, the Nash equilibrium strategy for any individual is to place all their tokens in their private account.

The stylized facts emerging from this type of experiment are that allocations to the group account exceed zero tokens on average, but are substantially below the Pareto optimal level of 100%. Initially, allocations to the group account tend to average close to 50% of the endowment. There is, however, considerable heterogeneity across individuals in their allocations. Further, when the game is repeated over a number of decision rounds, average group allocations tend to diminish.[1]

Previous VCM studies suggest that reciprocity considerations play an important role in explaining allocations to the group account.[2] In the repeated VCM environment, expectations of reciprocity by other group members may lead a subject to make a group-account allocation in one decision round in order to induce larger group-account allocations from other group members in future rounds. This paper reports experiments that add to the traditional repeated-VCM setting by allowing subjects to make binding multi-round commitments (MRC) to the group account, before subjects choose their final allocation. These commitments are made simultaneously within the group, and the aggregate group commitment is made public before final allocations are made. This process is repeated at five-round intervals.

The MRC environment we are investigating, while essentially artificial, has similarities to naturally occurring examples of public-goods fund raising. The multi-round nature of commitments is similar to mechanisms of public-goods provision in which contributors commit to contribute a minimum amount at repeating intervals of time. For example, The Public Broadcasting System operates fund drives that regularly announce the current level of pledges, which are often collected through regular payroll deductions. Similarly, religious organizations rely significantly on members making pledges toward regular, weekly or monthly, donations. Such pledges are often made public as part of "real time" fund drives.[3]

We find that subjects on average tend to make commitments in the range of one quarter to one third of endowments. However, commitments do not increase overall average group-account allocations relative to a control VCM environment without commitment opportunities. On the other hand, further analysis reveals that commitments affect within-group behavior differentially. We find that the variance of outcomes across groups is larger in MRC experiments than in control experiments.

The paper is structured as follows. Section 2 discusses previous experimental research of a similar nature to this study. Section 3 provides a description of the experimental design. Section 4 provides several conjectures of behavior based on subjects following norms of reciprocity. Section 5 presents the experimental results. Finally, Section 6 contains concluding remarks.

2. PREVIOUS EXPERIMENTAL RESEARCH

Chen and Komorita (1994) examine several forms of commitment mechanisms in a two-stage game that is repeated for 10 decision rounds. In the first stage of each round, subjects in a five-person group are given the opportunity to make a commitment. The second stage of each round is a VCM game. Their "binding pledge" condition is most analogous to the commitment mechanism of this study. In each decision round, subjects make a binding minimum commitment to the group account. In this condition, they find that subjects tend to commit between 20% and 30% of their endowments. [4] However, levels of group allocations are not increased relative to experiments without commitment opportunities. The MRC design of this study allows further examination of Chen and Komorita's conclusions, and examination of the extent to which MRCs have a different impact than single-round commitment mechanisms. In addition, Chen and Komorita do not report results related to how the impact of commitments may vary across decision-making groups or decision rounds. As discussed below, such behavior is important in understanding the role of commitment mechanisms more fully.

Bochet and Putterman (2004) examine a treatment condition with non-binding single-period promises to allocate a certain amount to the group account before each round. They find that group-account allocations are not significantly increased relative to control experiments unless subjects also have the ability to sanction each other. However, similar to our results, Bochet and Putterman (2004) also found that non-binding promises lead to a larger dispersion of outcomes across groups than in control experiments. Moreover, comparing average group allocations between groups in the control experiments and those in the treatment experiments, they find that those groups with the highest group allocations and those with the lowest group allocations are observed in the condition with non-binding numerical promises.

Other studies have employed some aspect of a "real time" public goods environment developed by Dorsey (1991). In Dorsey's "real time" VCM environment, a decision round begins with subjects simultaneously making individual allocation decisions to the group account. The decision round continues for a publicly announced time interval. During this time, subjects are able to adjust their group-account allocation, with adjustments becoming public information. In the *increase only* treatment subjects can only increase their group allocation. In the *increase/decrease* treatment, subjects can either increase or decrease their allocation. In the *increase only* treatment, group-account allocations increase relative to the allocations observed in control experiments, and allocations do not tend to decay across decision rounds. In the *increase/decrease* treatment, group allocations tend to rapidly decay over time.[5]

Kurzban and Houser (2001) study a variation of Dorsey's environment they refer to as a "circular" public goods game. At the beginning of each decision round, subjects make a simultaneous allocation of tokens between their private and group accounts. Subsequently, one subject at a time is informed of the aggregate group allocation and given the option of changing their allocation. Each round ends at a randomly chosen end-point unknown to the subjects. At the end of each round, payoffs are determined by the final allocation of tokens to the group and private accounts. Kurzban and Houser find that some groups in this environment are able to achieve substantial levels of cooperation over a large number of rounds, without encountering the decay in contributions that often occurs in the repeated VCM.[6]

3. EXPERIMENTAL DESIGN

A total of 23 decision-making groups, comprised of 92 participants recruited from Indiana University undergraduate economics courses, were studied.

Eighteen four-person groups participated in nine experimental sessions conducted in Spring 2004 in the Interdisciplinary Experimental Laboratory at Indiana University, using software developed on the NovaNET computer network. Of these, ten groups participated in the treatment condition that allowed for MRCs and eight groups participated in the control experiments without commitments. In addition, data is used from five four-person groups from a previous study by Laury, Walker, and Williams (1995) that used the same VCM procedures and parameters as the control experiments. This yields a total of 13 control experiments.

The VCM procedures implemented in both the MRC and the control experiments are based on those used by Isaac, Walker, and Williams (1994). The instructions were identical across experiments except for a one-page addition describing the MRC mechanism in the MRC experiments.[7] Participants completed a sequence of 30 decision-making rounds. At the start of each round, individual i was endowed with Z_i tokens which were divided between a private account, earning a constant return of p_i per token, and a group account, earning a return based upon the total number of tokens allocated by the group. Tokens could not be carried across rounds. For a given round, let m_i represent individual i's allocation of tokens to the group account and $\sum m_j$ represent the sum of tokens placed in the group account by all other individuals ($j \neq i$). Each individual earned $\left[G(m_i + \sum m_j) \right]/N$ cents from the group account. Because each individual received a $1/N$ share of the total earnings from the group account, the group account was a pure public good. The experiments were parameterized so that participants in groups of size $N = 4$ were each endowed with 40 tokens per round. The return from each individual's private account was 1 cent per token. Defining the marginal per capita return from the group account (MPCR) as the ratio of benefits to costs for moving a single token from the private account to the group account, or $G'(\cdot)/N$, the group account earned 2.2 cents per token allocated, yielding an MPCR $= 0.55$.

The return from the private account, and the function $G(\cdot)$ were chosen so that the Pareto Optimum (the outcome that maximizes group earnings) was for each individual to place all tokens in the group account. However, under the assumption of individual earnings maximization and common information, the Nash equilibrium required each individual to place zero tokens in the group account.

Each individual was informed of the number of rounds, the token endowment, the group's aggregate token endowment, and the returns from the private and group accounts. Subjects also knew that they would be randomly assigned to groups of size 4 and would remain in those groups for the duration of the experiment. It was explained that the decisions for each round were binding and that end-of-experiment earnings would be the sum of individual earnings from all rounds. Prior to the start of each round, participants were shown information on their own earnings for the previous round as well as the total number of tokens placed by the entire group in the group account. During each round, subjects could view their personal token allocations, earnings, and total tokens placed in the group account for all the previous rounds.

Prior to the 1st, 6th, 11th, 16th, 21st and 26th round of the MRC experiments, subjects were given the option of making a binding five-round commitment.[8] The aggregate group commitment of tokens to the group account was made public. Subjects were shown both their individual commitment and the aggregate group commitment on the computerized display used for eliciting their allocation decision in each round.

4. CONJECTURES

Under the assumption that all subjects act to maximize earnings and this is common knowledge, the Nash equilibrium in the game studied here is zero allocations to the group account. The addition of opportunities to make MRCs binding does not change this prediction.

Building on the discussion presented in Bochet and Putterman (2004), suppose some subjects follow norms of behavior in which they prefer to cooperate when they believe others are cooperating, and to be less cooperative when they believe that others are not cooperating. These subjects would have utility based upon their monetary earnings as well as a reciprocity component. Finally, it has to be assumed that subjects begin with prior beliefs about the prevalence of reciprocating subjects. In this case, the repeated VCM game becomes a Bayesian game of the type analyzed in Kreps, Milgrom, Roberts, and Wilson (1982) in which subjects adjust their choices as they update their prior beliefs about others as the game progresses.

Many types of alternative preferences have been suggested to explain positive group allocations in VCM experiments, for example, unconditional altruism, or individuals that receive a "warm glow" from giving. We have chosen to focus on reciprocity because it is best suited to explain the dynamics of contributions across rounds in our experiment. Also, past research has indicated that reciprocity has more predictive power than altruism related theories. Similar to other studies, Croson (1999) finds that group-account allocations are significantly positively related to both the group allocations of other subjects, and to beliefs about those allocations, providing strong support for reciprocity theories.

In the control experiments, in the presence of reciprocating subjects, a group may be able to sustain significant levels of cooperation across rounds if large group-account allocations made in the first round are reciprocated in future rounds, as observed in Gunnthorsdottir, Houser, and McCabe (2005). On the other hand, if subjects are paired with individuals who make low initial allocations to the group account, reciprocity may lead to decay in group allocations across rounds, as is often observed in finitely repeated VCM experiments. Clearly, a similar result could be observed if some subjects do not follow norms of reciprocity and do not reciprocate the positive group allocations of other group members.

Binding MRC opportunities may have implications for reciprocal behavior. Subjects have more reliable information about the future behavior of the other subjects in their group, and importantly, about the extent to which cooperative behavior can be exploited in future rounds. Further, binding commitments allow subjects to make more public their intentions toward cooperation. A reciprocating subject may signal intentions to be cooperative by making a large commitment, and if large commitments by other group members are observed, the subject may reciprocate by increasing his group-account allocation above his commitment. This process could potentially continue in future rounds in which new commitments are solicited, leading to sustained high levels of cooperation. However, if a reciprocating subject encounters commitments by others that are small compared to his own, the subject may respond by making no group allocations above his commitment, and by decreasing his commitment at the next opportunity. Following this logic, in the presence of reciprocators, the following outcomes may be supportable.

- In both control and MRC experiments, when a subject encounters group allocations by other group members that are large relative to his own, he will increase his group allocation in the following round, and when a subject encounters group allocations that are small relative to his own, he will decrease his group allocation in the following round.
- In MRC experiments, a subset of subjects will be observed making positive commitments. Further, a subject will increase his allocation above his commitment by a larger amount when encountering commitments by other group members that are large relative to his own, and will increase his allocation above his commitment less when encountering commitments by other group members that are small relative to his own.

- In MRC experiments, a subject will increase his current commitment above his prior commitment in the previous five-round commitment block if the commitments of other group members were large relative to his own in the previous block, and decrease his commitment below his commitment in the previous block if the commitments of other group members were small relative to his own in the previous block.
- Due to the fact that MRCs allow subjects to acquire more reliable information about the future behavior of other group members than is possible in the control experiments, a larger dispersion of outcomes across groups will be observed in the MRC experiments than in the control experiments. High levels of cooperation may be more easily maintained in the MRC experiments, while low levels of cooperation may be more extreme.

5. RESULTS

We begin the empirical analysis by considering aggregate allocations in the MRC and control experiments. This analysis is followed by a more detailed focus on individual behavior in both the MRC and control experiments. The final results turn to an examination of the variation of within-group and across-group behavior in the MRC and control experiments.

5.1. Group-Account Allocations across Treatment Conditions

Result 1. Average group-account allocations across rounds are similar in the MRC and control experiments. However, the decay in the average group-account allocation observed in the control experiments is not evident in the MRC experiments.

Fig. 1 displays average group-account allocations for each round in the MRC experiments and the control experiments. Behavior in the control experiments is similar to behavior in similarly parameterized linear public goods experiments. Average group-account allocations decay from 53.32% in the first round to 29.76% in the final round. This change is statistically significant.[9] Consistent with previous studies decay is not monotonic across rounds.

In the MRC experiments, the average group-account allocation pooled across all rounds is 45.77% of endowment. In the control experiments it is 45.83%. A t-test and a Wilcoxon test confirm that the average difference in group-account allocations is not significantly different.[10] However, as one

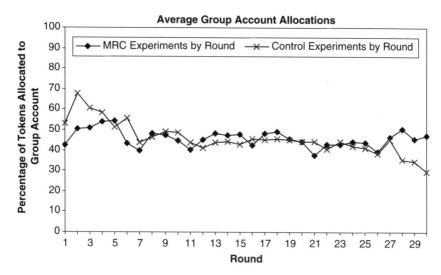

Fig. 1. Average Group-Account Allocations: MRC and Control Experiments.

can observe from Fig. 1, there is an interesting difference in the behavior across decision rounds in the MRC experiments relative to the control experiments. In early rounds, average group-account allocations are actually higher in the control experiments. However, unlike the control experiments, average group-account allocations do not decay across rounds in the MRC experiments. In fact, average group-account allocations are higher in the last round of the MRC experiments, 47.25%, than in the first round, 42.31%.[11] Clearly, we cannot conclude that group-account allocations decline as rounds advance in the MRC experiments. By the last three rounds of the experiments, the average group-account allocations in the MRC experiments are well above those in the control experiments, although the difference is not statistically significant.

5.2. Prevalence of Commitments in MRC Experiments

Result 2. Subjects on average make positive commitments at each opportunity and there is no sign of decay in average commitments. A large portion of group allocations are pre-committed in every round.

Fig. 2 displays the average commitment of tokens for each round, and the average group-account allocation in each round of the MRC treatment. Commitments average between 25% and 33% of endowments.[12] Further,

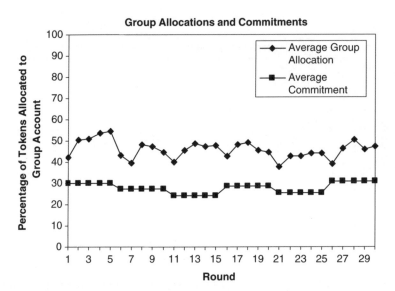

Fig. 2.   Average Individual Commitments and Group-Account Allocations: MRC
Experiments.

there is no noticeable decay in average commitments. In fact, average commitments are highest at the final opportunity before round 26. The large variation of individual commitment decisions is a second general feature of the data. Fig. 3, which displays the distribution of individual commitments pooled across the 6 commitment blocks illustrates. Less than 14% of individual commitments are for zero tokens. On the other hand, over 80% of commitments are for 50% or less of the token endowment. The average individual commitment when pooling across all commitment opportunities, is 27.72% of the token endowment, the median is 25% of the endowment.

Returning to the aggregate treatment results shown in Fig. 2, it can be observed that more than 50% of total group allocations in every round are pre-committed. A maximum of 71% of group allocations are pre-committed in round 1.

5.3. Evidence of Reciprocity in MRC and Control Experiments

To examine the extent of reciprocity, we investigate how individuals respond to deviations from the behavior of other group members in the case of both group allocations and commitments. We begin with analysis of the MRC experiments, and conclude with analysis of the control experiments.

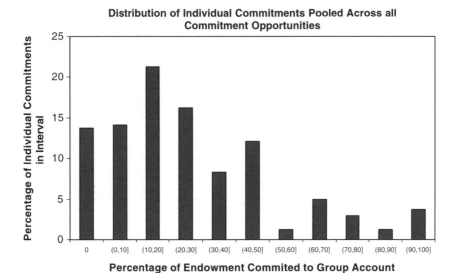

Fig. 3. Distribution of Individual Commitments.

Result 3. In the first round of each commitment block of the MRC experiments, a subject makes his additional group-account allocation above his commitment larger or smaller in response to the deviation of his commitment from the mean commitment of other group members.

Define A_{ijt1} as individual i's allocation to the group j group account in round 1 of block t, and C_{ijt} as i's commitment to the group j group account in block t. Then, the additional group allocation a subject makes above his commitment in round 1 of block t can be defined as $\Delta AC_{itj1} = A_{ijt1} - C_{ijt}$. Further, define $\bar{C}_{-ijt}$ as the mean commitment of other group j members in block t. The deviation of a subject i's commitment from the mean commitment of other group j members can then be defined as $\Omega C_{ijt} = C_{ijt} - \bar{C}_{-ijt}$.

Table 1 displays estimates of the following subject-specific random effects model:

$$\Delta AC_{ijt1} = \beta_0 + \beta_c \Omega C_{ijt} + \beta_B \text{BLOCK} + \sum_{j=2}^{10} \beta_{gj} D_j + u_i + \varepsilon_{ijt1}$$

BLOCK is the commitment block number added to the regression to control for inter-temporal effects. Dummy variables, D_j, for experimental groups 2 through 10 are also added. A Tobit specification is used for estimation purposes because ΔAC_{ijt1} is bounded from below at 0.

Table 1.   Reciprocity and Group-Account Allocations – First Round of
Each Commitment Block.

	Coefficient	SE	p	Marginal effect	SE	p
ΩC_{ijt}	−0.522	0.127	0.000	−0.281	0.068	0.000
Block	−0.748	0.395	0.058	−0.402	0.233	0.084
Constant	7.667	2.333	0.001	4.123	1.645	0.012
Group 2	−5.435	2.973	0.068	−2.922	1.690	0.084
Group 3	−6.951	5.054	0.169	−3.738	2.639	0.157
Group 4	−1.838	9.432	0.846	−0.988	5.035	0.844
Group 5	−0.206	6.026	0.973	−0.112	3.234	0.973
Group 6	6.699	11.697	0.567	3.602	6.723	0.592
Group 7	−9.806	2.863	0.001	−5.273	1.868	0.005
Group 8	−12.587	4.105	0.002	−6.768	2.547	0.008
Group 9	−6.426	4.601	0.163	−3.455	2.486	0.165
Group 10	−4.998	16.934	0.768	−2.687	8.744	0.759

Log likelihood = −574.380

Note: ΔAC_{ijt1} = 0 for 103 observations. N = 240, Individuals = 40, Dependent Variable: ΔAC_{ijt1}.

Providing strong evidence for reciprocity, β_c is negative and strongly significant. The estimated marginal effect of −0.281 for the β_c coefficient reflects a strong tendency for participants to reciprocate commitment decisions with group-account allocation responses. When their commitments are less than the average commitment of others, individuals tend to choose larger additional group-account allocations in the first round of each block. When individuals commit more than the average commitment of others, they tend to choose smaller additional group-account allocations in round 1 of each block. Also, the sign of β_B, the commitment block coefficient, is negative, meaning that as commitment blocks advance, subjects tend to increase group-account allocations above commitments less.[13] β_B is marginally statistically significant.

Result 4. In rounds 2 through 5 of each of the 5 round commitment blocks, a subject makes his additional group-account allocation above his commitment larger or smaller in response to the deviation of his commitment from the mean commitment of other group members. At the same time, a subject responds reciprocally to how much other members of his group increased their group-account allocations above their commitments in the previous round.

Define $A_{-itjk-1}$ as the total amount other group j members besides subject i allocated to the group account in round $k-1$ of commitment block t, and $C_{-itjk-1}$ as the total commitment of other group j members besides subject i

in round $k-1$ of commitment block t. Then, $\Delta AC_{-itk-1} = A_{-itjk-1} - C_{-itjk-1}$ is the total amount that other group j members besides subject i increased their group-account allocations above their commitments in round $k-1$ of block t. Table 2 displays Tobit estimates of the following regression model with subject specific random effects:

$$\Delta AC_{ijtk} = \beta_0 + \beta_c \Omega C_{ijtk} + \beta_{Ac} \Delta AC_{-itk-1}$$

$$+ \beta_B \text{BLOCK} + \sum_{j=2}^{10} \beta_{gj} D_j + u_i + \varepsilon_{ijtk}$$

The index on round, k, can take the values of 2 through 5, as there are 5 rounds in each commitment block, and in the case of the dependent variable, data from the first round are omitted.

β_c is negative and strongly significant with a marginal effect of -0.383. Therefore, similar to Result 3, when their commitments are less than the average of the commitments of others, individuals tend to offer larger additional group-account allocations, and when individuals commit more than the average commitment of others, they tend to offer smaller additional group-account allocations. At the same time, β_{Ac} is positive and statistically significant with a marginal effect of 0.122, meaning that the more that other group members

Table 2. Reciprocity and Group-Account Allocations – Rounds 2–5 of Each Commitment Block.

	Coefficient	SE	p	Marginal Effect	SE	p
ΩC_{ijtk}	−0.569	0.034	0.000	−0.383	0.036	0.000
ΔAC_{-itk-1}	0.182	0.028	0.000	0.122	0.016	0.000
Block	−0.416	0.150	0.006	−0.281	0.101	0.006
Constant	6.951	2.200	0.002	4.679	1.540	0.002
Group 2	−2.919	2.980	0.327	−1.965	1.998	0.326
Group 3	−4.293	4.076	0.292	−2.890	2.693	0.283
Group 4	−2.455	3.526	0.486	−1.653	2.345	0.481
Group 5	−3.523	3.772	0.350	−2.378	2.511	0.344
Group 6	0.996	4.667	0.831	0.671	3.157	0.832
Group 7	−9.560	3.953	0.016	−6.435	2.586	0.0128
Group 8	−14.634	5.761	0.011	−9.851	3.562	0.006
Group 9	−8.735	3.610	0.016	−5.880	2.392	0.014
Group 10	−3.132	3.794	0.409	−2.108	2.529	0.405

Log Likelihood $= -2578.910$

Note: $\Delta AC_{ijtk} = 0$ for 341 observations. $N = 960$, Individuals $= 40$, Dependent Variable: ΔAC_{ijtk}.

increased their group-account allocations above their commitments in the previous round, the more a subject increases his group-account allocation above his commitment in the current round. β_B is negative and statistically significant in this case, meaning that as commitment blocks advance, subjects tend to increase group-account allocations above commitments less.

Result 5. In the MRC experiments, subjects adjust their commitments at each opportunity in response to the difference between their previous commitment and the average previous commitment of other group members, and in response to how much other group members increased their group allocations above their commitments in the previous commitment block.

Define $\Delta C_{ijt} = C_{ijt} - C_{ijt-1}$ as the difference between subject i's commitment in block t and his commitment in block $t-1$. Second, define $\overline{\Delta AC}_{-ijt-1}$ as the total amount that other group j members besides subject i increased their group-account allocations above their commitments averaged over the previous 5 round commitment block. Table 3 displays GLS estimates of the following regression model with subject specific random effects:

$$\Delta C_{ijt} = \beta_o + \beta_c \Omega C_{ijt-1} + \beta_{\overline{Ac}}\overline{\Delta AC}_{-ijt-1} + \beta_B \text{BLOCK} + \sum_{j=2}^{10} \beta_{gj}D_j + u_i + \varepsilon_{ijt}$$

GLS estimates are used because in this case the dependent variable is not bounded from below at zero. $\beta_c = -0.458$ is negative and significant,

Table 3. Reciprocity and Commitments.

	Coefficient	SE	p
ΩC_{ijt-1}	−0.458	0.053	0.000
$\overline{\Delta AC}_{-ijt-1}$	0.124	0.044	0.002
Block	0.772	0.315	0.014
Constant	−7.334	2.996	0.014
Group 2	1.381	2.896	0.634
Group 3	−0.115	2.965	0.969
Group 4	−0.150	2.931	0.959
Group 5	2.040	2.918	0.485
Group 6	2.066	2.853	0.469
Group 7	1.073	3.068	0.727
Group 8	3.114	3.206	0.803
Group 9	0.763	3.049	0.803
Group 10	2.951	2.957	0.318
$R^2 = 0.244$			

Note: $N = 200$, Number of Individuals = 40, Dependent Variable: ΔC_{ijt}.

implying that the larger the positive deviation of a subject's commitment from the average commitment of others in the previous commitment block, the less a subject increases his current commitment above his previous commitment. Also, $\beta_{\overline{Ac}} = 0.124$ is positive and significant, implying that the more that other members of the group increased their group-account allocations above their commitments over the five rounds of the previous commitment block, the more subjects tend to raise their commitments relative to the previous commitment opportunity. In this case the sign of β_B is positive, and weakly statistically significant.

The following analysis turns to an examination of individual behavior in the control experiments. In particular, the analysis examines the extent to which changes in subjects' group allocations across decisions rounds can be linked to the past decisions of other group members.

Result 6. In the control experiments, subjects reciprocate group allocation decisions in round $k-1$ with larger or smaller group allocations in round k.

Table 4 displays GLS estimates of the following regression model with subject specific random effects:

$$\Delta A_{ijk} = \beta_A \Omega A_{ijk-1} + \beta_R \text{ROUND} + \sum_{j=2}^{13} \beta_{gj} D_j + u_i + \varepsilon_{ijk}$$

Table 4. Reciprocity in Control Experiments.

	Coefficient	SE	p
ΩA_{ijk-1}	−0.535	0.022	0.000
Round	−0.025	0.033	0.454
Constant	−0.306	1.980	0.877
Group 2	0.190	2.696	0.944
Group 3	0.345	2.696	0.898
Group 4	−0.181	2.696	0.947
Group 5	−0.198	2.696	0.941
Group 6	0.784	2.696	0.771
Group 7	0.793	2.696	0.769
Group 8	0.888	2.696	0.742
Group 9	0.448	2.696	0.868
Group 10	0.983	2.696	0.716
Group 11	−0.241	2.696	0.929
Group 12	0.448	2.696	0.868
Group 13	0.707	2.696	0.793
$R^2 = 0.203$			

Note: $N = 1508$ Number of Individuals $= 40$, Dependent Variable: ΔA_{ijk}.

The dependent variable, $\Delta A_{ijk} = A_{ijk} - A_{ijk-1}$, is the difference between subject i in group j's group-account allocation in round k and his group-account allocation in round $k-1$. $\Omega A_{ijk-1} = A_{ijk-1} - \bar{A}_{-ijk-1}$ is the difference between subject i's group-account allocation in round $k-1$ and the average group-account allocation of the other members of subject i's group in round $k-1$. ROUND is the round number added to the regression to control for inter-temporal effects.

The results indicate that in the control experiments, subjects tend to increase their group-account allocation above their previous group-account allocation if their group-account allocation was below the average of other group members' allocations in the previous round, and to decrease their group-account allocation if their group-account allocation was above the average of other group members' allocations in the previous round. β_A is negative and strongly significant. The coefficient on round number, β_R, has a negative sign, but is not statistically significant.[14]

The analysis that relates to the final two results is designed to examine to what extent the dispersion of within-group individual behavior and across-group behavior varies between the MRC and control experiments.

5.4. Across-Group Dispersion in Group-Account Allocations

Result 7. Less variation in individual allocations to the group account is observed within groups in the MRC experiments than in the control experiments.

Within each decision round and each group, one can compute the standard deviation of individual allocations to the group account. Fig. 4 displays the average within-group standard deviation for the MRC and the control experiments. With the exception of the first five rounds, and the final five rounds, the average within-group standard deviation is smaller in the MRC treatment. This difference in average within-group standard deviations is statistically significant when pooling across rounds (two sample t-test and Wilcoxon two sample test, $p = 0.000$). This observation suggests that the commitment mechanism, by providing additional information, may have allowed individuals in each group to more closely reciprocate, and conform to the behavior of other group members.

Result 8. A larger variance in group outcomes is observed in the MRC experiments than the control experiments.

Earlier discussion conjectured that MRCs may allow subjects to acquire more reliable information about the future behavior of other group

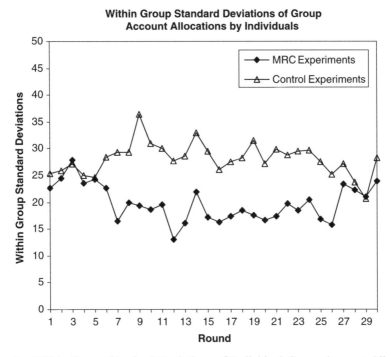

Fig. 4. Within-Group Standard Deviations of Individual Group-Account Allocations.

members than is possible in the control experiments. This may create a larger dispersion of allocations to the group account across groups in the MRC experiments relative to the control experiments. To investigate this possibility, we separate groups in the MRC and control experiments into two categories; those groups with an average group-account allocation higher than the overall average of groups in their treatment condition, "high groups," and those with a lower average group-account allocation, "low groups."

Fig. 5 displays the average difference between high groups and low groups in the MRC experiments and the average difference between high groups and low groups in the control experiments. The results are quite striking. The average difference between the high and low groups is larger for the MRC experiments than for the control experiments in the vast majority of rounds. This result is largely driven by the behavior of low groups in the MRC treatment; in 27 of 30 rounds the average allocation to the group

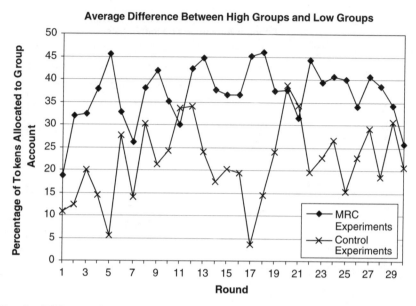

Fig. 5. Differences in Average Group Allocations: High Groups and Low Groups.

account is smaller in the MRC low groups than in the control low groups. In contrast, there is frequent overlap in the average allocation to the group account when comparing the high groups of the MRC and control experiments, although in late decision rounds the average group-account allocation in the high MRC groups tends to be above the average in the control experiments.

Fig. 6 provides further evidence in support of Result 8. Fig. 6 displays average commitments and average group-account allocations for an example high group and an example low group from the MRC experiments. It is quite apparent that the maintenance of cooperative outcomes is enhanced by increasing commitments as rounds advance in the high group. While in the low group, average commitments decrease across rounds, as do average group-account allocations.

6. CONCLUSIONS

This study examines the effects of allowing binding MRCs of tokens to the group account in a repeated VCM game. Subjects make binding

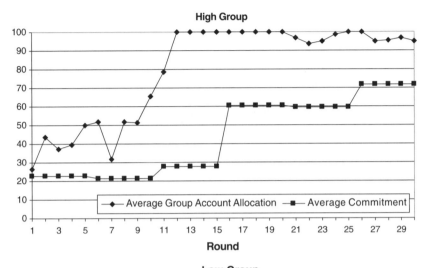

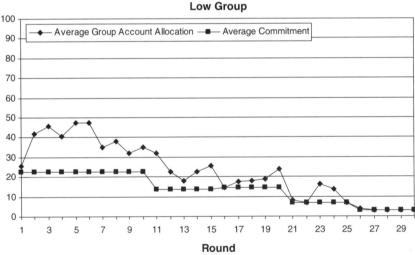

Fig. 6. Group-Account Allocations and Commitments in MRC Experiments – Example High Group and Example Low Group.

commitments averaging between 25% and 33% of their endowments. However, total group-account allocations are not systematically greater on average in the MRC experiments than those observed in the control experiments. In the final decision rounds, average group-account allocations in

MRC experiments tend to be higher than the control experiments due to the lack of decay in group allocations in the MRC treatment.

The study finds strong evidence of subjects following norms of reciprocity in the MRC experiments. Subjects respond reciprocally to other subjects when deciding how large a commitment to make before each commitment block, and also when deciding how much to increase their group-account allocation above their commitment in each round. Evidence for reciprocity was also found in the control experiments as group-account allocations responded to decisions in prior rounds.

The results of this study are largely consistent with Bochet and Putterman (2004) which studies non-binding numerical promises in the VCM. While binding MRCs have little effect on the average level of group-account allocations relative to the control experiments, commitments appear to promote more homogeneity within groups as subjects respond to commitments in a reciprocal manner. Further, there is a larger variance of group outcomes in the MRC experiments relative to the control experiments, leading to patterns of group cooperation that are more extreme.

NOTES

1. See Ledyard (1995) for a survey.
2. See Croson (1999) as an example.
3. Similarly, charities often announce a large "leadership" donation. List and Reilly (2002) present a field experiment confirming that "seed money" can significantly increase the effectiveness of fundraising by encouraging more frequent and larger contributions.
4. See Chen (1996) for further discussion of similar experiments.
5. Kurzban, McCabe, Smith, and Wilson (2001) find similar results in a study using Dorsey's "real time" environment.
6. Duffy, Ochs, and Vesterlund (2004) Duffy et al. (2004) also examine a dynamic voluntary contribution game in which subjects act sequentially. Their study finds similar results.
7. A copy of the instructions and the experimental data are provided at "mypage.iu.edu/~walkerj."
8. If a subject tried to make a group account allocation smaller than his commitment within any particular round, the subject received a message that he was in violation of his commitment and was prompted to reenter his allocation to the group account.
9. Matched pairs t-test ($p = 0.020$), matched pairs Wilcoxon test ($p = 0.034$), observations for 13 groups in each round.
10. t-test ($p = 0.977$), Wilcoxon test ($p = 0.904$), 390 observations in control experiments, 300 observations in MRC experiments.

11. Matched pairs *t*-test ($p = 0.629$), matched pairs Wilcoxon test ($p = 0.922$), 10 observations per round.

12. The size of commitments in percentage terms observed in the MRC experiments are consistent with the results observed in the previously referenced Chen and Komorita (1994) study on single-round commitments.

13. Regressions were also performed using separate dummy variables for each block instead of the commitment block number, with similar results.

14. Regressions were performed using separate dummy variables for each round instead of the round number, with similar results.

ACKNOWLEDGMENTS

We would like to thank the Center on Philanthropy at Indiana University for funding this project and the Interdisciplinary Experimental Laboratory at Indiana University for providing the facility in which the experiments where conducted. We would also like to thank an anonymous referee and the editor for very helpful suggestions.

REFERENCES

Bochet, O., & Putterman, L. (2004). *Not just babble: A voluntary contribution experiment with iterative numerical messages.* Working paper, Brown University.

Chen, X. P. (1996). The group-based binding pledge as a solution to public goods problems. *Organizational Behavior and Human Decision Processes, 66*(2), 192–202.

Chen, X. P., & Komorita, S. S. (1994). The effects of communication and commitment in a public goods social dilemma. *Organizational Behavior and Human Decision Processes, 60,* 367–386.

Croson, R. (1999). *Contributions to public goods: Altruism or reciprocity?* Working paper, University of Pennsylvania.

Dorsey, R. E. (1991). The voluntary contributions mechanism with real-time revisions. *Public Choice, 73,* 261–282.

Duffy, J., Ochs, J., & Vesterlund, L. (2004). *Giving little by little: Dynamic voluntary contribution games.* Working paper, University of Pittsburgh.

Gunnthorsdottir, A., Houser, D., & McCabe, K. (2005). Disposition, history, and contributions in a public goods experiment, forthcoming, *Journal of Economic Behavior and Organization.*

Isaac, R. M., Walker, J., & Williams, A. (1994). Group size and the voluntary provision of public goods: Experimental evidence utilizing large groups. *Journal of Public Economics, 54,* 1–36.

Kreps, D., Milgrom, P., Roberts, J., & Wilson, R. (1982). Rational cooperation in the repeated prisoner's dilemma. *Journal of Economic Theory, 27,* 245–252.

Kurzban, R., & Houser, D. (2001). Individual differences in cooperation in a circular public goods game. *European Journal of Personality, 15,* S37–S52.

Kurzban, R., McCabe, K., Smith, V. L., & Wilson, B. J. (2001). Incremental commitment and reciprocity in a real time public goods game. *Personality and Social Psychology Bulletin*, *27*(12), 1662–1673.

Ledyard, J. (1995). Public goods: A survey of experimental research. In: J. Kagel & A. Roth (Eds), *Handbook of Experimental Economics*. Princeton: Princeton University Press.

List, J. A., & Reilly, D. (2002). The effects of seed money and refunds on charitable giving: Experimental evidence from a university capital campaign. *Journal of Political Economy*, *110*(8), 215–233.

Laury, S. K., Walker, J., & Williams, A. (1995). Anonymity and the voluntary provision of public goods. *Journal of Economic Behavior and Organization*, *27*, 365–380.